Against Values

Against Values

How to Talk About the Good in a Postliberal Era

Philip J. Harold

ROWMAN & LITTLEFIELD
Lanham • Boulder • New York • London

Published by Rowman & Littlefield
An imprint of The Rowman & Littlefield Publishing Group, Inc.
4501 Forbes Boulevard, Suite 200, Lanham, Maryland 20706
www.rowman.com

86-90 Paul Street, London EC2A 4NE

British Library Cataloguing in Publication Information Available

Library of Congress Cataloging-in-Publication Data

Names: Harold, Philip J., author.
Title: Against values : how to talk about the good in a postliberal era / Philip J. Harold.
Description: Lanham : Rowman & Littlefield, [2022] | Includes bibliographical references and index. | Summary: "As a systematic introduction to the philosophical foundations of postliberalism, this timely book reveals how the idea of personal values have served to divide and segregate people rather than uniting them under a shared common good. Also discussed are the contemporary interplay of sovereignty and morality and religion and politics"-- Provided by publisher.
Identifiers: LCCN 2022030094 (print) | LCCN 2022030095 (ebook) | ISBN 9781538169803 (cloth) | ISBN 9781538174159 (paper) | ISBN 9781538169810 (ebook)
Subjects: LCSH: Postliberal theology. | Values. | Common good.
Classification: LCC BT83.595 .H37 2022 (print) | LCC BT83.595 (ebook) | DDC 230/.046--dc23/eng/20220808
LC record available at https://lccn.loc.gov/2022030094
LC ebook record available at https://lccn.loc.gov/2022030095

For Rachel

Mulierem fortem quis inveniet?
Procul et de ultimis finibus pretium eius.

Contents

Acknowledgments

Funding for this project was provided by the Fulbright Scholar Program, the Earhart Foundation, the Charles Koch Foundation, and the Axios Institute. Research was conducted at the *Zentralinstitute für Ehe und Familie in der Gesellschaft* (ZFG) at the Catholic University of Eichstätt-Ingolstadt in Bavaria, Germany, in 2010. I want to especially thank Jörg Althammer for hosting me at the ZFG, as well as my colleagues during my time there, Peter Wendl, Irina Sagel, Annika Hausner, and Susann Kunze. I also want to express my gratitude to Martin Groos, Jessica Hofmacher, Claudia Elenschneider, Bernhard Matschulla, Isabel Imhof, Anna Breitsameter, and especially to Hannah Elenschneider, and to Mathias and Mariele Hasselmeier. Thanks also to Titi Adewale, Monica VanDieren, Lindsey Sobolosky, David Jamison, Lawrence Tomei, Kathryn Dennick-Brecht, John Graham, Mary Ann Rafoth, Donna Reilly, Renee Augustine, Yvonne Miller, Rachel Farrell, and Morgan Zelkovic. Over the years I was blessed to have fantastic research assistants: Ellen Lichius, Anthony Gratter, Lara Will, Anna Hartwell, and Jake King. I wish to thank Anthony Giambrone for the gift of a crucial text I used during the pandemic of 2020 when all libraries were shut down. I also want to thank James Harold, Jason Bell, Annette Förster, and Mark Conlon for their helpful commentary, and Sarah Singh and Megan Furman for their editing. All the errors in this volume are my own. Gratitude for research assistance goes to Paul Harold, Ron Scrogham, Elizabeth Belyeu, Fran Caplan, Timothy Schlak, Bruce Johnston, Deb Martz, Jacqueline Klentzin, Kimberly Smith, Emily Paladino, Marcia Stevenson, Chloe Mills, Karen Fronzaglio, and Loretta Gossett. Thanks goes as well to Stephen Krason and Beata Engel-Doyle, as well as Natalie Mandziuk, Sylvia Landis, Anne Cushman, the copy-editor, and the anonymous reviewers of the manuscript. Many thanks to my wonderful parents and in-laws, James and Teresa Harold and Mike and Mary Ann Durbin, for all their love and support. I also want to thank Robert Morris University for the sabbatical semester and all the research support I have been given over the years. I have been very privileged to have held faculty appointments at Robert Morris and the University of Dallas, two wonderful places to work and teach in their own ways, oases of respectful and open dialogue, and I want to thank all my colleagues, the staff and administration, and the students I have had over the years at those two institutions.

Abbreviations

AA	The Academy Edition (*Academie-Ausgabe*) of the Collected Works of Immanuel Kant (*Kants Gesammelte Schriften*)
CE	Clarendon Edition of the Works of Thomas Hobbes
GA	The Collected Works (*Gesamtausgabe*) of Martin Heidegger
GW	The Collected Works (Gesammelte Werke) of Samuel Pufendorf
KGW	The Critical Edition of the Collected Works of Friedrich Nietzsche (*Kritische Gesamtausgabe*)
LW	The Collected Works of Martin Luther in English (*Luther's Works*)
Mic	Hermann Lotze, *Microcosmus*, 2 vols. (Edinburgh, 1885)
Mik	Hermann Lotze, *Mikrokosmus*, 3 vols. (Leipzig, 1856, 1858, 1864)
WA	The Weimar Edition (*Weimar Ausgabe*) of the Collected Works of Martin Luther

Preface

We no longer believe in the occult power of witches. Yet witchcraft was a significant part of our past. From 1450 to 1750, it was the reason over a hundred thousand people were tortured and fifty thousand people killed.[1] Though witch hunts themselves were propagated by locals and not central authorities, it was the intellectual elite of Europe whose conception of and belief in witchcraft laid the intellectual foundations without which the witch hunts could not have taken place.[2] Scapegoating witches served an important social function—namely, increasing a sense of communal unity and harmony.[3]

Ours is a great civilization. As with the great civilizations of the past, it contains elements that will intrigue and befuddle people hundreds of years from now—especially our very serious discussions about *values*.

As with the concept of witchcraft, our intellectual elite developed the idea of "value," which then filtered down to common people.[4] Also like the concept of witchcraft, the problem with value is that it promotes social unity through exclusion. "Values are always 'our' values, i.e., the values defining a group."[5] Since adhering to a value means opposing what degrades it, when it comes to values themselves, we cannot discuss and argue but only fight.[6] Those who believed in witchcraft did not even notice that it was a belief, but they saw it as just a part of the world; as a result, they were on the lookout for manifestations of it. Those who believe in values likewise never doubt their existence and, therefore, fail to notice how it makes them at odds with their fellow men. But if someone contradicts our values, we must oppose them—the result of this way of thinking is to set us against each other.

Political philosophy reflects on the meaning of terminal tropes in political discourse—the fundamental expressions that undergird persuasive speech, the basic symbols that are used to orient us politically.[7] *Value*, *fact*, and *morality* are words that come naturally to us moderns, but what do they mean? A lack of reflection on what we are saying risks mindlessly repeating ready-made language. Bad things happen when our language speaks us, rather than us speaking it. "Modern stupidity is not ignorance, but the *non-thought of received ideas.*"[8] George Orwell was right to maintain that languidly repeating meaningless words—a category in which he placed values—serves in political speech to defend the indefensible.[9] "Often held up as a source of illumination on the most difficult questions and choices," writes Langdon Winner, "the concept of 'values' is better seen as a symptom of deep-seated confusion, an inability to think and talk precisely about the most basic questions of human well-being and the future of our planet."[10]

It is time to put the concept of value itself in question. Failure to do so makes our discourse strange and hollow.[11] A number of great thinkers, including Martin Heidegger and Hannah Arendt, have criticized the concept of value; however, these scattered critiques have yet to be turned into a sustained argument. It is difficult to do so because the language of values is intimately bound up with the very foundational assumptions of modernity.[12] Valuation is esteem—that is to say, a flattening of what we mean when we speak of good and evil.[13] But when everyone is pursuing esteem, conflict is inevitable. Modernity's solution for this is the concept of sovereignty, wherein there is an "authoritative allocation of values for a society,"[14] a realm of "politics" opposed to something called "religion," with the concept of "morality" supposedly filling the gap between. All these terms are part of a self-reinforcing system, and we cannot critique the one without calling into question the others.

We need to get off modernity's perpetual motion machine and put its first principles in question. The most basic political concepts are justice and the common good, and they consist not in the triumph of our values but in our ability to be friends with each other.

NOTES

1. Jeffrey B. Russell and Brooks Alexander, *A History of Witchcraft: Sorcerers, Heretics and Pagans*, 2nd ed. (London: Thames & Hudson, 2007), 12.

2. Brian P. Levack, *The Witch-Hunt in Early Modern Europe,* 3rd ed. (Harlow, UK: Pearson Longman, 2006), 31–32.

3. Russell and Alexander, *A History of Witchcraft: Sorcerers, Heretics and Pagans*, 16.

4. The philosophical concept of value (from which we get contemporary values language) was invented in Germany during the late nineteenth century and was a product of the social and cultural German elite—the "mandarins"—as Jürgen Gebhardt has shown. Jürgen Gebhardt, "Die Werte," in *Anodos: Festschrift für Helmut Kuhn* (Weinheim: VCH, Acta humaniora, 1989), 35–54. See also Fritz K. Ringer, *The Decline of the German Mandarins: The German Academic Community, 1890–1933* (Cambridge: Harvard University Press, 1969).

5. Joel Backström, "Of Dictators and Greengrocers: On the Repressive Grammar of Values-Discourse," *Ethical Perspectives* 22, no. 1 (2015): 42.

6. Even value pluralism must rely on "fundamental" values that uphold the possibility of peaceful disagreement. These fundamental values are held sacred, as they are that for which we sacrifice and die. "Arguments about values often turn into fights over values," writes James Q. Wilson. He adds, disputing positivism's reduction of values to preferences, "That is not the way we discuss our taste for vanilla ice cream." James Q. Wilson, *The Moral Sense* (New York: The Free Press, 1993), xi.

7. "Words of great human significance," writes Michael Polanyi, "accumulate through the centuries an unfathomable fund of subsidiarily known connotations, which we can bring partly into focus by reflecting on the use of such words." Michael Polanyi, *Personal Knowledge: Towards a Post-Critical Philosophy* (Chicago: University of Chicago Press, 1958), 115.

8. Milan Kundera, *The Art of the Novel*, trans. Linda Asher (New York: Grove Press, 1988), 163.

9. It does this by allowing us to name things without calling up pictures of them. George Orwell, *All Art Is Propaganda*, ed. George Packer (Boston: Mariner Books, 2008), 276–82.

10. Langdon Winner, "Brandy, Cigars, and Human Values," in *The Whale and the Reactor: The Search for Limits in an Age of High Technology* (Chicago: University of Chicago Press, 1986), 156.

11. "All present value discourse, no matter how well-intentioned, shares this strangeness and hollowness given by the distinctly operative and at the same time obtrusively unquestionable character of the concept that empowers it." Ivo De Gennaro, "Preface," in *Value: Sources and Readings on a Key Concept of the Globalized World*, ed. Ivo De Gennaro (Leiden: Brill, 2012), xii.

12. Amy Wendling correctly speculates that the concept of value is a product of the bourgeois era. Amy E. Wendling, *The Ruling Ideas: Bourgeois Political Concepts* (Lanham: Lexington Books, 2012), 89. Values language is something unique to us. "'[V]alues' is a hard thing to put in a long diachronic frame," writes Justin Stover, "because it is not clear that there is any analogous notion in any culture besides our own." Justin Stover, "There Is No Case for the Humanities," *American Affairs* I, no. 4 (2017): 218.

13. The latter is bound up with the "possibilities of genuine human contact." Backström, "Of Dictators and Greengrocers: On the Repressive Grammar of Values-Discourse," 64.

14. David Easton, *The Political System: An Inquiry into the State of Political Science* (New York: Alfred A. Knopf, 1953), 129.

Introduction

Values originally meant monetary prices. Now the term refers, in an abstract way, to that which we think is good, worthwhile, estimable, and desirable.[1] Previously, we used the word *virtue* to describe something fundamental about an individual's or society's way of life; nowadays, we use values instead. "This transmutation is the great philosophical revolution of modernity" for Gertrude Himmelfarb, who insists that the shift to values language should be ranked in importance with the seventeenth-century revolt of the moderns against the ancients. "Yet unlike the earlier rebels, who were fully conscious of the import of their rebellion," she writes, "the later ones (with the notable exception of Nietzsche) seemed almost unaware of what they were doing. . . . [T]he new vocabulary, which was so radical a departure from the old and which in itself constituted a revolution in thought, passed without notice."[2]

This book is both a history of the concept of value and a critique of it. The concept as a philosophical category was created by the influential German philosopher Hermann Lotze in the nineteenth century. The term was popularized by the work of Friedrich Nietzsche starting in the 1890s, and as the twentieth century progressed, there was an explosion of the use of the word *values* in the plural that mirrored the corresponding decline of virtue, in English and German, and in a less pronounced way in the Romance languages.[3] The language of scholars a century ago became that of everyday speech: what puzzled and bored an educated audience during World War I was taken for granted and used to express hot topics in political campaigns seventy-five years later.[4]

The roots of value language reach back further, however, into the early modern period. The first instance of the new usage of "value" in the English language is found in Thomas Hobbes, whose book *Leviathan* (1651) is the progenitor of the new thinking. Values language is therefore not a surreptitious change as Himmelfarb claims, but it is part and parcel of modern political thought, or liberalism, and its project of diminishing the role of loyalty in political thought and of seeing in it only a source of corruption.[5] Modernity understands itself as advancing beyond the medieval political order, with the weight it gave to personal trust, loyalty, and friendship. These phenomena, however, can never be eliminated, only lost from view or misinterpreted.[6] This is what value does: it views the good as partial and impersonal. Instead of a common good understood as the increase of friendship—a good that is personal and comprehensive—liberalism frees individuals to pursue their values, which are competitive and divisive. Liberalism ends up undermining the types of relationships required for the functioning of its own institutions. Patrick Deneen writes that "liberal theory sought to educate people to think differently about themselves and their relationships"—namely, that we are "by nature, nonrelational creatures, separate and autonomous"—yet our liberation from our relationships renders us playthings of impersonal forces.[7]

Liberalism makes three moves. First, it replaces the idea of justice with *esteem*. Second, it understands political authority in terms of *sovereignty*. And third, it introduces the concept of *morality* as a substitute for sovereignty in order to make it more palatable (though no less inexorable). Necessary for all three is understanding the good as a value: gaining value for oneself crowds out the search for justice and supplies the reason to be moral, and the competition for value and resulting division justifies the imposition of order through sovereignty. This book will connect these dots while arguing for an alternative, postliberal political philosophy that would understand the common good in terms of real relationships and not an abstract morality.

This alternative is sketched right away in the first chapter. Values language is embedded in the language of morality, which goes beyond *mores*, the customs of a community, and are understood instead in modernity to be an abstract standard for esteem. Values are always pursued with reference to a system of morality; indeed, the whole point of following a moral system is to attain moral value. The terms *morally right* and *morally wrong* are poor substitutes for the language of *just* and *unjust*. A person is a constellation of relationships, and justice is the excellence of a person in his relationships. The arrow of causality when it comes to loyalty and our criteria for right and wrong therefore ought to be reversed: right and wrong arise on the back of loyalties, which are not chosen or subject to external criteria but enable us to have any criteria in the first place.

The next three chapters cover the three moves of liberalism. The first goes back to Martin Luther, who eliminates justice in favor of esteem, as is shown in chapter 2. We do not become just through a personal relationship with God, but rather are only given an external imputation of "just" by God. After Luther, justice becomes something extrinsic to a person, an imputation given prior to personal relationships, making them possible and coming from a ruler wielding overwhelming, sacred power. Luther thus also lays the groundwork for liberalism's second move, the creation of sovereignty, and chapter 3 covers the logical conclusion that the great political theorist Thomas Hobbes drew from Luther—namely, that sovereignty is magical and that the will of the sovereign *is* justice. Chapter 4 details how the thinkers who followed Hobbes desired to accept Hobbes's new science of politics, with its search for the transcendental ground of authority and rejection of justice as incarnated in personal relationships, while toning down its stark conclusion of the absolute power of the ruler to determine what is just. The result is modern morality, which searches for value apart from loyalty to others, and ends up diabolically undercutting that loyalty.

Finally, the last chapter shows how the philosophical concept of value as it was developed by nineteenth-century German thinkers recapitulates the basic tenets of liberalism going back to Luther and opposes the unique, irenic, personal good of friendship at every turn. The procrustean conceptualization of the good in terms of impersonal and partial values puts us at odds with each other. *The more values the less loyalty.* When life is a competition to be valued, we become paralyzed when we disagree: one man's morality is another's abomination.

What follows in the rest of this introduction is a review of the literature on values language, as well as on the concepts of loyalty, trust, and friendship. Scholars have typically focused on the creation of the philosophical concept of value in the nineteenth century, while ignoring the prehistory of the term.[8] The philosophers of value in the early twentieth century, the heyday of value theory, saw themselves as continuing the classical philosophical discourse on the good going back to the ancient Greeks.[9] But this misses what was new and different with this language. It was Martin Heidegger, in *Being and Time* and in other works, who first drew attention to the distortions in the concept of value.[10] A critique of values was at the very core of Heidegger's project; he wrote his habilitation thesis at the University of Freiburg in 1915 under Heinrich Rickert, one of the creators of the philosophical concept of value, and his first lectures after joining the philosophical faculty there—the courses that were the source of his enduring fame—were devoted to a consideration of value philosophy.[11]

For Heidegger, modernity has failed to attend to the ways in which the things we encounter become present to us and affect us. The qualitative differences of different types of being have a meaning on their own terms and as part of our lives as a whole. When we level them down to the lowest common denominator of bare existence, we miss the fundamental questions they pose to us and fall into an unreflective prejudice, aptly named by Heidegger as the mathematical prejudice. Then, only quantity matters as well as the (mathematical) method that produces it. The attempt to utilize a precise method to gain scientific control over present-at-hand "facts" by starting from axioms in a deductive system bypasses significance as it shows up in human life. It also leads to the hubristic pretention that we could attain a total grasp of facts, that everything could be laid out before us in the light of universal principles, or values in the modern sense (we get our term *axiom* from the equivalent for "value" in ancient Greek, ἄξιος). Heidegger traces this problem of value back to Plato. We will not engage that claim here, except to note in passing that it is perhaps not without significance that the community of wives and children under the name of political unity in the *Republic* indicates a very different approach to human loyalty than ours.

Heidegger's student Hans-Georg Gadamer (1900–2002) also studied under the great value philosopher Nicolai Hartmann (1882–1950). Gadamer gave a critique of the ethics of value in his inaugural lecture at Marburg in 1929, and he returned to the question in a number of later essays, arguing that the idea of values is disconnected from practical reality.[12] Talking about values gives us false expectations of being able to work out in advance correct arguments about action. Properly speaking, practical philosophy "does not claim to raise us to the point where we can freely survey an overarching heaven of values," he writes, but "rather, it exposes the supposed search for such a thing as a self-deception."[13] Values language subverts *ethos*—namely, a concrete network of friendships.[14]

A number of other thinkers have also expressed reservations with values.[15] There are, however, only three monographs on the topic. Edward Andrew sees that a critique of values must involve a critique of liberal pluralism, and he suggests employing a language of "principle" and "need" to more accurately express the common good.[16] Folke Werner shows how value language leaves no room for moral commandments or duties that are validated apart from human desires, and he decries how it has crowded out the more adequate language of goods and virtues.[17] Christof Breitsameter praises values discourse as upholding the individualism of the modern period yet wants both to restrict it to the legitimization of social norms and to avoid seeing values as ethical guides to action.[18]

Perhaps the best presentation of the case against values, however, has been sketched by Gadamer's collaborator Helmut Kuhn (1899–1991) in two rich essays.[19] Kuhn acknowledges that is helpful to speak of values because it awakens the question of purpose, unlike the language of facts or of exact science. Values can be thought of as primitive givenness; they are something we discover, not create, yet they have roots in the subject, not the object, in human nature as a form of being-for-another. Value is more concrete and durable, however, when we leave the realm of economic value and move to the realm of justice and, ultimately, to the sphere of personal relationships, though we are less able to define and rank-order them in this higher sphere. Ordering values apart from the whole of life is an artificial separation of action from its lived context. Life cannot be completely teleological; friendship, for instance, is a matter of sharing oneself with another person, not of creating a product. So ultimately *value* cannot replace *good*, because the former cannot express how being and the human being go together. Value language tends to make us satisfied with superficial explanations for our action, particularly questions of motivation, which involve not just correct desire but also the indirect question of how the world is constituted. These two questions are necessarily connected, since we encounter the good in living a life that is not just among and with others but also *for* others. An "in order to . . . " account of my actions—an account in value terms, a ready and clear explanation—has to be grounded in a deeper "because I . . . " explanation, for which there are no easy, pregiven paradigms. Figuring out who I am in relation to others is unique, personal, and more than a clear and present preference. Here the insufficiency of the term *values* is a symptom of a larger philosophical confusion. Values reflect an unjustified prejudice of modernity, the demand that everything be forced to appear as a phenomenon to consciousness.

Kuhn is right on the mark. Central phenomena of human life cannot be accommodated in the language of subject and object and of fact and value. "The category of 'values' acts like a lawn mower that cuts flat whole fields of meaning and leaves them characterless."[20] A betrayal of trust, for example, is an important and common phenomenon that is ignored by theorists.[21] Things like greetings, invitations, presents, and caresses all "reveal a logic of the gift that is quite different from mere factuality," as Hans Joas writes; he tells us we must confront the question "whether we can and ought to regard our lives as mere fact."[22] A "good" can be a gift, but not a "value," as Hermann von Coelln points out, and the categories of "empirical" and "transcendental" are inadequate to capture the former.[23] For von Coelln, modernity sees being as neutral facticity rather than as self-evidently good, so that even bodily organs can become seen as raw material that only become valuable when they serve the desires of a society.[24]

It is not enough to indict wrong or misleading language use. What is the alternative way of thinking and speaking about our fundamental commitments? "One obvious cure for the hollowness of 'values' talk is to seek out terms that are more concrete, more specific."[25] The Heideggerian language of the "clearing" is suggestive but abstract. At the end of his life, however, Heidegger wrote a letter to a French philosopher Henri Mongis that was reprinted as the preface to his *Heidegger et la critique de la notion de valeur*. There Heidegger defines the clearing, with reference to the poet Friedrich Hölderlin, as "the realm where we can be together trusting one another."[26] This book will take up this insight. That which is responsible for signification is our relationship to other people. It is our personal trust relationships that allow things to manifest themselves to us, an idea developed by Emmanuel Levinas, a student of Heidegger's.[27]

For us, the substance of the common good and human flourishing is found in personal relationships. The central insight of the emerging tradition of postliberalism is that politics is primarily a matter of "trust, dignity, and human relationships" rather than impersonal ideology.[28]

There is already a growing body of literature on *loyalty*, *trust*, and *friendship*. These concepts form a continuum: loyalty results in trust, which is necessary for friendship. The indispensability of friendship for the good life and for politics has been recognized since the dawn of Western reason.[29] Friendship is the measure of political success—"the isolated politician is the failed politician"[30]—and makes creativity in politics possible.[31] Certainly practical politicians still know the importance of friendship.[32] Political theorists, however, have forgotten it over the past five hundred years.[33] There was nothing written in English for over a hundred years on friendship; however, there has been a revival of interest since the 1980s in philosophy and other disciplines.[34] The word *trust* likewise suffered a protracted decline from 1850 to 1970 in American English, yet in the last half-century there has been a significant uptick in the use of the word.[35] The last decades have seen a renewed scholarly interest in these topics.[36] Current trust research, however, often views it superficially as the comportment of an individual subject, as "an attitude, an intention, a behavior and a dispositional orientation."[37] But in reality, it will be argued here, the phenomenon cannot be separated from a certain quality of personal relationships.

Awareness has grown concerning the importance of relationships to our thinking about morality.[38] Speaking only of interests and principles (as exemplified in the political theory of John Rawls) misses the allegiances that generate duties we do not choose. John Perry calls this a "turn to loyalty" and sees Michael Sandel, Stanley Fish, and William Galston as representative of such a turn, to which we could add Charles Taylor and Robert Putnam.[39] Kwame Appiah is right when he says that the "rigorous abjuration of partiality, the discarding of all local loyalties . . . is a hard sell. It is a position that has little grip upon our hearts,"[40] as is Perry when he writes, "We can better understand the conflicts like those of the culture wars if we see them as instances of conflicted loyalties."[41]

Our current language of morality and values fails to describe the world in which we actually live, act, and develop friendships. The first serious work on friendship since Emerson, a 1971 essay by Elizabeth Telfer, points to the self-defeating nature of treating friendship like a value, since "we attain the valuable relationship of friendship only when we cease to think about it and concentrate on the friend himself."[42] If Telfer is right, something is deeply wrong with our language. "The purpose of true morality is to eliminate certain conditions (suffering and grievous wrongs)," Saul Smilansky writes. "Yet only if those conditions exist can they call forth the moral actions that uniquely confer moral value." Since we would not wish for the bad conditions to exist just so moral value could be created, the resulting paradox entails that "morality is an 'enemy' of moral worth. Valuable moral behavior ends up resembling one of those mythological animals that eat their own tails, thus putting an end to the very condition for their own existence."[43] Michael Stocker famously viewed modern ethical theories as "schizophrenic" because they give reasons for acting that do not coincide with the motivations of people in real life, who act for the sake of and out of friendship. "It is perhaps clear enough by now," writes Stocker, "that recent ethicists have ignored large and extremely important areas of morality—e.g., that of personal relations."[44]

Up until recently there has not been a general follow-through on these insights, however. Stocker, for instance, never fulfilled the promise of his essay on modern ethical theories' schizophrenia and, not coincidentally, remains enthralled by value language.[45] To give another example, in George Fletcher's argument for the centrality of loyalty, the bedrock idea is not relationship but membership. Yet the deconstructive potential of loyalty is lost, though when it is turned into a static insider–outsider identity that is inevitably exclusive and violent, this does not entirely escape Fletcher: "Because the ethic of loyalty is so clearly at odds with universalist moral theory," he writes, "it becomes difficult to think of the latter as a corrective to the excesses of the former. It is almost as though one wished to apply the Copernican vision of the universe as a corrective for the weaknesses of the Ptolemaic system."[46]

In recent years there has been growing recognition of these failures of modern political thought to deal with personal relationships.[47] The rejection of liberalism's narrowness and the recovery of loyalty, trust, and friendship will enable us to recover a full understanding of the political. Politics—the element of suggestion and response in human action—is inescapable.[48] It cannot be replaced by morality, and we cannot evade the question, "Whom are we to trust?"[49] Politics is animated by the art of friendship.[50] The more we think in terms of morality, the less we understand our political situation. As Reinhardt Koselleck has shown in his essential *Critique and Crisis*, after the Enlightenment the real heirs to religion were moral doctrines, and since then, the tendency has been to conceive of politics in moral terms.[51] We cannot grasp something as basic as a political doctrine when we approach it in terms of "the old and barren" fact/value distinction.[52] Glen Newey is correct when he contends that much of contemporary Anglophone political philosophy is really antipolitical moral theory, which not only fails to understand how politics really operates but even aspires to a world without politics, with morality superseding it.[53] Our language and our theory need to reflect the vital importance of something of which political actors are to some degree already aware.[54] After all, loyalty and trust play a significant role both in democratization and the actual functioning of democracies.[55]

Recovering them will help us overcome the false impression given by values language. In the British context, political elites' use of the term "values" comes off as coercive and hectoring.[56] In America, values speak is the most prevalent in the so-called social issues, of which abortion is the most prominent. In no arena is the tendency more prevalent for people of opposing views to see each other as split into irreconcilable camps. Each side has its own values—on the one side, life and protection of the most vulnerable, on the other, individual autonomy and freedom of choice—facing each other as enemies in a culture war. No matter one's views, it is a lamentable situation for citizens to divide up into groups with mutual animosity for each other. The degree to which America is actually divided in a culture war is contested.[57] Nevertheless, the language of values and morality certainly encourages us to think that we are this divided, making it is more difficult to show loyalty to our fellow citizens. With a friend, we can be motivated to convince them of their error; with an enemy camp, on the other hand, we have every excuse to disengage. We thus rest content with our pet arguments, desiring only that a third-party power (in the United States, the courts) would enforce them on those who disagree.[58]

The less we see ourselves as enemies divided by opposing values and, instead, as fellow citizens to whom we ought to show loyalty even when we disagree, the less the liberal justification for sovereignty and morality seem plausible. The emerging school of postliberal political theory must emphasize a language of loyalty, trust, and friendship in an effort to overcome a view of politics as an ideological war.[59]

NOTES

1. See also Jan Nilbock, *Was Sind Werte? Philosophische Grundlagen zur Wertedebatte* (Norderstedt: GRIN, 2007), 5.

2. Gertrude Himmelfarb, *The De-Moralization of Society: From Victorian Virtues to Modern Values* (New York: Alfred A. Knopf, 1995), 9–10.

3. Google Ngram Viewer search performed June 17, 2021, https://books.google.com/ngrams.

4. Edmund Husserl's first North American student, Winthrop Bell, spent the Great War in a prisoner of war camp, Ruhleben, in Berlin, where he gave lectures on the philosophy of values for the other prisoners. In his diary, he noted that forty people were at the first session, but he noticed a lot of them looking bored. Diary entry for Thursday, May 23, 1918, "Notebooks—[ca. 1914]–1918," Winthrop Pickard Bell fonds, Mt. Allison University Archives. I am grateful to Jason Bell for alerting me to this item.

In the postwar era, the use of "values" was noticeably more frequent. Mentions of "American values" in the *New York Times* shows a sharp increase from 1965 (when it was not used) to 2001 (when the phrase was used in 0.1 percent of all articles). NY Times Chronicle, http://chronicle.nytlabs.com/, accessed May 13, 2016. The phrase "family values" showed an increase in the 1980s after it was an issue in the 1980 presidential campaign. Betty Friedan, *The Second Stage* (Cambridge: Harvard University Press, 1998), 98. The 1980 Republican platform stated, "We will work for the appointment of judges at all levels of the judiciary who respect traditional family values and the sanctity of innocent human life." Republican Party Platform of 1980 Online, The American Presidency Project, https://www.presidency.ucsb.edu/node/273420.

5. "A modern statesman is supposed to keep his 'private' concerns strictly separate from his 'public' responsibilities. And friendship is supposed to be strictly private. An act of power exerted on behalf of a friend, if publicly known, might bring indignation upon the power-holder." Horst Hutter, *Politics as Friendship: The Origins of Classical Notions of Politics in the Theory and Practice of Friendship* (Waterloo, Ontario: Wilfrid Laurier University Press, 1978), 1. "To be moral is to respect others as having equal value to oneself, and as having an equal right to pursue their own interests. One acts contrary to morality in preferring one's own interests, or the interests of those whom one likes and is connected to, simply because they are one's own, or one's friends', interests. Moral principles must be universal, or universalizable. They must be valid for all and compelling to any rational moral agent." Lawrence A. Blum, *Friendship, Altruism, and Morality* (London: Routledge & Kegan Paul, 1980), 3. "[W]e hardly even lament loyalty nowadays. We're inclined to look at it with suspicion, leery that loyalty is an excuse for nepotism and other varieties of corrupt favoritism." Felten, *Loyalty: The Vexing Virtue* (New York: Simon & Schuster, 2011), 267.

6. Gerd Althoff writes that "despite all the changes in the political and mental landscape since the Middle Ages, we can still observe the basic phenomenon of friendship networks, and the mutual support which they provide, everywhere around us today. It seems almost to represent something like an anthropological constant." Gerd Althoff, "Friendship and Political Order," in *Friendship and Medieval Europe*, ed. Julian Haseldine (Thrupp: Sutton, 1999), 100.

7. Namely, that of the state and the market, "inevitabilities to which we have no choice but to submit." Patrick J. Deneen, *Why Liberalism Failed* (New Haven: Yale University Press, 2018), 16, 32, 34.

8. E.g., Herbert Schnädelbach, *Philosophy in Germany, 1831–1933*, trans. Eric Matthews (Cambridge: Cambridge University Press, 1984), chap. 6: "Values." Hermann T. Krobath, *Werte: Ein Streifzug Durch Philosophie und Wissenschaft* (Würzburg: Königshausen & Neumann, 2009). Abraham Edel, "The Concept of Value and Its Travels in Twentieth-Century America," in *Values and Value Theory in Twentieth-Century America: Essays in Honor of Elizabeth Flower*, ed. Murray G. Murphey and Ivar Berg (Philadelphia: Temple University Press, 1988), 12–36.

9. Folke Werner, *Vom Wert der Werte: Die Tauglichkeit des Wertbegriffs als Orientierung gebende Kategorie menschlicher Lebensführung Eine Studie aus evangelischer Perspektive* (Münster: LIT, 2002), 36. Two representative examples include John Laird, *The Idea of Value* (Cambridge: Cambridge University Press, 1929) and

Oskar Kraus, *Die Werttheorien: Geschichte und Kritik* (Brünn: Rudolf M. Rohrer, 1937).

10. Martin Heidegger, *Sein und Zeit*, 4th ed. (Tübingen: Max Niemeyer, 1977), 99–100. Martin Heidegger, *Being and Time*, trans. John Macquarrie and Edward Robinson (New York: Harper & Row, 1962), 131–33. Martin Heidegger, *Pathmarks* (Cambridge: Cambridge University Press, 1998), 174, GA9 227. Martin Heidegger, *The Question Concerning Technology and Other Essays*, trans. William Lovitt (New York: Harper & Row, 1977), 80–108, 142; GA5 237–63, 101–2.

11. Martin Heidegger, *Towards the Definition of Philosophy*, trans. Ted Sadler (New York: Continuum, 2008), GA56/57 121–203. Heidegger's reputation was based on the courses he taught in the eight years before *Being and Time* appeared, starting with this one. Theodore Kisiel, *The Genesis of Heidegger's Being and Time* (Berkeley: University of California Press, 1993), 15–16.

12. The essays—"The Ontological Problem of Value" (1971), "The Ethics of Value and Practical Philosophy" (1982), and "Friendship and Self-Knowledge: Reflections on the Role of Friendship in Greek Ethics" (1985)—are collected in Hans-Georg Gadamer, *Hermeneutics, Religion, and Ethics* (New Haven: Yale University Press, 1999). "This is the decisive charge against the kind of being that the realm of value possesses," he writes, that "normative power does not accrue to it in the universality of phenomenological intuition but in a concretization appropriate to the situation, one that always finds the agent in the midst of doing something and from there determines appropriate behavior." Gadamer, *Hermeneutics, Religion, and Ethics,* 71.

13. Gadamer, *Hermeneutics, Religion, and Ethics*, 75.

14. "Starting from modern concepts it is admittedly difficult to define the place of friendship," Gadamer writes. "It is a good bestowed on us, not a 'value' of which we are conscious." Gadamer, *Hermeneutics, Religion, and Ethics*, 117.

15. For example, Hannah Arendt, *The Human Condition*, 2nd ed. (Chicago: University of Chicago Press, 1958), 163–66. (When she would use the term, Arendt would put it in scare quotes, e.g. in "Thinking and Moral Considerations," in *Responsibility and Judgment*, ed. Jerome Kohn [New York: Schocken Books, 2003], 159–89.) Maurice Blanchot, *Friendship*, trans. Elizabeth Rottenberg (Stanford: Stanford University Press, 1971), 93–97. Robert Sokolowski, *Phenomenology of the Human Person* (Cambridge: Cambridge University Press, 2008), 189. Allan Bloom, *The Closing of the American Mind: How Higher Education Has Failed Democracy and Impoverished the Souls of Today's Students* (New York: Simon and Schuster, 1987) 60–61, 141–48, 194–216. Rémi Brague, *The Kingdom of Man: Genesis and Failure of the Modern Project*, trans. Paul Seaton (Notre Dame: University of Notre Dame Press, 2018), 98–100. Harvey C. Mansfield, Jr., *America's Constitutional Soul* (Baltimore: John Hopkins University Press, 1991), 13. Robert Spaemann, "The Dictatorship of Values," *Project Syndicate*, 2001, https://www.project-syndicate.org/commentary/-the-dictatorship-of-values. Iain T. Benson, "Acton Lecture 2017: Civic Virtues and the Politics of 'Full Drift Ahead'" (Sydney: The Centre for Independent Studies, 2017), https://www.cis.org.au/app/uploads/2017/06/op155.pdf?. George Grant, *Time as History*, ed. William Christian (Toronto: University of Toronto Press, 1995), 58. Pierre Manent, *Beyond Radical Secularism: How France and the Christian*

West Should Respond to the Islamic Challenge, trans. Ralph C. Hancock (South Bend: St. Augustine's Press, 2016), 95–97. Hermann von Coelln, *Von den Gütern zu den Werten: Versuch einer Kritik aller Wertphilosophie* (Essen: Die Blaue Eule, 1996); Eberhard Straub, *Zur Tyrannei der Werte* (Stuttgart: Klett-Cotta, 2010). Nigel Walter, "From Values to Narrative: A New Foundation for the Conservation of Historic Buildings," *International Journal of Heritage Studies* 20, no. 6 (2014): 634–50, http://www.tandfonline.com/doi/abs/10.1080/13527258.2013.828649. Also cf. Frederick Beiser's exposition of Heinrich Rickert's philosophy of value, Frederick C. Beiser, *The German Historicist Tradition* (Oxford: Oxford University Press, 2011), 414–29, 439–41. Oddly, Beiser gives Max Weber a pass in the last chapter of that book, even though his theory is heavily indebted to Rickert and has the same problems. For a better take on Weber, see also Eric Voegelin, *The New Science of Politics: An Introduction* (Chicago: University of Chicago Press, 1987), 13–22.

16. Edward G. Andrew, *The Genealogy of Values* (Lanham: Rowman and Littlefield, 1995).

17. Werner, *Vom Wert der Werte*.

18. Christof Breitsameter, *Individualisierte Perfektion: Vom Wert der Werte* (Paderborn: Ferdinand Schöningh, 2009).

19. Kuhn, "Werte—Eine Urgegebenheit," in *Philosophische Anthropologie, Zweiter Teil*, ed. Hans-Georg Gadamer and Paul Vogler (Stuttgart, 1975), 343–73. Helmut Kuhn, "Fact and Value in Ethics," *Philosophy and Phenomenological Research* 2, no. 4 (1942): 501–510.

20. Langdon Winner, "Brandy, Cigars, and Human Values," in *The Whale and the Reactor: The Search for Limits in an Age of High Technology* (Chicago: University of Chicago Press, 1986), 158.

21. Cf. Collin O'Neil, "Betraying Trust," in *The Philosophy of Trust*, ed. Paul Faulkner and Thomas Simpson (Oxford: Oxford University Press, 2017), 70.

22. Hans Joas, *The Sacredness of the Person: A New Genealogy of Human Rights*, trans. Alex Skinner (Washington, DC: Georgetown University Press, 2013), 158–59.

23. von Coelln, *Von Den Gütern Zu Den Werten*, 21.

24. von Coelln, 24–26.

25. "Whenever we feel the urge to say 'human values' or 'social values,' perhaps we should immediately substitute a phrase closer to our intended meaning. If we mean 'motives,' then let's talk about them. If we mean 'consumer preferences,' then say so. . . . But this superficial cure sidesteps the larger malady. A great many people, including some with considerable social power, seem to have lost the ability to link the specific, concrete conditions of their own work to any reasonable conception of human well-being. The question just never seems to come up." Winner, "Brandy, Cigars, and Human Values," 162.

26. Martin Heidegger, "Letter—Forward," in Henri Mongis, *Heidegger et la critique de la notion de valeur: la destruction de la fondation métaphysique* (The Hague: Martinus Nijhoff, 1976), viii.

27. Levinas maintained that *Being and Time* was one of the best five philosophical texts of all time. His sharp words for his former teacher have led many scholars to misinterpret his work. Emmanuel Levinas, *Ethics and Infinity: Conversations with*

Philippe Nemo, trans. Richard Cohen (Pittsburgh: Duquesne University Press, 1985), 37. The clearing for Heidegger is that which gives the world of manifestation but which itself cannot be made manifest. This is insofar as our human situation is one in which total, intimate trust—"proximity" for Levinas—is lacking. It cannot come to light because everyone—what Levinas calls the "third"—is untrustworthy to some degree. Trust or the clearing withdraws; we therefore have to make do with discursive rationality. The concealing of this withdrawal is evident in the modern project, which tries to fashion a rational substitute for total trust, the transcendental.

28. Adrian Pabst, *Postliberal Politics* (Cambridge: Polity, 2021), 6.

29. Especially Aristotle's incomparable chapter 8 on friendship in the *Nicomachean Ethics*, in *The Basic Works of Aristotle*, ed. Richard McKeon, trans. W. D. Ross (New York: Random House, 1941), 1155a–1163b.

30. John von Heyking, *The Form of Politics: Aristotle and Plato on Friendship* (Montreal: McGill-Queen's University Press, 2016), 7. Tilo Schabert argues that friendship is necessary for political success and gives examples from presidential politics. Tilo Schabert, *Boston Politics: The Creativity of Power* (Berlin: Walter de Gruyter, 1989), 120–21n34.

31. Cf. John von Heyking, "Friendship as Precondition and Consequence of Creativity in Politics," in *The Primacy of Persons in Politics: Empiricism and Political Philosophy*, ed. John von Heyking and Thomas Heilke (Washington DC: The Catholic University of America Press, 2013), 79–106. "Our everyday friendships provide a vital link to the world which is part of us and of which we are a part. To lose that link is to lose our potential for collective action." Jon Nixon, *Hannah Arendt and the Politics of Friendship* (London: Bloomsbury, 2015), 189.

32. Pennsylvania Senator and US Senate Minority Leader Hugh Scott gave this advice to aspiring politicians: "One of the greatest assets you can have is friends—and lots of them." Hugh D. Scott, Jr., *How to Go into Politics* (New York: John Day, 1949), 50.

33. John von Heyking and Richard Avramenko, "Introduction: The Persistence of Friendship in Political Life," in *Friendship and Politics: Essays in Political Thought*, ed. John von Heyking and Richard Avramenko (Notre Dame: University of Notre Dame Press, 2008), 1. P. E. Digeser writes that "there is a modern theoretical neglect of friendship in the West and this neglect was probably overdetermined by such factors as the emergence of the large, impersonal state, industrialization, Weberian rationalism, a culture of rights, the increased mobility of individuals, and nationalism." P. E. Digeser, *Friendship Reconsidered: What It Means, and How It Matters to Politics* (New York: Columbia University Press, 2016), 283–84n1.

34. Michael Pakaluk, "Introduction," in *Other Selves: Philosophers on Friendship*, ed. Michael Pakaluk (Indianapolis: Hackett, 1991), 248. Heather Devere, "Amity Update: The Academic Debate on Friendship and Politics" 1 (2013): 5–33.

35. Google Ngram Viewer search performed March 8, 2017, https://books.google.com/ngrams.

36. The watershed was a Cambridge seminar that was published as an edited volume in 1988. Diego Gambetta, ed., *Trust: Making and Breaking Cooperative Relations* (New York: Basil Blackwell, 1988). The *Russell Sage Foundation Series*

on Trust has been publishing monographs since 2008, the *Routledge Studies in Trust Research* since 2018, and new books and journals have appeared in this decade; for example, Paul Faulkner and Thomas Simpson, eds., *The Philosophy of Trust* (Oxford: Oxford University Press, 2017). Since 2011, there is a *Journal for Trust Research* that publishes biannually. *Amity: The Journal of Friendship Studies* started in 2013.

37. Jared D. Harris, Adrian A. C. Keevil, and Andrew C. Wicks, "Public Trust in the Institution of Business," in *Handbook of Advances in Trust Research*, ed. Reinhard Bachmann and Akbar Zaheer (Cheltenham, UK: Edward Elgar, 2013), 205.

38. For reviews of this work, cf. Samuel Scheffler, "Morality and Reasonable Partiality," in *Partiality and Impartiality: Morality, Special Relationships, and the Wider World*, ed. Brian Feltham and John Cottingham (Oxford: Oxford University Press, 2010), 114–24, and Simon Keller, *Partiality* (Princeton: Princeton University Press, 2013), 12–13, 46–48.

39. John Perry, *The Pretenses of Loyalty: Locke, Liberal Theology, and American Political Theology* (Oxford: Oxford University Press, 2011), 17–47.

40. Kwame Anthony Appiah, *The Ethics of Identity* (Princeton: Princeton University Press, 2005), 221.

41. Perry, *The Pretenses of Loyalty: Locke, Liberal Theology, and American Political Theology*, 23.

42. Elizabeth Telfer, "Friendship," in *Other Selves: Philosophers on Friendship*, ed. Michael Pakaluk (Indianapolis: Hackett, 1991), 267.

43. Saul Smilansky, *10 Moral Paradoxes* (Malden, MA: Blackwell, 2007), 88.

44. Michael Stocker, "The Schizophrenia of Modern Ethical Theories," *The Journal of Philosophy* 73, no. 14 (1976): 464.

45. Cf. Michael Stocker, *Plural and Conflicting Values* (Oxford: Clarendon Press, 1990).

46. George P. Fletcher, *Loyalty: An Essay on the Morality of Relationships* (New York: Oxford University Press, 1993), 165.

47. Patrick Deneen's *Why Liberalism Failed* is notable, as is Alasdair MacIntyre's *Ethics in the Conflicts of Modernity*. Alasdair MacIntyre, *Ethics in the Conflicts of Modernity: An Essay on Desire, Practical Reasoning, and Narrative* (Cambridge: Cambridge University Press, 2016). Another exception is Karen Jones. Karen Jones, "'But I Was Counting On You!,'" in *The Philosophy of Trust*, ed. Paul Faulkner and Thomas Simpson (Oxford: Oxford University Press, 2017), 90–108. The thinkers of radical Orthodoxy—John Milbank, William Cavanaugh, and Andrew Jones—have also begun to show positively how human constructions can be revelatory of a common good not based on exclusion and violence. John Milbank, *Theology and Social Theory: Beyond Secular Reason*, 2nd ed. (Malden, MA: Blackwell, 2006). William T. Cavanaugh, *The Myth of Religious Violence: Secular Ideology and the Roots of Modern Conflict* (Oxford: Oxford University Press, 2009). Andrew Willard Jones, *Before Church and State: A Study of Social Order in the Sacramental Kingdom of St. Louis IX* (Steubenville, Ohio: Emmaus Academic, 2017). Only when taking this positive turn can we see how helpful the postmodern deconstruction of the fundamental concepts of modernity really is. Cf. Milbank, *Theology and Social Theory: Beyond Secular Reason*, 312–14.

48. This is Bertrand de Jouvenel's definition of politics in the most underrated book of twentieth century political theory. Bertrand de Jouvenel, *The Pure Theory of Politics* (Indianapolis: Liberty Fund, 2000), 91–125.

49. Cf. Harry Collins and Robert Evans, *Rethinking Expertise* (Chicago: University of Chicago Press, 2007), 139. While trust has been a theme in the literature on voting behavior, a lot of it has been on the aggregate level. Aaron Martin, *Young People and Politics: Political Engagement in the Anglo-American Democracies* (New York: Routledge, 2012), 11–12. There has not been a lot of discussion in political science of social trust as a *political good*, as a goal and measure of political action. As Mark Warren put it in 1999, "It was not self-evident until recently that there might be important questions to be asked about the relationship between democracy and trust." Mark E. Warren, ed., *Democracy and Trust* (Cambridge: Cambridge University Press, 1999), 1. Russell Hardin writes, "Philosophers, economists, psychologists, and political theorists, especially those in the tradition of John Locke, had addressed trust and have given interesting insights; but there is surprisingly little in all of these disciplines. Discussions of trust are almost entirely missing from moral philosophy." Russell Hardin, *Trust and Trustworthiness* (New York: Russell Sage Foundation, 2002), xix. Sociology has addressed it, most notably in Robert Putnam's classic *Bowling Alone*. Robert D. Putnam, *Bowling Alone: The Collapse and Revival of American Community* (New York: Simon & Schuster, 2000).

50. Schabert, *Boston Politics: The Creativity of Power*, 112.

51. Reinhart Koselleck, *Critique and Crisis: Enlightenment and the Pathogenesis of Modern Society* (Cambridge: The MIT Press, 1988).

52. Bernard Crick, *In Defence of Politics* (London: Bloomsbury, 2013), 17.

53. Glen Newey, *After Politics: The Rejection of Politics in Contemporary Liberal Philosophy* (New York: Palgrave, 2001), 2.

54. It could be argued that politicians already follow the advice to take values less seriously. While it is true that politicians in the United States "would rather discuss national values than anything else," an analysis of campaign speech showed that their words were more centered on human relationships than the rhetoric of citizens or the press. It concludes that "political campaigners are more buoyant, more grounded, and more relationally concerned than either the people or the press. . . . Campaigners eschew genuinely philosophical discussions by offering solutions to problems they can solve rather than discussing those they cannot." Roderick P. Hart, *Campaign Talk: Why Elections Are Good For Us* (Princeton: Princeton University Press, 2000), 142. Politicians are one thing, elites generally another, however. In the United States, elites "have either not cared about or been remarkably oblivious to the group identities that matter most to large segments of ordinary Americans, including people they are trying to help." Amy Chua, *Political Tribes: Group Instinct and the Fate of Nations* (New York: Penguin, 2018), 3.

55. Charles Tilly has shown how trust networks need to be integrated with public politics for democratization to occur. Charles Tilly, *Contention and Democracy in Europe, 1650–2000* (Cambridge: Cambridge University Press, 2004), 15–17, and Charles Tilly, *Trust and Rule* (Cambridge: Cambridge University Press, 2005), 12–17. The political field in democracies remains constituted by loyalties and reliant on trust.

"No claim can be complete without an argument; yet, even with the best arguments, no claim can go very far in politics without some connection to a particular social group, some way of life that generates particular needs and aspirations." Russell Muirhead, "The Case For Party Loyalty," in *Loyalty*, ed. Sanford Levinson, Joel Parker, and Paul Woodruff (New York: New York University Press, 2013), 252. "A number of studies have shown that when legislators are deciding how to vote on bills, they rely most heavily on information conveyed orally by colleagues whom they trust and whom they regard as particularly well-informed, such as bill sponsors and committee chairs. More sophisticated information probably influences legislative voting through the medium of these well-informed legislators more than through direct access by individual legislators to technological tools." Richard A. Stafford et al., *The Temple Papers on the Pennsylvania General Assembly, vol. IV: A Discussion of Topics Related to the Continuing Evolution of the Pennsylvania General Assembly* (Philadelphia: Temple Institute for Public Affairs, 2012), 41. Even superficial, generalized trust is associated with easier political decision making. Eric Uslaner writes that "trust in others helps make governments work better. Congress was more productive when the American public was more trusting." Eric M. Uslaner, *The Moral Foundations of Trust* (Cambridge: Cambridge University Press, 2002), 8.

56. "Precisely because liberalism seeks to keep specific conceptions of the good out of political discourse, its version of 'British values' can only be a set of fairly abstract universals that float free from specific, embedded relationships and from any substantive moral vision. In consequence, integration policy develops a coercive aspect. It will have to police the adherence of diverse ethnic and religious groups to a set of abstract 'values' they have had little or no role in formulating. Not surprisingly, this leads to politicians' being experienced as hectoring and superior." Angus Ritchie, *Inclusive Populism: Creating Citizens in the Global Age* (Notre Dame: University of Notre Dame Press, 2019), 106–107. Ritchie advocates for "negotiated pluralism," which focuses "not on abstract norms but on concrete relationships, that is, on the ways in which citizens, in particular times and places, seek to build a common life and discern a common good." Ritchie, *Inclusive Populism,* 107. A focus on values in England over the past two decades "side-lined and replaced," the idea of the "citizen as a participatory member of their communities, and of Citizenship education as concerned with forming core moral and civic virtues needed for such participation." Andrew Peterson and David Civil, "Virtues, values and the fracturing of civic and moral virtue in citizenship education policy in England," *Educational Review*, 12. DOI: 10.1080/00131911.2021.2023105.

57. Cf. Morris P. Fiorina, *Culture War?: The Myth of a Polarized America* (New York: Longman, 2004).

58. The program of judicial activism in the U.S. has its roots, however, in political incentives. Cf. Keith E. Whittington, *Political Foundations of Judicial Supremacy: The Presidency, the Supreme Court, and Constitutional Leadership in U.S. History* (Princeton: Princeton University Press, 2007). A lot of money is made on keeping Americans divided, which prevents a political solution (which could come through the Exceptions Clause of the U.S. Constitution). "You know, I always said there were some battles that nobody wanted to win," said one of the most powerful figures in

modern Pennsylvania politics, Vince Fumo, "and abortion was one of them because both factions—one side or the other—were making a damn good living at wrapping up their base and making big salaries as executive directors." Brad Bumsted and Paula Knudsen, "Powering Down: Former State Sen. Vincent J. Fumo Talks about Changes in the Political Climate since His Time Spent in Prison," *The Caucus* (July 17, 2018), 7.

59. Postliberalism has emerged in the last half decade as a school of political theory. In 2016 two important books were published: Alasdair MacIntyre's *Ethics in the Conflicts of Modernity*, and John Milbank and Adrian Pabst's *The Politics of Virtue: Post-Liberalism and the Human Future* (London: Rowman & Littlefield, 2016). A year later, British journalist David Goodhart published *The Road to Somewhere: The Populist Revolt and the Future of Politics* (London: Hurst, 2017), where he contrasted the mobile elites from "Anywhere" with the marginalized Trump and Brexit voters from "Somewhere." In 2018 Patrick Deneen published a book to wide acclaim, *Why Liberalism Failed*, and New Polity was founded—a think tank dedicated to developing a postliberal worldview. In 2019 Fred Dallmayr published *Post-Liberalism: Recovering a Shared World* (Oxford: Oxford University Press, 2019), and 2021 saw the publication of both D. C. Schindler's *The Politics of the Real* (Steubenville, Ohio: New Polity, 2021), and Adrian Pabst's *Postliberal Politics: The Coming Era of Renewal* (Cambridge: Polity, 2021).

Chapter 1

"Morality" and Personal Relationships

We speak about "values" today in large part because of Friedrich Nietzsche (1844–1900).[1] As Martin Heidegger writes, "[O]nly after the dissemination of the writings of Nietzsche did talk of values become popular."[2] During most of his lifetime, Nietzsche was ignored and his books sold very poorly. Only in 1888 did he start attracting attention after a Danish literary critic gave a series of lectures on his thought.[3] After he went insane the following year, Nietzsche's story captured the imaginations of the reading public; his publisher reissued his books, and they finally started selling well, to the point where, by the start of World War I, Nietzsche was so popular that thousands of copies of his magnum opus *Thus Spoke Zarathustra* were printed and handed out to German troops.[4] Nietzsche's rise explains the entry of value language into the scholarly and popular lexicon.[5] More specifically, he popularized the term in the *plural*; prior to Nietzsche, no one would understand values to express moral beliefs or social excellences; the term "virtue" was used instead.[6] After Nietzsche, "Good and evil now for the first time appeared as 'values.'"[7]

Nietzsche also famously opposed the concept of morality, a campaign that began with his 1881 book *Daybreak* and came to full fruition with his influential *Genealogy of Morals* in 1887. The power of Nietzsche's arguments has to do with his focus on the type of relationships involved in morality. In particular, he exposes how moralism involves envy coupled with impotence, *ressentiment* against another person who has what I desire. When I am in competition with another person but lack the power to get the better of him, it is natural to look for another way to satisfy my rancor—namely, by redefining what he does as immoral. This redescription is the "slave revolt in morals." The more we have this type of slavish relationship with others, the more we will believe in the concept of morality.

This chapter will develop this line of thought and show that morality leads us into various illusions. Far from escaping these illusions, however, Nietzsche's campaign against morality failed because of his attachment to values, which are the core of morality. Far from overcoming morality, Nietzsche is the consummate moralist, revaluing values to try to move us to the true morality, rather than moving beyond it altogether. Nietzsche's noble morality clarifies what is at the core of all moral thinking—namely, the domination of the high over the low. Morality stops with this domination and is unable to integrate high and low into one common good.

THE INSUFFICIENCY OF MORALITY

After Nietzsche, the insufficiency of the language of morality has not escaped the sharpest minds. Hannah Arendt, for instance, confronted us with how strange it should seem to us that "morality" is the word we use to distinguish between good and evil, and Elizabeth Anscombe famously wanted us to stop using the word "moral" to mean "good."[8]

When we refer to *morality* today, we mean a universal standard of correct conduct which makes someone good. This meaning is only found in modern times.[9] Classically, the concept of moral virtue referred to a *part* of what it means to be a good person; namely, checking one's appetites, which cannot be the sum total of human excellence, since we are not controlling our impulses just for the sake of it but rather for the sake of intellectual virtue and, ultimately, for the sake of our common life in the city. The Latin root *mores* meant habits or customs of individuals or communities. In antiquity, the term combined two senses that we separate out today, descriptive and prescriptive: *mores* were the actual customs or practices that are in place; the word could be used to designate those practices as well as to praise or condemn them. To describe the customs and practices of a people is, at the same time, to say that which *should* be assimilated to, were someone to go there to live among them. The *ought* is not separate from the *is*; the ways of a people are not a neutral facticity, since insofar as we interact with them, we cannot be indifferent to their customs. *Mores* are not neutral, because we cannot be neutral to other people. Nor are they perfect, the sum total of everything, since they can be bad and are therefore subject to criticism and improvement by relating them to a greater whole—namely, the greater social ordering which includes still other people. The Medieval period kept this usage of antiquity; moral philosophy studied a part of human life while orienting itself towards the whole of social and human existence, including politics and economics and, ultimately, theology.[10]

Our term *morality* comes from a technical philosophical term found in Aristotle, namely his coining the word *ethics*. However, as Oscar Wilde reminds us, "τα ηθικα does not mean Ethics, nor τα πολιτικα politics" for Aristotle; "rather we should say that he took a comprehensive view of life as an entirety, a whole . . . ηθικα [is] not Ethics but the formation of character, and to produce good citizens of excellent character is the object of the statesman (πολιτικὸς νομοθέτης)."[11] Cicero translated Aristotle's word "ethics" as *philosophia moralis*, and this is the provenance of our term *morality*. It is notable that in order to talk about human character, it is not necessary to have this word. The term *ethics* was not used by Plato, who nevertheless had a lot to say about human character and habits.[12] In addition, the term *moral* traditionally referred to fitting our character to the society we live in, to the acceptable standards of behavior. It meant something that is social, or related to the common good.[13] In English, the earliest use of the term came in the phrase "moral virtue," a translation of the post-classical Latin term *virtus moralis*, which came from Aristotle's ἀρετὴ ἠθική, which he contrasted with "intellectual excellence" (ἀρετὴ διανοητική). Moral virtue for Aristotle is impulse control, a necessary part of living a good life—but only a part: controlling one's inclinations is not the sum and purpose of life, but rather, it is for the sake of developing one's higher talents.[14] Moral excellence, character-related virtues, are but one element of human goodness; it is not that goodness itself *tout court*. It cannot therefore be contrasted with evil, but rather with other types of excellence, be they intellectual virtue or theological virtue, which are also needed for a person to be good.

For classical thinkers such as Plato, Aristotle, or Augustine, man is never considered good because he is related to an abstract code of conduct. For them the city is man writ large; the order of the soul and the order in the city are the same.[15] Man is a political being; there is no human excellence apart from the city in which one lives and the consequences of his behavior within and for the city.[16] The Indo-European root of the word "ethics," **swedh*, referred to the whole ways of being of a people.[17] In ancient Greece, "morality meant the goodness of the community."[18] To achieve full excellence as a human being, and not just partial excellence at a specific task, one had to be *just*.

Justice is the virtue that enables us to act correctly no matter the set of relationships within which we happen to find ourselves. Both the Hebrew and Greek traditions converge on this understanding. The Hebrew understanding of justice—the terms are *tzedakah* (צְדָקָה) and *mishpat* (מִשְׁפָּט)—refers to fulfilling the obligations that a relationship involves.[19] It is likewise noteworthy that the term "faith," *emunah* (אֱמוּנָה), does not mean believing a proposition is true, but trusting and showing fidelity to a person.[20] God counted Abraham as just because Abraham trusted in him. "Nowhere else but in ancient Israel has there been found such persistent and insistent emphasis on doing, on carrying out, not merely on believing in, the teachings of God's spokesmen."[21] The Greek notion of virtue or excellence (ἀρετή) for the human being as such, viz. justice (δικαιοσύνη), is acting well given your situation vis-à-vis others. In the fictional city of Plato's *Republic*, the content of virtue changes according to the relationships involved: the virtue of the productive class, shared with the ruling class, is temperance; of the warrior class, courage; and of the ruling class, wisdom. Justice is the proper ordering of all three. For Aristotle, in politics natural justice is changeable, something that makes no sense if we consider justice as abstracted from relationships, a matter of the content of the suggestion and not the person doing the suggestion.[22] For both the Hebrew and Greek conceptions, in order to be just, one must first learn what the set of relationships is within which one must act, in order then to act well given these relationships. The proper object of justice is the community, since the outcome of justice, the excellent performance, is necessarily always a communal performance. The authors of the biblical texts always contextualize justice in terms of personal relationships. The obligation to use our gifts for the benefit of all is brought out in the parable of the talents in the gospels of Matthew and Luke; the obligation to forgive others is at the center of the parable of the unforgiving servant in Matthew. Justice as the quality of personal relationships is intensified for the followers of Jesus, as God is now revealed as having taken on a human face, called his followers "friends," and made the mark of his disciples the way in which they treat their neighboring human beings, even to the point of embracing a loving relationship with their enemies.

Being a good person does not just mean controlling one's passions; it means being a part of a whole network of relationships and justly balancing them. Justice, the excellence of a person as such, is always a matter of personal relationships. A person is a constellation of relationships.[23] Who a person is, as a whole, is always a matter of all of these relationships. Any attempt to fully know someone's character requires getting the testimony of the people who interact with him. If a person has a good relationship with some people, but an abusive relationship with others, for instance, then making out his character requires coming to terms with both data points. If I treat some people very well, people who have power over me perhaps, but I treat others terribly, people over whom I have power, then any honest assessment of my behavior will have to take that into account.

"The realm of human affairs," writes Hannah Arendt, "consists of the web of human relationships which exists wherever men live together."[24] In a social order, each person depends on others. "Without ties of loyalty, authority, and fraternity, no society as a whole, and none of its institutions, could long function."[25] This task engages a person on many different levels, not just that of self-control. What matters in social relationships is always the question,

"To which community do I belong?" The big questions of life—who am I going to marry, how am I to deal with a dysfunctional family, what am I going to do with my life and the basic questions of religion and politics and economics—are all bound up with the question, "To whom should I grant my loyalty?" This is a question that matters, that of my concrete loyalties and their nature. Is such and such a relationship healthy? Does it contribute to my overall happiness? Does it exclude or persecute marginal third parties? Does it contribute or detract from the wider social order? The question, "To whom am I going to be loyal?" is never easy or simple to answer, but it is always *meaningful*, much more so than my ranking according to an abstract morality. St. Augustine, for instance, never speaks of human goodness as summed up in a moral code, but rather as a matter of membership in two different communities, the city of God and the earthly city.[26]

Anscombe therefore was right to conclude that using the terms "morally right" and "morally wrong" is a mistake, and that we should prefer instead the language of "just" and "unjust"—a language more appropriate to a communal context where it is not a matter of our individual behavior considered in the abstract but of our engagement with the people around us. When we act with and react to others, we can see that our actions have consequences; we can feel our responsibility only in the encounter with another person, not in an abstract theory. We can never really be responsible to a moral code, only to a person. "People act much worse under shelter of anonymity, as parts of a faceless mass, than they do when they are watched and made accountable as individuals."[27]

Morality is too general to deal with unrepeatable persons.[28] It can only be the measure of repeatable actions—perhaps fitting for the virtue of self-control, for example, but not at all for the complicated decisions that form a political biography. The biography of political actors is illustrative in this connection, since they can face the choice between bad options and worse options. How do we know they chose wisely? The verdict of documented history can miss the silent hero who prevents disaster that would otherwise have taken place.[29] Consequentialism is attractive precisely due to the failure of any moral code to account for unique acts.[30] Recent decades furnish examples of erroneous judgments. Who now castigates Saddam Hussein or Muammar Gaddafi? Yet absent the worse option (that unfortunately in these cases did take place), all we see is their dictatorships—that is, something condemnable when considered as repeatable in the abstract. One might say *après nous, le deluge*, but we can never know the truth of unique cases if we stick with morality.

Finally, the imperative force of morality is, at bottom, always personal solidarity. The question that haunts morality is always, "Why do I want to be moral at all?" The answer always comes back to loyalty. If a good friend of mine has an opinion on the best type of conduct, I will try to abide by it on some level. But if I do not have any loyalty to someone who is proffering a moral theory, I will ignore it or give it only academic attention.

In his great work *Formalism in Ethics*, Max Scheler had a line that did not make it into print: "[E]thics is 'damned bloody stuff,'" he wrote in the manuscript, "and if it gives me no directions about how 'I' should be and live in this social and historical context—well, what is it good for?"[31]

ESTEEM VERSUS LOYALTY

Abandoning morality, of course, does not mean that anything goes when it comes to human conduct. Clearly there is a difference in practice between a community in which people are generally treated with love and respect and one in which they are not.[32] In seminal lectures on moral philosophy, Hannah Arendt holds that (1) there is an absolute difference between good and evil, and (2) this difference "turns on the question of with whom I wish to be together, and not about 'objective' standards and rules."[33] Our "decisions about right and wrong" depend, for Arendt, "upon our choice of company, of those with whom we wish to spend our lives."[34] A just person is one who gives what is due to the other people with whom he is related.

"Man is a relational being."[35] There are many types of human relationships: we act differently when faced with different people. We do not relate in the same way to family members, friends, neighbors, colleagues, supervisors, business partners, officials, or acquaintances. At any point in time, our behavior is partially a function of those with whom we are interacting. We are *persons*, a word that comes from the ancient term for masks worn in the theater to indicate those roles.[36] We wear different masks in different social situations; we play different roles depending on those with whom we are interacting.

These relationships are not mutually exclusive. They coexist. Simply because I am someone's friend does not mean I cease to be a loyal son, colleague, neighbor, or spouse. Stifling another person with possessive love is bad because it pits one loyalty against another. We can be a good friend *and* a good spouse *and* a good co-worker. Loyalty for us means actual or potential friendship, and showing loyalty means showing solidarity or acting in ways that do not foreclose a future friendship with someone. Of course, our loyalties can come into conflict. "Our loyalties are always getting hopelessly tangled and compromised. Even if we want to commit ourselves to being true, we can never escape the conflicting demands that our contradictory loyalties create."[37] The ancient Greek concept of φιλία—which played a similar role to loyalty, a concept which they lacked—contained a similar problem.[38]

The coexistence of multiple loyalties is not easy. It takes intelligence, creativity, and hard work to maintain a network of human personalities. The nature of all meaningful human choice, nevertheless, comes down to the question, "To whom shall I be loyal?" Every single hypothetical moral dilemma in every textbook of moral philosophy is reducible to this question.[39] Ethics textbooks assume that the question "What should I do?" has a right answer independent of my particular loyalties. This assumption keeps professors of ethics employed.

But it isn't true. There is no right or wrong in the formation of human loyalties. We may in fact use criteria to form loyalties; however, this practice is inherently competitive and leads to problems. In particular, if there were correct criteria, this would mean that one particular type of loyalty would always be correct. We have multiple loyalties and friendships which coexist, and insisting that one type alone is always right is depersonalizing. "A friendship that—through its exclusivity—denies the possibility of other friendships becomes inward-looking and self-enclosed within the private realm."[40] There are horrible cases in which another person is enslaved, held captive, and cut off from all other relationships—and it is clear that such treatment denies the personhood of the other person, demanding as it does that one relationship alone define him.

Of course, it is possible to talk about *actions* being right or wrong. The basis on which we say this is, however, always broader than a description of the action. We can perceive the difference between right and wrong actions only when we consider the larger context of personal connections. To get a sense of actions that are right or wrong when it comes to a particular individual, we must consider how we are related to him, and this relation is always enmeshed in a context that includes all other actual and potential relationships. Sleeping with one's wife builds up the spousal relationship, and two people having a strong marriage benefits them, their children, the community in which they live, their country, and even the whole world. Sleeping with someone else's wife does the opposite.

Without considering the particular loyalties at stake, it becomes next to impossible to speak of "right" and "wrong" actions.[41] It would be silly to say it would be "right" to marry this or that person or to be loyal to this or that group before knowing who the people are and what the context is. It cannot be a matter of "right" before we consider the loyalties themselves. What is "right" depends on those loyalties. Our loyalties are the *nec plus ultra* and not our criteria. Any standard of "right" and "wrong" is always a *result* of human loyalty. Is a person "right" to be loyal to the United States? Well, if that person is an American, it does make sense. Is someone "wrong" to refuse affection to an older person? If it is their mother, then that salient detail must enter into any attempt at an answer.

Once we know something about a person, taking his loyalties into account, we can then begin to see a difference between "right" and "wrong" modes of conduct—that is to say, a difference between that which serves and promotes those relationships and that which poisons and destroys them. To say that loyalties should be formed according to a standard of right is putting the cart before the horse. What is right and wrong comes on the back of human loyalties.

Ethics cannot tell me which person to marry. It cannot tell me who is lying or those whom I can trust. It cannot tell me my vocation in life. The language of "right" and "wrong" does not apply to the *formation* of human loyalties, but comes into play only afterwards.

Loyalty is not for its own sake; rather, it finds its terminus in friendship. In Aristotle's classic explication of friendship in the *Nicomachean Ethics*, there is a teleology of human relationships: a friendship comes from goodwill that is noticed and reciprocated through living together—or in our formulation, loyalty is reciprocated, resulting in mutual trust and ultimately friendship. Personal relationships require this alternate vocabulary. The term *loyalty* is particularly useful because it is so flexible. People have to know each other to trust each other; but a person can be loyal to another both before meeting them, as well as after their death.[42] Loyalty can even be stretched to refer to artifacts of human relationships, like principles or philosophies. (There is a danger here. Without a language of trust and friendship, we might think that loyalty is properly loyalty to a cause, when actually it is our relationships that produce any and all devotion to an abstractly defined "cause" in the first place.[43])

People are capable of multiple loyalties because they are capable of multiple relationships with other people and groups. One way of viewing action is as a contest of loyalties; the way I act comes down to which loyalty is the strongest part of my identity. But are loyalties competitive? Must we throw other people under the bus in order to assert our identity? A readiness to sacrifice lower-level loyalties simplifies matters: if a person knows precisely where their loyalties lie, then they can be confident that their actions are always right. They can simply jettison any semblance of loyalty to those they consider less important, whenever they need to.[44] If action is a matter of finding the correct loyalty and sacrificing everything else to it, then we can make decisions relatively easily. The only difficulty would be steeling oneself so as to remain hard enough to do it. This would be less a case of acting with others, however, than remaining true to my values.

Action with others is more difficult if we seek to maintain our crosscutting relationships such that they are not in competition with each other. After all, my loyalties need not be mutually exclusive. A family that has another child does not thereby start loving the rest of the children less. Patriotism does not mean looking down on foreigners. Even rivalries between organizations or groups can be friendly. There are no restrictions on the loyalty I can give out, as if it were a stock room with a limited inventory. Loyalty is a common good—indeed, it is *the* common good. The more people to whom I am loyal, the better for me and for society. When a population has crosscutting loyalties, it makes civil war less likely.[45] St. Augustine wrote that the reason for the development of the custom prohibiting cousin marriage was so that "the social tie would not be confined to a small group but would extend more widely to connect a large number with the multiplying links of kinship."[46]

Deeper loyalties are not competitive. "The essence of friendship is entireness, a total magnanimity and trust," as Emerson writes. Once I start thinking that I have to economize my loyalty, the loyalty I do show becomes impoverished. Only narrow loyalties see themselves this way: the mafia asks the new recruit to kill someone to prove his commitment, the possessive girlfriend forbids her boyfriend from talking to other girls, the political partisan does not see anything the other party might have to offer the country.[47] Deeper and stronger loyalties do not see a competitor around every corner nor insist on excluding other types of loyalty. Rather, strong personal relationships have positive, reciprocal effects on each other and on others. "My portion of friendship is not diminished when another's is increased; instead, my portion is increased by sharing it more."[48]

Matters are different when we view ourselves as competitors for esteem. People filled with admiration for someone else, while lacking the capacity for a relationship with him, admire only their own imaginings. Living in their own world, they inevitably esteem an idea, not a person. A stalker is not in a relationship. There is no give-and-take and no trust. "[T]o discover that no friendly attitudes are returned, is to discover that what one thought was a friendship in fact was not."[49] A personal relationship is never a matter of one person's sentiment alone. As Aristotle noted, friendship not only has to be reciprocal, it also has to be recognized as reciprocal.[50] Friends trust each other, and the basis for trust is always a relationship. "My trust of you grows out of my relationship with you,"[51] since trust "aims at mutuality."[52]

Relationships can never be reduced to esteem, explained in terms of esteem, or even explained at all, for that matter, unless both people are doing the explaining, for starters. Otherwise, you are just getting one side of the story.

Esteem requires no relationship. Too much esteem even precludes it; filled with admiration in the present, pure esteem does not have a future, because it is so one-sided. It puts a person up on a pedestal, considering him apart from his other relationships. When I am removed from a thing, I can esteem it, comparing and contrasting it with its competitors. I have to be at a distance to do this, so I cannot do that with the relationships close to me. Deeper relationships, on the other hand, involve people who are not our competitors, but who form a part of us. Consider a spouse, for example; here the distance necessary for pure esteem is impossible: "I always loved her far too much to observe her."[53]

Because esteem is one-sided and takes place at a distance, it can never form an answer to the question, "Am I a good person?" The best answer to any question is given by an expert, the person most thoroughly acquainted with the subject matter. When it comes to me and my life, the same thing applies: we need to know who the experts are. The answer is the people who know me well. Answering a question about me must involve consulting the people who know me, the people with whom I am in relationship. Those who observe someone from a distance, that is to say, the esteem other people have for a person, is irrelevant, as they lack the necessary expertise to get a handle on whether he is a good person or not. Esteem for the accomplishments of someone is only partial. You might as well try to get the character of a movie star by asking their stalker about them. If we think of morality as making a person worthy of esteem, we are placing the testimony of the stalker before the spouse, the novice before the expert. What do we get out of being moral? What the stalker has to offer: esteem.[54] As we have seen, the Achilles' heel of morality is the question, "Why we should care to be moral in the first place?" In the absence of personal solidarity with the person espousing a moral code, our motivation could only be to win the esteem of others, or to gain justified self-esteem.

This is why a focus on justice as the upholding and balancing of loyalties is not another moral theory, because the aim is not gaining esteem but rather strengthening and balancing the personal relationships themselves. If justice were thought of in terms of the basis for estimating or imputing the label "just" upon someone, such that they deserve our esteem, then it would be a matter of morality.[55] We will see this conception of justice take hold with Martin Luther in the next chapter; for now, we can say that it is external, perspectival, conflictual, and exclusive. If I am concerned that other people esteem me as just, I am necessarily going to be concerned with what other people think rather than what I find to be essentially just. How can I win the esteem of other people? I need to know what their frame of reference is, what their views of justice are. Not everyone will have the same views, however; different people will have different perspectives. Which view should I choose? Logically, I cannot choose all the competing ideas, since to some degree they will be mutually exclusive. This puts us at loggerheads with others, forcing the choice as to who is right and who is wrong.

A personal relationship, by contrast, involves loyalty that does not have to operate through competition and exclusion: it is a *common* good. A relationship is something which I participate in but do not unilaterally control.

In other words, it has its own integral form. When I act for the sake of a relationship, and it is deepened and strengthened, it is not just myself and my friend who benefit. A strong friendship benefits the other friends and associates of the two friends in a myriad of ways, as it increases their social trust and social capital. Likewise, the isolation and loneliness of individuals has negative effects on those whom they encounter, as this privation manifests itself in distrust and hostility. When social trust spreads, everyone benefits; where it disintegrates, it negatively affects everyone. The integral form of a friendship does not exclude other social forms and their corresponding loyalties but finds its place within the larger comprehensive whole that it supports.

It has been remarked that the hatred of Americans for each other comes from our lack of support networks.[56] Another example is the village in southern Italy studied by Edward Banfield in the 1950s, where no one was concerned with the common good and everyone avoided close attachments. While there were strong loyalties to the immediate family, everyone else was viewed suspiciously and there was no trust in authority. As a result, there was exact reciprocity: anyone who did any favors for anyone else kept a careful record of them and expected to be repaid. As a result, people avoided asking for favors. The lack of social trust prohibited the most efficient economic organization, and the village was grindingly poor. Interestingly, the person who could be considered the most public-spirited leader in the town gave the following reason for why he did not get involved in politics: "You must make more friends than you want and you must act like a friend to many people you don't want to be friends with."[57] He labeled this "falsity in politics." By contrast, take the documented "Roseto effect," referring to a tight-knit town of Italian immigrants in eastern Pennsylvania in the decades before 1965. The supportive and friendly nature of the community resulted in a significantly lower rate of heart attacks in younger men and a much lower morality rate.[58]

THE NATURE OF POLITICS

The modern conception of morality rests on fundamentally competitive relationships. Competition for esteem cannot be the basis for friendship and other relationships of loyalty, however. If following a moral code is what it means to be a good person, then personal relationships would be extraneous to action rather than being their end: action would be properly individual. That is indeed how we see morality—as the regulation of individual action. Collective action is a different matter; it is seen as "political," defined as seeking the power to push a policy or law that would be imposed on others.[59] Both spheres, morality and politics, view action as unilateral and fragmented, failing to aim at a common good that includes the other person, presuming instead an indifferent or antagonistic relationship. The fact that there are two irreducible spheres, "two truths," manifests the disintegrated nature of the modern conception of action.

We propose here an integrated view, which would see action as always properly aiming at a common good, a good that includes the other with whom I am acting, rather than aiming at esteem.

To begin, action in its most proper sense is always action with others. The Greek term πρᾶξις meant acting with regard to the collective potential for action. A case of pure *praxis* would be, for example, the setting up of an organization by soliciting interested parties, having meetings, drafting bylaws, electing officers, etcetera—activity that is not producing anything external to itself but rather developing the capability of a social aggregate to function. This is action in the fullest sense. Individual action is not primary, and it is always inescapably embedded in and contributes to the social structures that make it possible.

The full reality of human action is always *political* in the broad sense. The basic political phenomenon is suggestion-response, in which one person suggests a course of action to someone else, who can respond or not. We should jettison the conception of power as a matter of imposing one's will on someone else. This is *force*. By contrast, "political power is power in the subjunctive mood."[60] No one has brought this out better than Bertrand de Jouvenel, in his classic work *The Pure Theory of Politics*. For de Jouvenel, everything that happens in human life is the result of someone taking the initiative. While the instigator appears to be the leader who is in control, in reality, the one responding has the last word. In the last analysis, it is my action in responding that makes the leader a leader, not any force brought to bear by him. While there can be every reason to expect compliance in a circumstance, it is never a given, and the reasons for response are complicated. We might think of compliance with a suggestion as stemming from a regard for the pure content of the suggestion; however, this turns out to be exceedingly difficult. In reality, compliance has to involve an assessment of the person making the suggestion; even if we try to evaluate a suggestion on its merits alone, this will mean consulting an expert, and this is only substituting one assessment of authorship for another. Most of the time, then, we respond on the grounds of authorship, that is, because of the credit we give the person who suggests the action. This credit given to an author of an explicit suggestion is their *authority*. Although de Jouvenel does not mention it, we could also consider *inspiration* as a phenomenon of implicit suggestion. I can be inspired to follow someone's example without them explicitly instigating an action from me. The inspirational figure could be long dead, yet his impact on others continues in the future through followers modelling their behavior on his example.

Authority is not an attribute of a person but a quality of a relationship. There are two types of it for de Jouvenel: formal and informal. The latter is the authority of a person holding a particular office, while the former is outside of these formal structures of compliance and involves a group freely following a charismatic figure. Formal authority is limited in scope, involves the right to command and a corresponding duty to obey, and has the role of eliminating suggestions that are inconsistent at the level of the set (e.g., everyone drive on the right side of the road) by issuing suggestions much stronger in intensity, that is, commands. Formal authority originates from and regularizes the informal authority that is necessary at the founding of an aggregate. It tends to efface the suggestion-response characteristic of all politics, cultivating the illusion of inevitable compliance, since it is useful, when issuing commands, if people think they must obey.

Formal authority is impressive; however, informal authority is actually more frightening. The raw power of an instigator leading respondents who want to be led has no inherent limits, and the group can, in principle, do anything. That is, there is no way to say that this form of suggestion-response oversteps its bounds, because the force in this relationship obeys no laws. It would be like complaining that a lightning bolt is out of line when it hits my house. We inevitably prefer involuntary authority because we follow it voluntarily. It is the "natural" authority of a charismatic person whom we enjoy following, feeling like we are just obeying ourselves. This is impossible to feel with obedience to formal authority.

Whether or not authority—the credit given the author of a suggestion—is formal or informal, however, the suggestion-response structure is still the same. Seemingly powerful entities, like a giant car manufacturer, ultimately derive its appearance of power from individuals responding to its suggestions of which vehicles to purchase. Response always has the last word; political power is always mutual, even the commands of the state. The external trappings, the majesty of the ruler, serve the purpose of distinguishing commands from mere suggestions and impress upon citizens that they really should obey. But this is because the people have the last word, and compliance cannot be taken for granted. Good leaders recognize this mutuality to authority. They want to only give commands that will be followed, to maintain the illusion of their authority, which has a cumulative effect—people tend to be more likely to comply with someone's suggestions the more they are in the habit of it and the more they see other people complying as well. Commands are never really unilateral, outside the structure of suggestion-response, because compliance is not automatic, even though leaders might work hard to maintain that illusion. "It is a terrible thing to look over your shoulder when you are trying to lead—and to find no one there," Franklin Delano Roosevelt once remarked.[61]

We should separate illusion from reality. There is no such thing as unilateral authority. While formal authority tends to cultivate an illusion of inevitability about its commands, it is, nevertheless, not a given. To think so is depersonalizing, as it takes away the reciprocal nature of politics as suggestion-response. If, instead of understanding ourselves as responding to a person who is in a certain role as the instigator of an action, we respond as if he is not there, we would then not be able to account for the interplay of person and role, of informal and formal authority, as well as the overlapping loyalties of the leader which now include care for the common good of the aggregate and the dilemmas and difficulties resulting from the interaction of both of these for the person in a position of authority. In short, we would not consider the personal element of authority and, therefore, would not be able to see the separation of the person and the office.

This leads to another blindness, which supposes that it is the magic of the office that confers automatic power on its holder. It is not the case that the holder of the office, whoever it may be, wields the power of the office as a matter of course. Authority is more than a matter of formal commands alone.

These illusions coalesce in the error of seeing formal authority as a seat of power, a prize to be won, as if the power were automatic and impersonal and not, ultimately, reciprocal. This is a characteristically modern view. Modernity arose as feudalism declined. Invented in the seventeenth century to describe something that was passing away, the term *feudalism* refers to the decentralized political system of Europe which began in the early ninth century. The decline of the Carolingian Empire in the late ninth century and the corresponding need for protection from marauders resulted in a political and economic system that was based around personal ties. What mattered was one's allegiance, not territorial borders that demarcated exclusive sovereign authorities.[62] Feudalism simply did not have the characteristics of the modern state of territoriality and sovereignty; it was built instead upon the personal loyalty of vassals to lords, and cooperative alliances of friendship.[63] Whatever the shortcomings of feudalism, it could never have been confused about the embeddedness of political power and personal responsibility in the mutual give-and-take between persons. In the sixteenth and seventeenth centuries, however, the conception of political life changed. Supreme rule no longer meant responsibility for a common good, and the tendency was towards absolutism. The desire to concentrate power in an absolute monarch ruling through extralegal means only originates if power is viewed as a possession, outside of suggestion and response. Insofar as liberalism and democracy resisted absolutism, they did so on the basis of a language of morality, values, and human rights.[64]

These abstract languages themselves tend to reproduce the error. When St. Thomas Aquinas writes about tyranny, he follows Plato in seeing the distinguishing mark of the tyrant as his inability to be friends with his subjects.[65] Modern political theory looks at things differently. In Niccolò Machiavelli's (1469–1527) book *The Prince*, for example, the context is a *new* ruler of a "state" (which at that time was just becoming conceived as detached from the authority of the ruler).[66] Machiavelli's focus on maintaining one's position illuminates the effects of treating power like a possession, as his stress is on acting and gaining esteem in the present.[67] There is less room for error for a new prince; the horizon is shortened to the challenging, short-term goal of staying in power. As a means to that end, the new prince needs to take care to be esteemed by the many, that is, to appear to have certain virtues. Those who know what the prince really is will not dare oppose the many and the majesty of the state.

Machiavelli shows that the more one's horizon is constricted, the more we take the good of our action to be a narrow grasping for power, then the more the appearance of excellence, being esteemed for it, becomes indistinguishable for all intents and purposes from actually having the excellent quality and, while reality and appearance are not convertible over the long run, the counterfeit can be accepted initially before the rule of the new prince gains habitual acceptance. Even in that precarious initial situation, the two are not fully fungible, since the prince must avoid relationship-destroying action that would incur hatred and contempt at all costs.

Machiavelli is therefore not fully "Machiavellian." He knows that well-established loyalties are more resilient and so preferable. His prescriptions for a ruler who cannot rely on customary loyalty are insightful precisely because there *is* a good greater than the temporary success of one leader—namely, the durability of the political order. Machiavelli is not saying that the unstable rule of the new prince is the desirable situation for all social orders—rather, the opposite—and he helps us see that the narrower our horizon and the more instrumental our grasping for power, the less personal relationships matter and the more esteem waxes in importance.

More modern is the view of authority as impersonal, as "the state." This term, meaning an abstract entity rather than personal rule of a monarch, became common in the sixteenth century. Thomas Hobbes (1588–1679) provides a theory of it in the seventeenth century.[68] For him, it does not matter who the leaders are and what their capabilities are. Hobbes writes in the dedication to *Leviathan*, "I speak not of the men, but (in the Abstract) of the Seat of Power, (like to those simple and unpartial creatures in the Roman Capitol that with the noyse defended those within it, not because they were they, but there)."[69] This is a reference to the Capitoline geese, which alerted the Romans to the attack of Gauls climbing up the cliff to their fortification. It sums up nicely the entire book, which creates the idea of a seat of power exercising unilateral authority and deserving of exclusive loyalty.

We will cover Hobbes's theory of sovereignty extensively in chapter 3. For now, it can be noted that his theory of impersonal power excludes the person holding the office from the common good that is served by the role. The exercise of authority might be good for everyone else, but not for the person in the position of command himself. For Hobbes, as we shall see, the Sovereign is still in the state of war with his subjects, even as he makes peace possible for everyone else. Setting the person who exercises power apart from everyone else sacralizes him and puts him beyond good and evil. Such unilateral, transcendental power is seen as that which ought to be obeyed whether or not it is good.

The modern conceptualization of morality separates it from politics. Morality regulates individual actions; politics, understood as state commands, regulates collective action. In both cases, authority is unilateral either as the content of a suggestion or the form of a command. But as we have seen, in reality, authority is always a back-and-forth between persons. It cannot be unilateral because it cannot exclude the free response of the person subject to it. Politics aims at a common good, not an exclusive good, and a common good is never a term in a syllogism or the form of a command but is always a communion of persons. Even a formal command is never issued in the abstract but always by a person who has more or less informal authority. That person is likewise always included in political action. It matters for the person who is in authority whether or not his own exercise of power is good or not, and our response to authority must take the person who is exercising it into account as part of a common good and as a consideration when it comes to our obedience. For the person in office, it really matters whether or not he exercises his authority well, as that determines the friendships he can enjoy with those responding to him. The bad exercise of power hurts the possibility of friendly relations with those negatively affected; the mark of a tyrant is that he is not friends with his subjects. That is bad *for the tyrant*. Our response to the exercise of power must include the good of the authority figure himself—and, once we do that, the right can never be separate from the good, nor politics from ethics. Only when we aim at an exclusive good, a good that excludes the authority figure—even though it might include everyone else—does there appear a neutral realm that mediates between squabbling conceptions of the good: the realm of the state. But what is good is not exclusive and fragmentary, unless we take competitive relationships as our model. Once we accept noncompetitive human relationships as the end and measure of action, the illusion of unilateral authority dissolves.

NIETZSCHE, THE CONSUMMATE MORALIST

Morality purports to measure individual human conduct according to an abstract standard, rather than seeing persons as embedded in a network of relationships and tasked with harmonizing them. Instead of the happiness of friendship, it offers instead a competition for esteem. Action is thus unilateral rather than collaborative, a matter of following a moral code rather than deepening one's relationships. As personal relationships lose their authority, collective action likewise becomes unilateral. Rather than the pursuit of a common good that includes leader and followers, political action is thought of as the powerful imposing their will on others. Instead of widespread friendship, the measure of politics is thought to be morality. However, morality is indisputably contestable. Everyone does not automatically agree. There is a contest between rival moralities, a polytheism of values. What is of value to one person might be seen as only a neutral fact by another person. "A work of art is worth a diamond to some, a pebble to others."[70] This is the problem of values, the Böckenförde dilemma: values are plural, and the choice among them cannot be rationally grounded.[71] We can point them out through ostension, but we are unable to rationally argue about them with someone who does not accept them, just as we cannot argue with someone who does not speak our language.[72] People inevitably select the morality that fits their habits, occupation, manner of life, beliefs, etcetera. We hold to the values that make us comfortable, that affirm our place in society.[73] "As long as the reason of man continues fallible, and he is at liberty to exercise it, different opinions will be formed," writes James Madison in *Federalist #10*.[74]

The solution in a case of deep disagreement is always loyalty to another person, which alone can make frank discussion and effective suggestion-response possible. The more we are attached to morality and its self-evident truths, the less we see this, however. Then the only way out of deep disagreement and the impossibility of discussion is to fight over it, with the victorious imposing their will. The dilemma of values inevitably leads to war. Every man puts a high value on himself, as Thomas Hobbes writes, and then "every man looketh that his companion should value him, at the same rate he sets upon himselfe: And upon all signes of contempt, or undervaluing, naturally endeavours, as far as he dares (which amongst them that have no common power, to keep them in quiet, is far enough to make them destroy each other,) to extort a greater value from his contemners, by dommage; and from others, by the example."[75] Unlike personal relationships in which we can be friends even when we disagree, with morality, we must first agree on what is right in order to effectively coordinate our actions and not work at cross-purposes. The competition for esteem recapitulates itself as a competition for power to determine what is esteemed. Moralities clash, and the solution can only be to get everyone on the same page and assenting to the same moral values. The most fundamental political competition therefore will always concern which morality to impose; persons are able to cooperate towards a collective goal only if they agree on what is estimable and what is not. Disagreements must be settled through a power struggle. Personal relationships no longer have authority, so we cannot rely on reciprocal political action, obtaining compliance for suggestions, but rather have recourse only to unilateral, impersonal force in order to form a social aggregate. As Hobbes saw, there must be a common power to keep people quiet who are otherwise at one another's throats.

Morality requires a sovereign whose commands settle disputes about morality, and this is justified because a people are better off when war between them is forestalled. The sovereign acts for the benefit of the people by imposing morality. But what about the benefit for the sovereign himself? There is a distinction—seen in book I of Plato's *Republic*—between the exercise of expertise, which is always for the good of the subject who benefits from it, and the advantage of the expert himself, which requires an additional art of moneymaking. The good of the sovereign ruler and the good for the people are separate. Sovereign morality aims at a benefit for the people but does not consider what benefits the sovereign. The sovereign is beyond morality.

Moral thinking offers individuals esteem for action which benefits the people. But is this really the correct scale of values? It is not the only one. In addition to the moral code imposed by the powers that be, there is also the will to power of those rulers themselves. It is undoubtedly estimable to gain enough power and have the creativity to impose a morality in the first place. It is their creativity that is responsible for the scale of values that measures the benefits for everyone else, a force which brought about a change in the way people esteem things and that, therefore, cannot be measured by any conventional morality at all. As a result, we now have two competing estimations, the will to power, and conventional morality. The latter is operative only after the former has successfully cleared a zone free of deadly conflict, enabling us to pursue moral value at all. It is easy to forget this and take our peaceful situation of equality for granted. Morality can take itself to be the sole standard only by deluding itself; in reality, the will to power makes it possible and is therefore primary.

Any serious philosophical reflection on morality must reconcile these two competing standards for esteem—the will to power and conventional morality. In the end it must concede that one is primary and foundational for the other. Therefore, our estimations must reflect this. The will to power must be acknowledged as the true, natural value and not the conventional morality of any given, taken-for-granted peaceful life, which would operate in ignorance of the conditions of its own existence. Nietzsche is thus not abolishing morality—far from it. "It goes without saying that I do not deny—unless I am a fool—that many actions called immoral ought to be avoided and resisted, or that many called moral ought to be done and encouraged," he writes, "but I think the one should be encouraged and the other avoided *for other reasons than hitherto*."[76] Those "other reasons" are precisely another morality, and Nietzsche calls it this.[77] Nietzsche's preference is for a different moral system, but for a moral system nonetheless, viz. a unilateral standard of esteem that is not seeking a common good but rather differentiating high from low. Morality itself requires the will to power to be workable in practice, and Nietzsche simply wants to incorporate this truth into our moral thinking. He is not changing the essence of morality but returning it to its roots, expanding it to include the conditions for its possibility.

This expansion reveals the unpleasant truths that conventional morality would like to keep hidden. Nietzsche's morality thus seems very different from the doctrines of conventional morality. Nevertheless, Nietzsche is only taking morality to its decisive conclusion. Ultimately, morality must valorize the powerful and justify the subjection and exploitation of the weak. "The essential characteristic of a good and healthy aristocracy," he writes, "is that it experiences itself *not* as a function (whether of the monarchy or the commonwealth) but as their *meaning* and highest justification—that it therefore accepts with a good conscience the sacrifice of untold human beings who, *for its sake*, must be reduced and lowered to incomplete human beings, to slaves, to instruments."[78] The purpose of morality is to orient esteem; conflicts over morality are settled by power. Therefore, before anything else, power should be esteemed. This has the unsightly consequence that those who are not powerful are trampled upon. Nietzsche spares no detail when it comes to how figures unimportant to his "noble" individuals are treated by them. Outside of their social circle, these noble ones "revert to the innocence of wild animals: we can imagine them returning from an orgy of murder, arson, rape, and torture, jubilant and at peace with themselves as though they had committed a fraternity prank—convinced, moreover, that the poets for a long time to come will have something to sing about and to praise. Deep within all these noble races there lurks the beast of prey, bent on spoil and conquest."[79]

Nietzsche is not launching an attack on the universality of morality and reducing morality to the *mores* of a community. Rather, he is defending morality as universal and transcendental and based on truth. The noble creators of morality, the Zarathustras who are required for morality to exist at all, do not rethink the unilateral nature of authority found in adherence to an abstract moral code. The antagonism that exists between the sovereign nobles and the weak does not deviate from the necessarily competitive relationships of morality. And since it will always be universally true that moral conflicts will require creative interventions of the powerful, any true scale of estimations must accommodate this. Nature *is* cruel. The most natural morality must be the tyrannical domination of some over others. Conventional morality pretends to be universal, but in reality, we must admit that it necessarily relies on the will to power of those who create new customs and estimations.

Nietzsche consummates liberalism. He is the "last metaphysician," as Martin Heidegger calls him. His view that life is a will to power, and his idolization of the strong, great, noble souls who are able to impose their values on others is a final recapitulation of the modern tradition.

We sense that we have reached an end point today. Liberalism is exhausted, its myths played out. This includes morality: it must be judged as pernicious, for example, that a significant segment of the college-educated population in our country are in a competition for moral righteousness on social media. Morality is a myth because our problems will never be solved by fine-tuning a moral doctrine. In the end what matters is how we treat each other, the quality of the personal relationships we share. Our loyalties are the anti-morality because they bind us to others rather than putting us in competition with each other. Particular rather than universal, they nevertheless can be expanded and harmonized with other loyalties without limit. Regard for loyalties respects the true political nature of all action, which includes the other person in the question of right conduct.

We now go back to the beginning, and turn to the origin of modernity and the progenitor of the liberal tradition, Martin Luther.

NOTES

1. According to Herbert Schnädelbach, "All historians of philosophy, however, are in agreement with the contemporaries of the philosophy of values in thinking that it was Nietzsche's provocative slogan of the 'revaluation of all values' which first led to the boom-period of the concept of value; this boom was then further intensified by the value-theoretical interpretation of the cultural sciences in Rickert and Max Weber and also by the debate about value-judgments in the social sciences." Herbert Schnädelbach, *Philosophy in Germany, 1831–1933*, trans. Eric Matthews (Cambridge: Cambridge University Press, 1984), 161.

2. Martin Heidegger, *The Question Concerning Technology and Other Essays*, trans. William Lovitt (New York: Harper & Row, 1977), 70.

3. Jennifer Ratner-Rosenhagen, *American Nietzsche: A History of an Icon and His Ideas* (Chicago: University of Chicago Press, 2012), 32.

4. Rüdiger Safranski, *Nietzsche: A Philosophical Biography*, trans. Shelley Frisch (New York: W. W. Norton and Company, 2002), 318, 329.

5. A seminal work that brought values language into English was Wilbur Marshall Urban's *Valuation: Its Nature and Laws, Being an Introduction to the General Theory*

of Value, published in 1909. Urban coined the term *axiology* in it. Nietzsche was decisive; Urban found the *Genealogy of Morals* browsing through a bookshop in Jena, and reading it he described as "the greatest single spiritual adventure of my life." Ratner-Rosenhagen, *American Nietzsche: A History of an Icon and His Ideas*, 29.

6. John Heenan, "Putting the Plural Noun Values in Context," *Keynote Address to the Eighth National Character Education Symposium* (Wellington, 2010), http://www.pnbhs.school.nz/wp-content/uploads/2015/11/John-Heenan-Putting-Values-in-Context.pdf.

7. Allan Bloom, "How Nietzsche Conquered America," *Wilson's Quarterly*, vol. 11, no. 3 (Summer 1987), 82.

8. Hannah Arendt, "Some Questions of Moral Philosophy," in *Responsibility and Judgment*, ed. Jerome Kohn (New York: Schocken Books, 2003), 50–52. G. E. M. Anscombe, *Human Life, Action and Ethics* (Charlottesville: Imprint Academic, 2005), 190.

9. With the exception of the ancient Stoic and Epicurean philosophers, the concept of morality separated out from political life is more or less unknown in the vast swath of the philosophical tradition. "If you look back to traditional, premodern philosophy," writes Hannah Arendt, "there existed no moral subdivision within philosophy." Ethical questions in the medieval period, for example, were discussed "in the fashion of antiquity, where ethics was part and parcel of political philosophy—defining the conduct of man insofar as he was a citizen." Arendt, "Some Questions of Moral Philosophy," 64. Philosophers in later antiquity after the rise of empire withdrew from public life and transformed philosophy into moral teachings in a sense not found in Aristotle. Nicholas White, "Indifferenz und der nicht peripatetische stoische Begriff des Guten," in *Zur Ethik der Älteren Stoa*, ed. Barbara Guckes (Göttingen: Vandenhoeck & Ruprecht, 2004), 184–85. It is no accident that the birth of morality in the early modern period takes place concomitantly with a revival of Stoicism. However, even the Stoics did not think ethics was a self-standing discipline; it was only a part of philosophy, which meant it had to be strongly unified with the other branches to understand itself. Julia Annas, "Ethics in Stoic Philosophy," *Phronesis* 52, no. 1 (2007): 60–61.

10. G. Jüssen, "Moral, Moralisch, Moralphilosophie: Lateinische Antike," in *Historisches Wörterbuch der Philosophie*, ed. Joachim Ritter (Basel/Stuttgart: Schwabe & Co., 1974). G. Jüssen, "Moral, Moralisch, Moralphilosophie: Lateinische Patristik Und Lateinisches Mittelalter," in *Historisches Wörterbuch der Philosophie*, ed. Joachim Ritter (Basel/Stuttgart: Schwabe & Co., 1974). G. Wieland, "Moral, Moralisch, Moralphilosophie: 12. Jahrhundert, Hoch- und Spätscholastik," in *Historisches Wörterbuch der Philosophie*, ed. Joachim Ritter (Basel/Stuttgart: Schwabe & Co., 1974).

11. Iain Ross, *Oscar Wilde and Ancient Greece* (Cambridge: Cambridge University Press, 2013), 205.

12. Hans Fink, "Against Ethical Exceptionalism—Through Critical Reflection on the History of Use of the Terms 'Ethics' and 'Morals' in Philosophy," *SATS* 21, no. 2 (2020): 87–90.

13. Arash Abizadeh, *Hobbes and the Two Faces of Ethics* (Cambridge: Cambridge University Press, 2018), 219–20.

14. "Moral Virtue, N.," OED Online (Oxford University Press, 2017).

15. Cf. Eric Voegelin, *The New Science of Politics: An Introduction* (Chicago: University of Chicago Press, 1987), 61–62.

16. As Augustine puts it, "the source of a community's felicity is no different from that of one man, since a community is simply a united multitude of individuals," and "the individual man is, like a single letter in a statement, an element, as it were, out of which a community or a realm is built up." Saint Augustine, *Concerning the City of God against the Pagans*, trans. Henry Bettenson (New York: Penguin, 2003), 25, 138.

17. Fink, "Against Ethical Exceptionalism—Through Critical Reflection on the History of Use of the Terms 'Ethics' and 'Morals' in Philosophy," 87.

18. Bettany Hughes, *The Hemlock Cup: Socrates, Athens and the Search for the Good Life* (New York: Alfred A. Knopf, 2001), 9.

19. Millard J. Erickson, *Introducing Christian Doctrine*, ed. L. Arnold Hustad, 2nd ed. (Grand Rapids, Michigan: Baker Academic, 2001), 318. D. D. Raphael, *Concepts of Justice* (Oxford: Clarendon Press, 2001), 11–18.

20. Martin Buber, *Two Types of Faith*, trans. Norman P. Goldhawk (New York: Macmillan, 1951), 28–29.

21. Harry M. Orlinsky, *Ancient Israel*, 2nd ed. (Ithaca: Cornell University Press, 1960), 129.

22. Aristotle, *Nicomachean Ethics*, in *The Basic Works of Aristotle*, ed. Richard McKeon, trans. W. D. Ross (New York: Random House, 1941), 1134b18–1135a4.

23. The culture of South and East Asia has recognized this to a much greater degree. "Asian culture (on the whole) has resisted the neat division or demarcation of domains, preferring to see human and social life instead as a complex web of relationships, as a holistic fabric of elements held together by some kind of inner balance," while the "self" for Confucius "is a *relational* self or a 'self as center of relationships' rather than an 'isolable individual' pursuing random goals." Fred Dallmayr, *Horizons of Difference: Engaging With Others* (Notre Dame: University of Notre Dame Press, 2020), 88, 91.

24. Hannah Arendt, *The Human Condition*, 2nd ed. (Chicago: University of Chicago Press, 1958), 184.

25. Richard Sennett, *Authority* (New York: Alfred A. Knopf, 1980), 3. Sennett is nevertheless part of the modern tradition of searching for "legitimate" authority that is justified by an impersonal image. For us, power is not synonymous with strength as Sennett contends (170), but rather, as Jouvenel shows, has the structure of suggestion-response where the follower has the last word. As a result, it is inherently a matter of personal relationships, not impersonal arguments and images.

26. These two cities are "created by two kinds of love: the earthly city . . . created by self-love reaching the point of contempt for God," which "looks for glory from men," and the "Heavenly City [created] by the love of God carried as far as contempt of self," which "finds its highest glory in God, the witness of a good conscience." Augustine, *Concerning the City of God against the Pagans*, 593.

27. Martha C. Nussbaum, *Not For Profit* (Princeton: Princeton University Press, 2010), 43.

28. Cf. John F. Crosby, *The Selfhood of the Human Person* (Washington, DC: The Catholic University of America Press, 1996), 41–81.

29. Nassim Nicholas Taleb, *The Black Swan: The Impact of the Highly Improbable* (New York: Random House, 2007), xxvii–xxviii.

30. Though it also fails to go far enough along these lines. Cf. Roger Scruton, "Parfit the Perfectionist," *Philosophy* 89, no. 350 (2014): 621–34.

31. Quoted in Hans-Georg Gadamer, *Hermeneutics, Religion, and Ethics* (New Haven: Yale University Press, 1999), 72.

32. We can add to this that it is good when my friends are friends with other people: when my good aligns with the greater common good, competition or possessiveness with friendship or loyalty are out of place.

33. Arendt, "Some Questions of Moral Philosophy," in *Responsibility and Judgment*, ed. Jerome Kohn (New York: Schocken Books, 2003), 125.

34. Arendt, "Some Questions of Moral Philosophy,"145–46.

35. Joseph Ratzinger, *Jesus of Nazareth: The Infancy Narratives*, trans. Philip J. Whitmore (New York: Image, 2012), 44.

36. Barbara Cassin, Marc Crépon, and François Prost, "Morals/Ethics," in *Dictionary of Untranslatables: A Philosophical Lexicon*, ed. Barbara Cassin, trans. Steven Rendall et al. (Princeton: Princeton University Press, 2014), 694. John von Heyking, *Augustine and Politics as Longing in the World* (Columbia: University of Missouri Press, 2001), 124–25. Christian theology transformed the term *person* to mean "relation." "[T]his word 'person' signifies 'relation,'" as St. Thomas Aquinas puts it. Thomas Aquinas, *Summa theologiae*, I, q. 29, a. 4, *in Summa Theologica: Complete English Edition in Five Volumes*, vol. 1, trans. Fathers of the English Dominican Province (Notre Dame, IN: Christian Classics, 1981), 159. Cf. Joseph Ratzinger, "Concerning the Notion of Person in Theology," *Communio* 17, (Fall 1990): 439–54.

37. Eric Felten, *Loyalty: The Vexing Virtue* (New York: Simon & Schuster, 2011), 6.

38. "The ancient city, then, was fixed between the two poles of friendship that sought to tear it asunder both from within and without: on the one side, the friendship (or kinship) formed in households and in clans; and from the other pole, those guest-friendships between citizens and foreigners, formed by elites out of private interest." Patrick J. Deneen, "Friendship and Politics: Ancient and American," in *Friends and Citizens: Essays in Honor of Wilson Carey McWilliams*, ed. Peter Dennis Bathory and Nancy L. Schwartz (Lanham: Rowman & Littlefield Publishers, 2001), 52. "*Philia* has one of two foundations: family connection, or an exchange of services. . . . The weakness of *philia* as any kind of bond is that its double foundation makes it fundamentally unstable." Paul Woodruff, "In Place of Loyalty: Friendship and Adversary Politics in Classical Greece," in *Loyalty*, ed. Sanford Levinson, Joel Parker, and Paul Woodruff (New York: New York University Press, 2013), 44.

39. "A moral dilemma is a complex situation that involves a conflict between moral imperatives, such that choosing one would violate the other." Christian Smith, *Lost in Transition: The Dark Side of Emerging Adulthood* (Oxford: Oxford University Press, 2011), 56.

40. Jon Nixon, *Hannah Arendt and the Politics of Friendship* (London: Bloomsbury, 2015), 188.

41. Avery Kolers gets this partially correct, as he insists that figuring out whose side you are on is prior to figuring out what the right thing to do is. However, he views loyalty as commitment to a collective regardless of right and wrong, rather than as a personal relationship, and he still seeks the mirage of an agent-neutral ethics that would "guide us through divisive and even excruciatingly difficult political challenges." Avery Kolers, *A Moral Theory of Solidarity* (Oxford: Oxford University Press, 2016), 166.

42. For example, to one's future spouse or to the memory of loved ones. The phrase that so-and-so "is turning over in his grave" is another example. Cf. the beautiful reflections in the first chapter of Derrida's *Politics of Friendship*. Jacques Derrida, *Politics of Friendship*, trans. George Collins (London: Verso, 1997), 1–25.

43. Josiah Royce makes this mistake in *The Philosophy of Loyalty*. Josiah Royce, *The Basic Writings of Josiah Royce: Logic, Loyalty, and Community*, ed. John Joseph McDermott (New York: Fordham University Press, 2005), 855–1013. John Stuart Mill had a personal revelation that loyalty to causes is not enough to give life meaning. John Stuart Mill, *Autobiography*, ed. John M. Robson; John M. (New York: Penguin, 1989), 111–16. Royce's vision of "loyalty to loyalty" is nevertheless similar to the theory of non-competitive loyalty advanced here. Jason Bell writes, "Loyalties that harmonize individual actions for a brief time, while disrupting the social and individual conditions that allow for loyalty, eventually prove disharmonious, whereas in loyalty to loyalty, the individual loyalist seeks, by his or her service, to establish a long-enduring cooperative and rational form of service of both individual loyalties as a coherent system within an individual loyalist, and a harmonious system of loyal corporate 'bodies' in relation to one another." Jason Matthew Bell, "The Relevance of Royce's Applied Ethics: Studies in War, Business, and Environmental Ethics" (Vanderbilt University, 2009), 25. But while Royce seeks the conventional task of the ethicist—to tell us what to do—for us, non-exclusive loyalty is a quality of a personal relationship, not a theoretical principle that could be applied. The latter is, in any case, hard for anyone to create, including Royce, who "has little advice as to how we may best practically apply the test of *loyalty to loyalty*. We must simply look in each case and attempt to ascertain which cause serves the greater loyalty." W. J. Mander, *Idealist Ethics* (Oxford: Oxford University Press, 2016), 151.

44. This is much easier to do if loyalties are reinterpreted as emotions. For example, Lawrence Wilde defines "solidarity" as "a feeling of sympathy shared by subjects within and between groups, impelling supportive action and pursuing social inclusion." Lawrence Wilde, *Global Solidarity* (Edinburgh: Edinburgh University Press, 2013), 1. Pursuing ever-widening social inclusion is certainly a laudable goal. Yet we short-circuit the difficulties of this if we look at abstract position-taking, rather than concrete relationships, and run the risk of new type of exclusion in the name of inclusiveness. And indeed, Wilde brandishes "solidarity" like a club to advance a partial political agenda over and against his political enemies: for example, rich individuals and large businesses, whose resources he believes the state should take away and redistribute. Wilde, *Global Solidarity*, 246–47. If solidarity is a new principle, then it

can be used to crush those who stand against it, but then (like all principles) it is just a new justification for exclusion.

45. Cf. Joel Sawat Selway, "Cross-Cuttingness, Cleavage Structures and Civil War Onset," *British Journal of Political Science* 41, no. 1 (2011): 111–38.

46. Augustine, *Concerning the City of God against the Pagans*, 624.

47. Sandra Lynch reflects on the "friendship" of mafia bosses: "The word 'friend' is derived from the Old English words *freon*—which meant 'free'—and *freo*—which meant 'love.' . . . There is a bond between the Mafiosi; they exhibit commitment to a shared relationship, but not the passion or freedom of choice which are the desiderata of the etymological account." Sandra Lynch, *Philosophy and Friendship* (Edinburgh: Edinburgh University Press, 2005), 4–5.

48. Jeremy Holmes, *Cur Deus Verba: Why the Word Became Words* (San Francisco: Ignatius Press, 2021), 17.

49. Jacopo Domenicucci and Richard Holton, "Trust as a Two-Place Relation," in *The Philosophy of Trust*, ed. Paul Faulkner and Thomas Simpson (Oxford: Oxford University Press, 2017), 158.

50. Aristotle, *Nicomachean Ethics*, in *The Basic Works of Aristotle*, ed. Richard McKeon, trans. W. D. Ross (New York: Random House, 1941), 1156a.

51. Russell Hardin, *Trust and Trustworthiness* (New York: Russell Sage Foundation, 2002), 198.

52. Stephen Darwall, "Trust as a Second-Personal Attitude (of the Heart)," in *The Philosophy of Trust*, ed. Paul Faulkner and Thomas Simpson (Oxford: Oxford University Press, 2017), 48. For Darwall, trust "is a species of second-personal attitude through which we lay ourselves open to others in a way that is distinctive of personal relationship and attachment." Darwall, 46.

53. In a letter of Goethe to Kestner, speaking of his youthful love. Emil Lucka, *Eros: The Development of the Sex Relation Through the Ages*, trans. Ellie Schleussner (New York: G. P. Putnam's Sons, 1915), 244.

54. This is not to say that esteem is not at all important. The prestige that goes with holding public office, for instance, is a very good thing, since those who have care for the common good should be held high in our estimation.

55. The root of *imputatio* and *reputatio*—*putatio*—means a reckoning or an esteeming.

56. "Increasingly, Americans live without deeper forms of what we now causally call 'support networks' that help and nourish us, both practically and emotionally." In 1985 a quarter of the U.S. population could be classified as isolated; by 2004 that was over half. Dick Meyer, *Why We Hate Us: American Discontent in the New Millennium* (New York: Crown, 2008), 20, 25–26.

57. Edward C. Banfield, *The Moral Basis of a Backward Society* (Glencoe, Illinois: The Free Press, 1958), 24.

58. John G. Bruhn and Stewart Wolf, *The Roseto Story: An Anatomy of Health* (Norman: University of Oklahoma Press, 1979). Brenda Egolf et al., "The Roseto Effect: A 50-Year Comparison of Mortality Rates," *American Journal of Public Health* 82, no. 8 (1992): 1089–92.

59. Expressed in the words of Richard Sennett: "Power between two people is the will of one person prevailing over the will of the other," and is therefore shortsighted. Sennett, *Authority*, 170.

60. Bernard Crick, *In Defence of Politics* (London: Bloomsbury, 2013), 120.

61. Jean Edward Smith, *FDR* (New York: Random House, 2008), 419.

62. Cf. Hendrik Spruyt, *The Sovereign State and Its Competitors: An Analysis of Systems Change* (Princeton: Princeton University Press, 1996), 36–39.

63. "Friendship was just as important for the functioning of medieval order as feudal bonds or kinship ties." Gerd Althoff, "Friendship and Political Order," in *Friendship and Medieval Europe*, ed. Julian Haseldine (Thrupp: Sutton, 1999), 92.

64. James Turner Johnson, *Sovereignty: Moral and Historical Perspectives* (Washington, DC: Georgetown University Press, 2014) 101–14.

65. Saint Thomas Aquinas, *On Kingship, to the King of Cyprus*, trans. Gerald B. Phelan (Toronto: Pontifical Institute of Mediaeval Studies, 1982), 44–45. Plato defines the tyrannical man as someone who never experienced true friendship and, as a result, describes his character as distrustful. "Throughout their life, then, they are never friends with anybody. They are always one man's master and another man's slave. The tyrannical nature never gets a taste of freedom or true friendship. . . . Wouldn't we be right in calling people like this distrustful?" Plato, *Republic*, in *The Collected Dialogues of Plato,* ed. Edith Hamilton and Huntington Cairns, trans. Paul Shorey (Princeton: Princeton University Press, 1989), 576a.

66. Alissa M. Ardito, *Machiavelli and the Modern State* (Cambridge: Cambridge University Press, 2015), 41–42.

67. Cf. J. G. A. Pocock, *The Machiavellian Moment* (Princeton: Princeton University Press, 1975), 160–61.

68. Quentin Skinner, *The Foundations of Modern Political Thought: Volume Two, The Age of Reformation* (Cambridge: Cambridge University Press, 1978), 352–58.

69. *Leviathan*, Epistle Dedicatory. CE 4, 4. Citations to the works of Hobbes will be given with chapter and paragraph number where available, followed by the volume and page number for the Clarendon Edition of the Works of Thomas Hobbes.

70. Paul Valéry, *History and Politics*, trans. Denise Folliot and Jackson Mathews (New York: Pantheon, 1962), 178.

71. Cf. Ernst Wolfgang Böckenförde, *State, Society, and Liberty: Studies in Political Theory and Constitutional Law*, trans. J. A. Underwood (New York: Berg, 1991).

72. *Ostension* is the bodily gesture which is the basis for initial word acquisition; its equivalent, in this case, is the suggestion of desire, setting in motion the mimetic desire of the other. Cf. Chad Engelland, *Ostension: Word Learning and the Embodied Mind* (Cambridge: MIT Press, 2014).

73. "The systems of stereotypes may be the core of our personal tradition, the defenses of our position in society. . . . It is the guarantee of our self-respect; it is the projection upon the world of our own sense of our own value, our own positions and our own rights." Walter Lippmann, *Public Opinion* (Mineola: Dover, 2004), 52.

74. Alexander Hamilton, James Madison, and John Jay, *The Federalist Papers*, ed. Clinton Rossiter (New York: Penguin, 1961), 73.

75. Thomas Hobbes, *Leviathan*, 13.5. CE 4, 190.

76. Friedrich Nietzsche, *Daybreak*, §103. KGW 5.1:103, 89–90. Citations to Nietzsche will give the English translation followed by the Critical Edition volume and page numbers.

77. "Two types of morality must not be confused: the morality with which the healthy instinct defends itself against incipient decadence—and another morality with which this very decadence defines and justifies itself and leads downwards. The former is usually stoical, hard, tyrannical (–*Stoicism* itself was such a brake-shoe morality); the latter is enthusiastic, sentimental, full of secrets; it has the women and 'beautiful feelings' on its side (–primitive *Christianity* was such a morality)." Nietzsche, *The Will to Power*, §268. KGW 8.3:15[29], 216.

78. Nietzsche, *Beyond Good and Evil*, §258. KGW 6.2:258, 216.

79. Nietzsche, *Genealogy of Morals*, I:11. KGW 6.2, 288–89.

Chapter 2

Martin Luther

Modern political thought, or liberalism, tries to bracket the deep philosophical questions concerning the meaning of life. These questions liberalism leaves each individual to answer on his own. When it comes to state law and policy, the thinking goes: attempting to answer such questions leads to dissention and violence, so the state should bracket them and focus on lower-level goods instead, for example, physical and economic goods. Individuals should be left free to choose for themselves how they will answer the big questions concerning the meaning of life; but, of course, when citizens harm each other, the state must step in. *Harm* must therefore be defined and this official definition enforced.

It is not obvious, however, what constitutes harm. The only way to know if I am harming someone is to be in relation to them, which is why, for us, personal relationships form the ultimate horizon for social norms. To do the opposite, to make a moral code the ultimate standard of harm, is to limit our recognition of violence and even our awareness of it to only certain manifestations—naturally, the violence from which the state protects us. Insofar as our definition of violence changes, then our conception of the scope of public order would change as well. The deployment of state power would follow upon moral ideas. Morality is meant to be enforced; the essence of morality would be the doctrine that the sovereign state imposes. The claim of the liberal state to be incompetent with respect to adjudicating deep philosophical questions of ultimate meaning is thus a smokescreen: by defining the nature of harm itself and not deferring to any other body of tradition, the state inevitably commits to certain answers to these questions, as D. C. Schindler shows.[1] The state that does not defer to any other authority is an absolute state. The doctrine which underlies the understanding of the purpose of its power for such a state is a *moral* doctrine. These two concepts are mutually reinforcing within liberalism. We will detail the creation of these in the next two chapters, starting with sovereignty in this chapter and chapter 3, and then taking up the creation of morality in chapter 4.

The content of any moral doctrine within liberalism is arbitrary. Harm is defined in a particular way; it may have widespread acceptance, but it is not based on any principle apart from that acceptance. To be just in a liberal state is to be *esteemed* as just. Liberalism cannot ask the question of different types of relationships and loyalties, asking what they are and what is due as a result of them. Liberalism is premised, instead, on public esteem replacing justice. This is the foundation of modern political thought. It comes from Martin Luther.

***

Martin Luther was a revolutionary thinker with an impact impossible to overstate.[2] At the core of Luther's thought is the solution to a personal dilemma he faced, revealed to him during his *Turmerlebnis* (tower experience), a kind of conversion he had when he was a monk and, by his own account, "hated the just God who punishes sinners."[3] As he explained at the end of his life, only with a certain interpretation of scripture was he relieved from his depression and felt as though he was "born again."[4] Luther's *Lectures on Romans*, delivered from spring of 1515 to the fall of 1516, illuminate both his difficulties and the decisive first formation of the new viewpoint at which he arrived.[5] In St. Paul's Letter to the Romans, variations of "justice" (δικαιοσύνη) appear over sixty times—and Luther's troubles had to do with the idea of justice.

WINNING GOD'S ESTEEM

Luther was troubled for two reasons. First, he held a philosophical conception of justice: justice is an active practice, and we can become just by doing just acts, as Aristotle taught. Second, as a person, Luther was scrupulous. Although he lived as a "monk without reproach," he writes that he felt "that I was a sinner before God with an extremely disturbed conscience. I could not believe that he was placated by my satisfaction."[6] He was hyperconscious of his sins and unable to feel assured that God accepted his reparation for them. Because of his acute awareness of his falling short, Luther felt burdened by the justice of God. Men are miserable sinners, God punishes them, and thus men can only feel threatened and sorrowful with regard to God and the gospel.

How to overcome the inevitable feeling of oppression? Was it by encountering God as a loving father, welcoming back the prodigal son by putting a ring on his finger and throwing a party—God as infinitely merciful, always forgiving us, and calling us to forgive each other? Was it, in other words, that God's love is greater than justice and that justice serves love? No. For Luther, it had to do instead with the way God "justifies" (*iustificat*) us. Justification, for Luther, is a gift of God that we passively possess and which remains external to us. He read Romans 1:17—"For in [the gospel] is revealed the justice of God from faith to faith; as it is written, 'The one who is just by faith will live'"—and writes: "There I began to understand that the justice of God is that by which the just lives by a gift of God, namely by faith. And this is the meaning: the justice of God is revealed by the gospel, namely, the passive justice with which merciful God justifies us by faith."[7]

This was the critical discovery for Luther. "Here I felt that I was altogether born again and had entered paradise itself through open gates."[8]

A passive justification remains external to us. We do not become just; we are only given an external imputation of being just. This is a matter of esteem, not of a personal relationship. In Luther's *Lectures on Romans*, justice does not have a positive meaning. He writes that the very meaning of the term justice is the same as the non-imputation of injustice.[9] To be just is not to have a virtue of acting in a good way towards others—to make sure to pay your debts, for instance, or to be honest and trustworthy. Rather, it is disconnected from a pattern of action and from the exercise of virtue in community. Justice is replaced by faith, defined as belief. For justice to be imputed to us, it is not a matter of being just but of confessing a belief. Justice is not a personal quality that becomes manifest in relationships but a status of being esteemed. As we know, I can esteem somebody without entering into a relationship with him, by looking at his good qualities and being enthralled with them, while downplaying any bad qualities.[10] Seeing someone in the static way required for esteem lacks the back-and-forth of a personal relationship in which two parties respond to each other.

Instead of a back-and-forth with God, seeking to show our love with our words and deeds—which would involve a personal relationship with a give-and-take like other relationships, with God leading us but also responding to our prayers and entering into conversation and communion with us—Luther wanted God's esteem. Unlike a relationship, where a pattern of action is built up that forges mutual trust between the parties, esteem is a passive *being regarded* in a certain way. Just as our admiration for others plays up their good qualities and downplays their bad qualities, we want God to regard us as "just," even when we know we are not. "'To be just before God' is the same as 'to be justified before God,'" writes Luther. "A man is not considered just by God because he is just; but because he is considered just by God, therefore he is just."[11]

As a result, "[W]here there had been an *acting* Christian, or a Christian *agent*, now there is simply a *believer*."[12] This is a replacement of justice with esteem. In his *Lectures on Romans*, there are three examples of political figures whose active pursuit of justice Luther thinks is wrongheaded. Instead of defending their rights, these figures should have endured the evils they suffered as punishments for their sins. They could not take their understanding of their rights to be equivalent to God's understanding of justice. God rules the world through universal justice.[13] We are only capable of knowing *particular* justice, however. "This is the reason (if I may speak of myself)," Luther writes, "why even hearing the word 'justice' nauseates me to the point that if someone robbed me, he would not bring me such grief. . . . For I in myself and with many others have had the experience that when we were just, God laughed at us in our justice."[14] No matter what we think about justice, God laughs at our little ideas, which always fall badly short of his universal standard. No wonder Luther hated the just God who punishes sinners—the deck is stacked against us and we can never win a clear conscience, since what human beings esteem as just is laughable compared to what God esteems as just. This must be the case when justice is interpreted in terms of esteem rather than personal relationships.[15]

Nevertheless, for Christians of all stripes, relationships clearly matter a great deal; how we treat the least of our fellow human beings is of the greatest concern to God according to the teachings of Jesus, and it is a highly debatable idea that the scriptures paint a picture of God laughing at human beings who are trying to treat each other well.

To think in terms of esteem rather than relationships means that God's justice is in competition with ours. For Luther, it had to be one or the other: either we are under the reign of sin or of God; the two systems of esteem are in opposition to each other. God crushes the system of human esteem and substitutes a different standard, but it is a standard that we can never live up to. The point is not to follow it, but rather, to be crushed by it and thus to abandon human esteem and passively accept the divine ascription of justice. God's glory is in competition with man's glory. If we allow men the ability to do anything, it takes away from God. Luther insists that "all the good in us is to be ascribed to God . . . the mercy of God alone does everything, and . . . our will does nothing, but rather is passive; otherwise all is not ascribed to God."[16] The only solution is for God to destroy the value system that is rivaling his. This is God's aim with the Mosaic law. God did not give the law so that he could enter into a special relationship with the Jewish people. God did not even give the law so that it would be followed. It was impossible to follow the law, Luther tells us, and this was indeed the point of it—to show man his impotence. To think that a law is given to be followed, such that we must have the power to follow it, is from "the arguments of human Reason, that she thinks man is mocked by an impossible precept."[17] Instead, Luther contends that the "blind, self-confident man may through them come to know his own diseased state of impotence if he attempts to do what is commanded."[18] The law was intended to crush our spirits and make us despair, because we are asked to do something that is impossible. Thus, we are made to realize that we are in need of God: "for Moses does not say, 'Thou has the strength or power to choose,' but, 'Choose, keep, do!' He issues commandments about doing, but does not describe man's ability to do."[19] Moses did not give the law with the intent that it be followed. After he gave it, he washed his hands of it.[20]

Not having access to God's justice works out to be the equivalent of saying that there is no standard of universal justice we can know. The standard for behavior is not the point of faith, and faith is not helping us live up to the standard. To think otherwise is to subject God to human esteem; if it were possible for me to follow the standard, I would then deserve God's esteem. God would be forced to esteem me as just. Such a Pelagian viewpoint would puff up our pride; in actuality, our pride and our human system of esteem needs to be crushed. The standard that God uses to predetermine who gets into heaven and who goes to hell is so far above us that it might as well be a secret. It is not for us to know; it goes against human reason. Love of neighbor, the state of all of our relationships with others, is not the standard. Justice does not have a positive meaning. Concerning the saints, Luther writes that "in their own sight and in truth they are unjust, but before God they are just because He reckons them so because of their confession of sin. They are actually sinners, but they are just by the imputation (*reputatione*) of a merciful God."[21]

GOD AS SOVEREIGN

God's pardon and condescending mercy towards us, such as it is, takes place in the absence of a personal relationship. The picture of God in Luther is not of a divine person who loves us and wants us to love him back, who bears our burdens and wants us to love our neighbor, since he loves everyone else infinitely as well. Rather, we have a picture of God as the source of an impersonal judgment, of giving or withholding esteem. Luther's image of God is of a wrathful avenger whom we must appease because we will otherwise be punished, not a father who cares for us and wants to win us over with his love. Luther never abandons the picture of God as an angry, all-powerful judge that he had when he was tortured by his scruples, going to confession for upwards of six hours at a time. No one really wants to have a personal relationship with an angry judge who knows what we did and has the power to smite us for it. The goal would be rather to get off the hook for our misdeeds.

Luther's conception of God as all-powerful, and that power consisting in his sovereign declaration of who is saved and who is damned, overshadows any possibility for a personal relationship with him. As he makes clear in *The Bondage of the Will,* Luther already holds the doctrine of predestination associated later with John Calvin. Since free will would conflict with the nature of God as all-knowing and all-powerful, there is no such thing as free will: "We do everything by necessity, and nothing by free choice."[22] All of the activity is God's, who chooses who is elect and who is damned. This doctrine of predestination is not a side issue. Even though contemporary Lutherans do not follow it, for Luther, all other Reformation initiatives flow from the central doctrine. Not only is it "religious, devout, and necessary a thing,"[23] he says it is "the question on which everything hinges," as opposed to other aspects of the Reformation, "irrelevancies about the papacy, purgatory, indulgences, and such like trifles (for trifles they are rather than basic issues)."[24] Luther said in 1537 that of all his books, only *The Bondage of the Will* and his *Catechism* satisfied him.[25] God is the sovereign; he is the dictator of my destiny. With regard to God, we lack the basic requirement of a personal relationship: freedom.[26] God is not leading us to transforming love. It is not a matter of being caught up in the love of the God who thinks we are worth dying for and of us wanting to return that love, to please him and not offend him. God is not offering us a dynamic relationship, a growing in intimacy, but rather the willingness to look at us in a certain static, one-sided way.

The cold logic of predestination means God is indifferent to our salvation. God could save everyone if he wanted—it certainly lies within his power—but he does not. "This is the highest degree of faith," according to Luther, "to believe him merciful when he saves so few and damns so many, and to believe him just when by his own will he makes us necessarily damnable."[27] Why does he not change the hearts of the wicked and make a good ending for everyone? Luther answers, "This belongs to the secrets of his majesty, where his judgments are incomprehensible. It is not our business to ask this question, but to adore these mysteries. And if flesh and blood is offended here and murmurs, by all means let it murmur; but it will achieve nothing; God will not change on that account."[28] We cannot question God's imputation of justice.[29]

Given this conception of the deity, it is not possible for us to have a personal relationship with God. We do not have the freedom to do that, but truth be told, we probably would not want to anyway, given God's nature. He is not only omnipotent but also insecure on Luther's telling, threatened by our human standards of esteem, which must be crushed by giving us impossible standards to live up to. We need God to overlook our sins and deem us worthy in spite of our transgressions. By passively accepting that God is in fact merciful, we will get his undeserved esteem. We can only hold onto this external justification if we continuously recognize that there is nothing we have done to earn it. It is like being in the entourage of a famous, mercurial athlete, flying around in his jet and staying in his summer homes—we have to remember who is the superstar and who is the sycophant. As long as we recognize that we are not worthy, we can take advantage of God's mercy.

The best formulation of the conception of God behind Luther's idea of justice as esteem is to say that God is sovereign. The term *sovereign* means the supreme authority which is not relatively higher than us, but absolutely higher.[30] There is a break, in other words, between us and the sovereign, such that a personal relationship is impossible. God's action is beyond justice and injustice.[31]

THE PERSPECTIVE OF OVERWHELMING POWER REPLACES JUSTICE

Only personal relationships can engage us on every level; only personal contact can provide the points of reference to assess our character. When we consider our lives apart from our relationships, we deal in opinionated viewpoints rather than testimony, which makes any judgment impossible. Testimonies can be weighted, compared, and pieced together to sketch a whole picture of a person's life. Viewpoints, on the other hand, are mutually exclusive; any assessment of a person would be relative to the frame of reference chosen. There is no way to get a comprehensive view of the whole if we are restricted to the metrics intrinsic to a particular viewpoint, because if we suddenly switch gears and adopt a different standard, everything might look different.

This kaleidoscopic effect does not occur with the testimonies of different people concerning someone's character for three reasons. First, testimonies can help us to accurately contextualize a person's character. While the relative weight of the metrics for an area of life is governed by a paradigm, the relative weights of paradigms vis-à-vis each other is up to idiosyncratic individual judgment. A testimony, by contrast, can provide not only data points but also judgments as to how the paradigms themselves should be weighed; in other words, they can offer an assessment of the *external* context: the circumstances as well as social milieu, *mores*, and standards that the person was facing. Second, because it involves a relationship, a testimony offers a fuller picture of a person, including observations about how a person treats third parties and deals with different circumstances. My assessment of someone's character—that is, his pattern of suggestion and response, not only to the *what* of a suggestion but also the *who*—is not only based on how the person directly treats me, but on how I observe him act towards others and speak about others. Testimony from a well-placed witness can offer a glimpse into a whole person; it is a vantaged perspective, but nevertheless one that concerns the whole. Finally, testimony enlightens us in a way that performance vis-à-vis an abstract standard does not, because it offers insight into the *internal* context. Knowing someone's backstory—the abuse they might have suffered, for example—tempers any assessment we might be tempted to give by adjusting our expectations for the individualized case. The old adage of walking a mile in someone's shoes is a plea for dropping depersonalized judgments in favor of understanding a unique personal situation.

By contrast, justice considered apart from personal relationships can only be a point of view, a way of seeing reality, which is inherently partial. As a static portrait, a person is a Rorschach test or a gestalt that can be viewed in two different manners; there is no truth itself, at least that to which we can have access, but rather only different perspectives. In the realm of esteem there is really no "truth," but a variety of evaluations.[32] If justice is inevitably a partial point of view, the key, then, would be to get the right perspective on justice—for Luther, this is a theological perspective rather than a philosophical one: the justice of God rather than the justice of man. The two perspectives are in competition with each other, and God's perspective wins.

Viewpoints must be adopted first in order to then be applied; they are deductive and never inductive. Faith for Luther is adherence to a viewpoint; this must come before works, so to speak. Works only have meaning because of the worldview under which they are assumed. The paradigm becomes the ultimate arbiter of meaning and not the personal interaction. We cannot then look at something and identify it is good. There always has to be an ideological filter. To whom is it good, that is to say, which class of people? Which worldview benefits? Goodness loses its quality as simple. A relationship of loyalty and friendship cannot just be good without there being some caveat attached. There is no good in itself: for example, a positive relationship that contributes to peace and harmony. On the contrary, a worldview would always determine what is good, and our relationships need to conform to that worldview—not the other way around. It is then not a matter of loving human love wherever it may be found and bringing that love to its perfection, for example, in gift of self by following Christ's example. Rather, sanctification only comes after a passive, external imputation of justice. There is no virtue, love, or friendship before that. If we think those things are good, we become prideful, and this makes them actually bad. Luther writes that "the loftiest virtues of the heathen, the best things in the philosophers, the most excellent things in men, which in the eyes of the world certainly appear to be, as they are said to be, honorable and good, are nonetheless in the sight of God truly flesh and subservient to the kingdom of Satan; that is to say, they are impious and sacrilegious and on all counts bad."[33] Philosophy and religion are competing ideologies. Something that seems good within the philosophical system is actually evil considered from a religious viewpoint.

Relationships can and should be noncompetitive, balanced over the short and long terms, and not pitted against each other. Without a personal relationship that could bridge the perspectives and bring them into dialogue with each other, we are left to our own resources choosing between competing worldviews. The victor in this struggle—the transcendental truth, the truth of the overwhelming power—might not be strictly coterminous with victory in a power struggle.[34] However, it is basically arbitrary. The rationality of it is inaccessible to us, such that may as well be, as far as we are concerned, reducible to raw will.[35]

THE VIEWPOINT OF OVERWHELMING POWER GUIDES ESTEEM

When justice is taken out of personal relationships, it is no longer the task of harmonizing different and potentially conflicting loyalties and responsibilities, but rather becomes a viewpoint. In order to secure our own happiness and power, we need to adopt the viewpoint of the one who has power over us. This holds both for godly and for merely human justice. If we do not want the magistrate to impute to us the quality of lawbreaker and deprive us of our liberty, then we need to follow his human directives; if we do not want God to impute to us the quality of unjust and send us to eternal damnation, then we need to follow his divine directives.

We think in terms of which viewpoint has the power, so that we can then adapt ourselves to it. For Luther, even serving God does not gain us true freedom.[36] Since justice is a viewpoint, it must precede works. One must know which viewpoint to follow in order to know which works have value. Before we can assess the value of the work, we have to know the viewpoint under which the work will be assumed. As Luther writes: "The justice of God is so named to distinguish it from the justice of man, which comes from works, as Aristotle describes it very clearly in Book III of the *Ethics*. According to him, justice follows upon actions and originates in them. But according to God, justice precedes works, and thus works are the result of justice."[37]

First, you have to adopt the correct viewpoint, and then, your works can have value. If we initially harmonize our viewpoint with God's viewpoint, then our works can be just. That harmonization with the divine viewpoint has to come first, otherwise the works fall under our human viewpoint and puff us up with pride.

If we exult works, this shows that we are captive to the human system of valuation. When a man acts in accord with human justice, and does just deeds, the problem is that he "seeks to be esteemed and to be honored for it . . . he does not do his good deed out of love and humility for God's sake but . . . he does it for his own sake and for the sake of his own reputation, from a hidden conceit and love of self."[38] The whole system of human esteem is rotten, for Luther, because it shuts out God. Human justice, justice as understood by the philosophers, must be rejected and seen as injustice. The two are in competition and are mutually exclusive: "the Word of God and the traditions of men are irreconcilably opposed to one another, precisely as God himself and Satan are mutually opposed, each destroying the works and subverting the dogmas of the other like two kings laying waste each other's kingdoms."[39] Man can only be seen as just when he repudiates his own justice, which God hates.[40]

The problem is not with doing works; works are fine. The problem is pride, thinking the works have any significance on their own. The problem for Luther is not doing works, but rather the *esteem* that we give them.[41] It is a category mistake to think our works have value in and of themselves. They cannot; they are facts which are good in reference to a viewpoint that gives them value. In themselves, works fall under the realm of the indifferent, the *adiaphora*. It is a viewpoint that gives things their value. What is precious when it comes to religion can only be determined starting from the Word through faith, which determines what should be valued. As Luther says, "the prudence of spiritual men knows neither good nor evil but always looks to the Word and not to the work, and weighs and estimates the dignity of the work on the basis of the Word, where even if the work is the lowliest of all, yet this prudence values it as most precious (*preciosissimum estimat*), for he always puts the highest value on (*preciosissimum semper reputat*) the Word."[42]

We do not have to agree with a certain point of view. In the case of divine justice, I might think it is crazy to both save and damn the unworthy. In both cases the solution is not to think, "I know better than the one who has the power," but rather to simply accede to the controlling viewpoint, as it enables me to get what I want (commodious living or eternal salvation). The viewpoint is controlling, not because it is *transcendent*—that is, represents a more comprehensive common good. As a viewpoint and not a loyalty, it is incapable of transcending other viewpoints but must clash with them. Viewpoints are rather *transcendental*, the impersonal condition for the possibility of what is lower. The condition for the possibility of my liberty and commodious living is adopting the viewpoint of the magistrate. The condition for the possibility of eternal life is adopting God's viewpoint. I prefer that God would use his power to save everyone and not damn many (if not most) people to eternal torment, but that is just my preference. It could, of course, be asked, "Why does God not cease from the very motion of omnipotence by which the will of the ungodly is moved to go on being evil and becoming worse?" Luther answers, "This is wanting God to cease to be God on account of the ungodly if you want his power and activity to cease, which implies that he should cease to be good lest they become worse."[43] Likewise, to prefer a different law is to desire that I should be the lawgiver, and that his "power and activity" should cease.

For us, truth is inseparable from personal relationships. Knowing that something is true, at least something of any consequence, is based on evidence that includes believing other people with whom we are in relation. Since people will have different ideas, different perspectives, different bases of knowledge, and different attachments to the truth, it is inevitable that we have to make judgments in whom to trust, assessments which cannot be entirely separated from an evaluation of the quality of the relationship we have with the person making a claim—for example, whether our relationship is strong enough for the other person to share with me an unpleasant truth. Communication does not require agreement.[44] There cannot be a pure judgment on a viewpoint as such, apart from a consideration of the types of relationships we have with people who espouse the viewpoint.

By contrast, a transcendental viewpoint is supposedly independent of all personal relationships. Transcendental truth functions as a litmus test, determining in advance whom we should follow. Community membership is at stake with the acknowledgment of a transcendental truth; for example, God is the overwhelming power that controls everything, including especially who goes to heaven and who goes to hell—the power to decide who is on the outside and who is on the inside. Why some people accept it and are saved and others do not and are damned is not really for us to know. The worldview is the basis for inclusion and exclusion, but it itself is unable to respond to rational challenges.

For Luther, adopting the viewpoint of the Word of God is all we have to do. The adoption of this metaphysical conviction is not subject to human influence: it is preached and then automatically accepted. Following God's commands is likewise simplistic.[45] There is a clear command—Luther always believed that scripture was clear[46]—and we either follow it or we do not. It does not involve any creativity or real responsibility, and in particular, we are responsible for ourselves and not for others. Salvation is an individual matter after all; this is the upshot of Luther's bedrock principles of *sola scriptura*, *sola fide*, and the priesthood of all believers. I can be saved without others being saved. Their salvation is up to them accepting it. Lack of responsibility means that our attitude towards others is one of indifference. Luther's description of the indifference of Moses as to whether or not the Israelites followed the law is paralleled with the attitude of the Christian towards the salvation of his fellow human being. *Sola fide* refers to individual salvation. It is complemented by *sola scriptura*: we do not need to be loyal to other people to gain salvation. All we need is faith in scripture. For Luther, scripture dictates our loyalties in advance. If the church goes against scripture, then we should leave the church and follow someone who has a correct understanding.[47]

ALTRUISM: THE MINIMUM-LOYALTY RELATIONSHIP

In a competition for esteem and under the power of a sovereign, human relations take on a character of indifference and altruism. In his sermon on two types of justice, Luther reduces the justice that belongs to us—as opposed to the alien justice imputed to us based on our faith—to altruism.[48] "Altruism" is the name of doing good without friendship and without loyalty, doing good outside the context of a relationship, doing good to others while remaining indifferent to them. We set an example for our neighbors, rather than building up our relationships with them.[49]

I am altruistic when I help someone without regard for myself. I am concerned for the other and not about me, which means that I am concerned for the other and not concerned for the relationship I have with the other. "Therefore he should be guided in all his works," Luther writes of a true Christian, "by this thought and contemplate this one thing alone, that he may serve and benefit others in all that he does, considering nothing except the need and the advantage of his neighbor."[50] Altruism pits regard for self and regard for the other against each other as two competing considerations. I look to the needs of the other person and not to my own needs. By contrast, if I were concerned with the relationship I have with another, I could not exclude myself and be solely other regarding; I would have to have appropriate regard for myself as well, as a necessary term in the relationship. Our relationships with others are deeply beneficial to ourselves. As Chad Engelland puts it,

> Jesus says, "Deny yourself." But he also says, "Love your neighbor *as yourself*." He takes self-love to be the measure and standard of loving another. . . . Yes, love involves sacrifice. A mother and father must sacrifice many things for the sake of their children. But this is not to act selflessly. For one of the greatest glories of being a person is being a great mother and father and having the company of children who have turned out well. This is among the most personally satisfying things the human being is capable of.[51]

Altruism, on the contrary, takes place outside a relationship; it is a random act of kindness rather than a sustained love affair. The theme of friendship is conspicuously absent in the writings of the Reformers.[52] For Luther, trust is the opposite principle of good government.[53]

If the Christian life is altruism, it makes sense for Luther to say that the law is impossible to fulfill. No one can be completely selfless, forgetting himself all the time. Likewise, it makes sense to deny merit to the saints, as Luther does, saying that "no saint has adequately fulfilled God's commandments in this life. Consequently the saints have done absolutely nothing which is superabundant."[54]

For Luther, friendship is utilitarian, while altruism is selfless.[55] He writes that "love of neighbor is not concerned about its own; it considers not how great or humble, but how profitable and needful the works are for neighbor or community."[56] This even applies to salvation. We are supposed to try to get into heaven, but it would be selfish to make that the motivation for all our actions.[57] The ultimate reward of heaven, or any reward, cannot form a motivation for acting; the just must seek only the glory of God, and forget themselves.

However, if our aim is a relationship with another person, we cannot entirely forget ourselves. "Love your enemies" is a very different prescription from "forget yourself." The one acknowledges the state of a relationship—whether someone is a friend or not—while the other does not. For the former commandment, if someone is our enemy, we are still called to love them; this is not easy, and the commandment does not pretend that it is easy. Altruism, on the other hand, is not aiming at friendship; it does good indiscriminately, without distinguishing between friends and enemies.[58] Love has its terminus in friendship, but for altruism, friendship is irrelevant, as we do good to others without regard for our relationship to them.

There is a question what doing good means exactly in this connection, especially if good is defined by a worldview. Doing good to another person might be selfless, but if it is outside of a dialogue with him, it may not be experienced by him as good, and it might not actually work for his benefit. He might resent humanitarian help, given without dialogue and without taking him seriously. If there is no terminus of friendship but just "good" that is done to those who "benefit" from altruism, it is unclear what they are getting out of it, other than perhaps taking advantage of a kindhearted soul in the short-term. Without a long-term aim for the action or an understanding of the benefit we are working to accrue for their sake, the whole enterprise lacks a criterion of success. This is why Luther defines it in terms of the intention and not the result: as long as it is done selflessly, it is worthwhile—for us, that is, and not necessarily for the person about whom we are supposedly concerned. Giving money to a drug addict to feed their addiction does not help them; were we in that situation, we would not want our friends to treat us this way. It actually manifests a lack of concern, not true concern. Someone who knows us and knows our situation is in the position to do good to us that will help us in the long run. Only a true friend can be motivated to give us what we really need, which on occasion might not be what we think we want.

For us, we need a relationship with others first, and only then can we do good to them. Altruism, however, is doing "good" to others while maintaining our indifference, keeping our loyalty to them to a minimum. I am loyal to you enough to not harm you, at least according to my definition of harm. I can even do good to you, though you will not necessarily experience it that way.

My good deed is all about me; it does not arise from an authentic concern with you, but means doing good to you without risking a relationship and stopping with minimum loyalty.

INDIFFERENCE TO THE COMMON GOOD: "RELIGION" AND "POLITICS"

Altruism turns indifference to others into a virtue. Such indifference at least grants others negative liberty. Under Luther's premises, consider what would happen if we took a strong interest in the salvation of others. Since salvation is the adoption of our worldview, the more our worldview would be adopted by other people, the more people would be saved. True concern for them would therefore entail getting them to adopt the worldview by any means necessary, including force. Refashioning society according to our viewpoint and eliminating freedom, which would only be freedom to do bad things as defined by our worldview, would be completely justified. Given this, it is clear that caring too much about building a godly society brings conflict and destruction.

This is indeed what many perceived to have happened. The Reformation started with Luther's questioning the practice of church indulgences in October of 1517, continued past his condemnation for denying church teaching in 1521, and inspired enormous popular enthusiasm among common people, for whom it promised liberation from oppressive authority and the financial burdens of supporting church institutions. This blossomed a few years later into the largest rebellion before the French Revolution: the most important event of that era, the German Peasants' War (1524–1526). Almost three hundred thousand townsmen and farmers rebelled against their lords, using scripture to justify their complaints about unjust treatment and their attempt to overthrow the feudal order. The causes of this attempted revolution were many, but there was, as Peter Blickle concludes, a "religious-legal dimension to the revolt's causes. A strong, if not the strongest, pillar of feudalism was the force of legitimacy, which impelled the peasants to present only such grievances as could be justified by law. . . . When, however, the ancient tradition was replaced by the religious-legal principle of the godly law, the effect was liberating and even revolutionary. Under the godly law, the peasants' needs could be expressed as morally justified demands."[59] This challenge to the whole social structure was violently repressed. Luther was horrified by the outbreak of the German Peasants' War and wrote a tract that justified a crackdown on the peasant rebels. In it he held that anyone in revolt against constituted authority should be killed by anyone else, bypassing normal judicial procedures.[60] After a hundred thousand peasants were massacred,

Luther came under pressure but refused to disavow his previous cheerleading for the violence against them.[61]

Indifference to our fellows and total obedience to our rulers seems preferable to the destruction of the German Peasants' War, which showed how Christianity as a metaphysical conviction could quickly be turned to revolutionary ends. Stopping the violence that results from turning Christianity into an ideology seemingly entails seeing Christianity as without effect on worldly justice, coexisting with indifference to our neighbors, and, additionally, as entailing obedience to the powers that be, who protect us from our neighbors and to whom we have minimum loyalty. This is the invention of what we know today as "religion" in contradistinction to "politics." *Religion* is the realm of interminable conflict over mutually exclusive metaphysical interpretations of the world, while *politics* is the realm of ultimate sovereignty for the sake of keeping the peace. This conceptualization did not exist before Luther; it was created by him and triumphed with the violent rise of the modern state, which used it to justify its own violence.

We will first explicate Luther's creation of "religion." Then we will show how it sacralizes the worldly sovereign and how this, in turn, fragments the common good.

The contemporary meaning of the term "religion" takes hold only after Luther. "Christianity," writes John Bossy, is "a word which until the seventeenth century meant a body of people, and has since then, as most European languages testify, meant an 'ism' or body of beliefs."[62] Nobody before Luther would have understood "religion" to be what we understand by the word today. Aristotle made "no real distinction between what we would call the 'religious' and the 'political.'"[63] In the medieval period, *religio* meant ceremonial worship, the virtue of honoring God, a part of justice.[64] It was not synonymous with Christianity and was not used in the plural. This is obviously very different from the current sense of the term. Today, religion in Western societies signifies a metaphysical conviction as opposed to science.[65] It is an alternate explanation of things, a story about the world that we believe in and credit as true. The religious or metaphysical story we are to believe in involves beings and actions for which there is no evidence and can never be evidence in the scientific sense. Explanations like Santa Claus or the Tooth Fairy bringing us presents are clearly made up, but children believe them; likewise, religion would have us believe stories that are metaphysical, that is, beyond our senses. They are alternate stories from the ones that can be proven based on evidence.

For Luther, metaphysical conviction stands apart from reason.[66] Faith and reason are in competition; the word of God and traditions of men are implacably opposed to each other.[67] This does not mean that metaphysical conviction is unclear; the opposite is the case. Clarity about the bible makes *sola fide* and *sola scriptura* possible—after all, if the bible were not clear, we would not be sure what we are believing in exactly, and we would need other people to help explain our faith to us. We can be certain about our salvation only if we are saved by faith alone, meaning a certainty of holding a clear belief by an individual, who has no need to delve into the traditions of rationality to settle perplexing questions. Likewise, when justice is a matter of imputed esteem, similar complications are removed. Am I a worthy person? As each human being has positive aspects along with shortcomings and misdeeds—some relationships or aspects of relationships that a person has with others may be positive, while others are not—to total up the whole picture for a single individual would require godlike intuition. In our own civilization, determining whether a person is guilty of violating a single criminal law beyond a reasonable doubt requires a long procedure and the interaction of multiple institutions, and it can still get the result wrong, so knowing with certainty whether a person as a whole is really "just" is *prima facie* impossible. However, if my justification as a valuable person is just a matter of my faith, my clear convictions, then my uncertainty about it can be overcome.

Most importantly, religious faith as we understand it today is a *part* of life only. This was not Christianity's previous understanding of itself. The term for *Christianity* amongst the earliest Christians was "the way"—that is, a way of life, shared together in a community with others. Brad Gregory coins the phrase "more-than-religion" to describe Christianity before the Reformation in the early sixteenth century, in which "religion was neither a matter of choice nor separate from the rest of life."[68] Christianity, considered as a relationship of God with man, makes a claim on the whole person and is not reducible to just following certain rules and ceremonies or assenting to certain doctrines. This understanding of Christianity is a bad fit with the modern category of *religion*, since, for the latter, certain tenets of faith and traditions delineate a particular realm of life vis-à-vis other realms and is potentially in competition with them.

The hallmark of religion as we understand it today is the doctrine of the afterlife, combined with prescriptions on how to get to heaven. The rest of life consists of matters indifferent to our salvation, a zone of freedom. An important topic for Luther's close associate Philip Melancthon was this realm of the *adiaphora* or "things indifferent." Even Luther, who does not believe in free will, allows that there is indeed something like free will in the nonreligious domain of life.[69]

It is by carving out a realm of salvation, hived off from the rest of life, that Luther turned Christianity into a religion.[70] Essential to such a move is the absence of a full personal relationship with God. Such a relationship would involve our whole being and our free consent. Freedom would not be a realm apart from God, but rather in living out of that back-and-forth relationship with God, which would fully engage us rather than only being a matter of part of our lives; for example, thinking that as long as we have the certainty of faith, our works are extraneous. Religion acts as if God is a company boss: someone who wants something out of us during the work day but does not care what we do with our private lives.

Such a division of life into separate spheres is incompatible with justice as the integration of life. The point of doing good works therefore cannot be to get to heaven; rather, they must have some other aim. "Luther horizontalized Christian ethics; he transferred its goal from Heaven to earth," writes Heiko Oberman. "Good works are not required for salvation but crucial for survival in a threatened world."[71] Oberman aptly says "survival" and not "justice." The Christian church does not work to bring about justice in the world; justification by faith alone has destroyed the concept of justice on earth and replaced it with esteem. We are not trying to work for justice or a peace based on justice; we just want to be left alone: a Christian obeys all authority and suffers in silence. "The true, persecuted Church," Oberman writes, "has no political ambitions that it would risk peace in the world to achieve."[72] That the Church has "no political ambitions" means that Christians obey unquestioningly the commands of the ruler as if they were the commands of God. This is not a secularization, but a *sacralization* of political authority, or better "political power/authority" (since Luther does not distinguish between the two).

Since Luther, we have understood the worldly realm gaining in popularity, adherence, and importance generally vis-à-vis religion as "secularization." However, it should be noted that our understanding of secularization is Luther's explicit teaching, that is to say, the way in which he set up the terms of the opposition in the first place: Luther always envisioned true Christianity as a tiny band in a hostile, secular sea, a situation to which he was resigned. Secularization is the *fulfillment* of his worldview, in which Christianity is turned into a religion—namely, something that the worldly authority/power can control.[73] We might also question whether the accepted story of the rise of secularization after the Protestant Reformation does not have it backwards. In particular, the past five hundred years have seen the rise of sacred political authority and grotesque moral and political ideologies: irreligious, but not exactly adhering to rational skepticism. Confusion reigns when it comes to defining basic terms in the secularization thesis.[74] Categories have to be anachronistically invented to understand pre-modern thinkers.[75] Comparing responses on a questionnaire about doctrinal attachments five hundred years ago with responses today would tell us something about changes in common cultural reference points, but reveal nothing about the real state of Christian faith, if the latter is actually a life-changing personal relationship. Measured in terms of a love of Christ deep enough to give up one's life, the twentieth century was the most Christian, not the least Christian, century.[76]

Christianity as a "religion" is opposed to the corresponding political realm of power/authority, which has the freedom to create its own justice. Enforcing it keeps the peace and thus allows us to survive. This is not something to which we can be indifferent, and actually, we must obey the powers that be because they stand in the place of God. Worldly justice therefore turns out not to be merely something hopelessly partial, something at which God laughs, a justice of works that God requires us to repudiate, and something that is definitively overcome with our justification by faith.[77] While it is Luther's starting point to denigrate worldly justice as steeped in sin, in the end he views it as the key to our survival and a direct expression of the will of God.

The worldly ruler has the right to enforce his standard of esteem. This is the difference between religion and politics. A religious leader has no right to force anyone to do or believe anything. There is no such thing as spiritual authority. "God cannot and will not permit anyone but himself to rule over the soul."[78] With religion, everything is radically democratic; there is no *Obrigkeit* or superiors. In stark contrast with the worldly realm—where abilities are unevenly distributed and the vast majority of people are in no way fit to rule—we are all equal.[79] Democratic consent is necessary for everything in the spiritual realm. To God all men are equal; the God's-eye view of mankind is an original position under a veil of ignorance, looking at people before their various talents, abilities, and blessings are conferred. We can depose our pastor, but not our ruler.[80] An external church only exists to expound scripture, but that is itself clear, so there is no need for there to be any fixed authority.[81]

Preachers can preach, generally, that the worldly power/authority should follow God. Preachers have no authority, however, to change the civil law, as this is simply not given to them but to the worldly rulers.[82] The same thing *seems* to be true in the other direction. However, we must read closely when Luther writes the following: "The same is true when spiritual or secular princes and lords want to change and correct the Word of God in a dictatorial and dominating fashion, when they themselves dictate what should be preached and taught, even though they have no more right to this than the lowest beggar. Such people want to be God themselves, and not to serve Him or to remain subordinate to Him."[83] The worldly rulers cannot interfere with the Word of God that is preached and taught, but *not* because it is the domain of spiritual authority. Rather, Luther says that they "have no more right to this than the lowest beggar"—in other words, *no one* has a right to interfere with it. God reigns exclusively over souls. There is no spiritual authority at all; what is preached and taught is just the Word of God: namely, scripture alone, which is clear. The limitation on the power/authority of the worldly rulers is, in the end, no restriction at all, as they only lack authority to do what no one can do.

That spiritual authority is otiose means that temporal authority gains considerably in importance, and indeed Luther ranks political leadership the most important and noble of all callings and lavishes praise on the blessings conferred by government.[84] Luther initially seems to want to make the worldly sphere appear unimportant in his initial description of the two kingdoms. However, when it is time to actually list that which Luther considers to be "external," outward goods, they turn out not to be restricted to bodily things, and government ends up controlling all the dealings men and women have with one another, including honor and respect, as well as knowledge, judgment, and evaluations.[85]

Luther splits up life into two domains, the religious and non-religious, the spiritual and the worldly, in order to stop preachers from dictating to rulers. Religion is a sacred metaphysical doctrine that cannot be enforced; politics is a sacred metaphysical doctrine which can and must be enforced. There is as a result of this a migration of the sacred to the worldly rulers; the ruler becomes the true mediator of God's action in the world.[86] God delegates princes their control over their kingdoms.[87] Rulers have authority over everything that it is possible for human beings to control. Turning Christianity into a religion makes it something able to be controlled by political rulers. In the end, no matter the separation of the worldly and the spiritual in Luther, princes even have power to determine which religion is true.

This conclusion is overdetermined in Luther. First, rulers have control over external things, which includes everything except a blunt attempt to compel belief. However, as soon as they are preached or published, doctrines interpreting scripture are inherently outward and thus subject to the worldly powers. They must be put into some kind of outward form if they will win followers and, therefore, will inevitably be regulated by the civil authority. In 1519 Luther addresses the Christian nobility and advises that first, "[T]he number of books on theology must be reduced and only the best ones published."[88] Second, rulers have to step in as soon as religious controversy leaves people divided. Worldly rulers should settle religious controversies when different sides are wrangling about scripture or about religious traditions.[89] The same thing holds for human custom in religion, "For what the Scriptures do not contain, the preachers ought not wrangle about in the presence of the people."[90] Third, there is no church with special rights separate from worldly rulers.[91] So there is no rigid separation of church and state, as the state can regulate external aspects of the church, like any other organization. Fourth, princes who themselves are Christians are free, just like other Christians, to follow scripture and to use their judgment in what should be done. Like anybody else, they can take up the cause of the reformation of Christendom. Luther in 1520 asks worldly authorities to take the lead in reforming the church: "It would be best—in fact it is the only way—if kings, princes, nobles, cities, and communities made a start, so that bishops and clergy (who are now afraid) would have reason to follow."[92] Fifth, the survival of true religion depends on the protection of worldly authority. In practice, the Reformation was accepted in many cities in Germany and Switzerland because of decisions of the political authorities not to suppress it. In Zwingli's Zürich, for example, the city council claimed the authority to determine what the true religion was, over the head of the bishop.

In his 1530 commentary on Psalm 82, Luther discriminates which teachings are heretical and should be suppressed by worldly authority. He concludes that heretics who are seditious, who preach communism, or who say that Christians cannot serve as worldly rulers are to be punished as rebels—also, those sects which preach against traditional, accepted Christian doctrine should be punished as blasphemers.[93] Luther concludes: "By this procedure no one is compelled to believe, for he can still believe what he will; but he is forbidden to teach and to blaspheme."[94] It is unsurprising, then, that the Reformation undermines Church authority, as Brad Gregory writes, "but not the authority, power, or control of political rulers."[95] "In Lutheran territories as elsewhere, what is idealized as a *partnership* between church and state plays out as a *subordination* of church to state."[96] The most decisive act of Luther's break with Rome was his burning of books of canon law in 1520; yet thirty-five years later, Luther and his followers had embraced canon law while giving power over it to worldly rulers rather than the church authorities.[97] "The Reformation, by splitting Christendom, made modern civil religions inevitable because the secular authority was now the guarantor of ecclesiastical authority rather than its rival."[98] By the 1530s, the thinker that Lutherans looked to in order to explain the relationship of religion and temporal power was Philip Melanchthon, who made it clear that civil rulers had to take care of religion, controlling it for the sake of good order.[99]

A big part of this is the simple falsity of Luther's insistence that scripture is clear. In reality, biblical exegesis gets very complicated very quickly.[100] Scripture interpreted through the Spirit "could come to mean almost anything," as Brad Gregory concludes. This "was true for the entire Reformation era, but it is often overlooked because two forms of Protestantism received ongoing political support while other expressions were routinely suppressed."[101] Magisterial Protestantism (Luther and Calvin) exercised great historical influence not because it had the correct interpretation of the bible, but because it gained the protection of princes, which, for example, the radical Reformation lacked. Lutheran and Reformed Protestantism were, in Gregory's phrase, "the great exceptions to the Reformation," rather than its archetypes, unless we believe there is a necessary connection between an accurate interpretation of the bible and having support from political leaders. Political leaders, of course, will naturally favor religious doctrines that confirm their authority.[102] Magisterial Protestantism needed the support of worldly rulers to survive, and as a result, writes Gregory, "[O]nly a carefully controlled and domesticated Reformation would be permitted to exert a widespread influence."[103] So controlled and domesticated was it that Luther and Melanchthon even gave Philip, landgrave of Hesse, permission for bigamy in 1540. This episode was not an instance of Luther giving way under pressure, but rather an indication "that his political theology had led him into a trap."[104] A decade earlier, Luther had already given way to pressure, when Elector John convinced him that his doctrine of passive resistance to authority did not apply to the Emperor.[105] While before the German Peasants' War, Luther published works that affirmed the rights of Christian congregations to choose their own pastors, he dropped this view after that bloody conflict, and "agreed that matters which had in the past been the concern of the Church—administering its landed wealth and providing for the payment of its clergy—should now become the business of the secular prince."[106] "All in all," writes a scholar of Luther's political thought, "Luther's arguments were an exercise in admitting the prince into the church by the back door while ostentatiously denying him entry through the front door."[107]

Not only does Luther admit the prince into the church, he assigns him the task of guarding the entrance. There is simply no one else to protect the purity of Christian doctrine from imposters if spiritual authority is reduced to leadership by example and the church to a radical democracy, with everyone being equal and having the right to resist. When there is no spiritual authority in practice, defenses are lacking against a charismatic person winning adherents for his own idiosyncratic vision of Christian teaching. In 1534, for example, John of Leiden proclaimed himself king and messiah of the German city of Münster, where he abolished private property, destroyed religious art, banned all books, and instituted polygamy. If a community of believers adheres to wacky beliefs, it should no longer be considered Christian. The doctrines of *sola scriptura* and *sola fide* make this matter of doctrinal content acute; if the very definition of Christianity is conviction, then when we adhere to a false conviction, we are not just misinformed or uninformed but lose the essence of the religion itself. The radically democratic nature of the church cannot be taken so far such that a group of believers could decide to believe something obviously heterodox; they have to be held within limits of traditional doctrines, and the leadership that is competent to enforce these limits can only be the civil authorities. There is no other authority left. If preachers start preaching their own preferences and opinions but nevertheless win followers through their charisma, they do not suddenly then transform the Word of God into something else. What guarantee do we have, then, that a preacher is preaching the Word of God and not misleading us? Preachers cannot self-validate that their words are from God; anyone can challenge them on anything, as everyone has the right to resist spiritual authority. There must be, then, an outside validation, a guarantee that spiritual authorities are preaching the Word of God and not their own views. Once that assurance is given, then the spiritual authorities can have influence, preaching within the boundary of correct doctrine. Validating that boundary is not up to the preachers but the prince.

Luther does not use the concept of validity, but this term does capture some of the connotations of his *Obrigkeit*, or "superiors." Both concepts combine power with impersonal authority. If we say a command is valid, we are not speaking of whether it is good.[108] Valid commands have to be obeyed no matter whether the ruler is good or bad. No matter how tyrannical he becomes, a person who goes against his ruler forfeits all his rights. This is the magic of sovereignty, of worldly power/authority. Worldly justice is both sinful and our salvation. It is *sacer*—a Latin word that means both "accursed, horrible, and detestable," as well as "sacred, holy, and consecrated." As that which faith humiliates and overcomes, human justice is accursed, horrible, and detestable, but as that which must always be obeyed because it upholds our existence and expresses the will of God, it is sacred, holy, and consecrated.

The task of preserving true Christian doctrine is a *sacred* task. The ruler has care over the whole community and not just a group of partisan believers. In Luther's vision, everyone is united together under the worldly ruler. He writes,

> For with respect to God and in the service of His authority (*Oberkeit*) everything should be identical and mixed together, whether it be called spiritual or secular—the pope as well as the emperor, the lord as well as the servant. No distinctions and no respect of persons applies here: one is as good before God as the other. For He is one God, the same Lord of all, of the one as well as of the other.[109]

God looks on everyone as individuals and as equals. This means there is no distinction between the worldly and spiritual when it comes to worship. "Therefore they should all be identical in their obedience and should even be mixed into one another like one cake, everyone of them helping the other to be obedient. Therefore in service or submission to God there can be no rebellion among the spiritual or the secular authorities (*geistlichen oder weltlichen Regiment*)."[110]

When Luther says "they should all be identical in their obedience," and describes "everyone of them helping the other to be obedient," we must ask *to whom* we ought to be obedient. There is no such thing as spiritual authority;

pastors who preach and serve are unable to give commands that would have to be obeyed. The only authority with reference to whom "obedience" could be due is the civil authority; therefore, everyone is to be united in obedience to the prince. The actions of the prince are the actions of God. For someone to oppose the civil authority would mean that they want people to follow them, not the ruler. If there are two legitimate authorities in their own spheres, then one opposing the other is a power struggle, not a revolutionary movement. To say, "On such and such a matter, people should defer to one constituted authority rather than another," is not a destabilizing challenge to all constituted authorities as such. However, matters are different when there is one sole authority, who is then challenged. When there is only one social power, uniformity is the only choice. This is the case in Luther. The political community becomes the "congregation of God," and the whole society is considered sacred. As Luther writes in his *Commentary on Psalm 82*, "Observe that he calls all communities or organized assemblies 'the congregation of God,' because they are God's own, and He accepts them as His own work, just as (Jonah 3:3) He calls Nineveh 'a city of God.'"[111] The ruler heads this congregation of God and provides the guarantee that preachers are preaching the Word of God. God himself acts through rulers to provide this assurance. Luther thus names rulers "gods": "Now because this is not a matter of human will or devising, but God Himself appoints and preserves all rulership, and if He no longer held it up, it would all fall down, even though all the world held it fast, therefore, it is rightly called a divine thing, a divine ordinance and such persons are rightly called divine, godlike, or gods."[112]

Luther liberates Christianity from the pope, only to subject it more tightly to a new overlord, the temporal ruler. The ruler is now invested with the powers of the pope. In the medieval period, the ruler could not "legislate" by unilaterally declaring a law. Rather, the ruler proclaimed what the law already was, the rights and obligations that preexisted the ruler.[113] The ruler was not there to "make" the law, and the will of the ruler had no magical quality that could turn his whim into justice. The idea of legislation was not unknown, but it had to be stimulated by events, like the rediscovery of Roman law and of Aristotle between the eleventh and the thirteenth centuries. This set the context within which the Gregorian Church Reform and the separation of canon law as a separate discipline starting at the end of the eleventh century could create the idea of legislation through the will of the pope. The ecclesiastical jurists came to see the authority of the pope as a plenitude of power with the ability to legislate, exercising the office of God on earth. After Luther, however, and the removal of the authority of the church, the prince took on the plenitude of power that the pope had possessed, including the ability to legislate as an exercise in God's power. The prince could legislate without being backed by anything other than his will.

Unconditional obedience to a will untethered to the common good of concrete, customary relationships again exhibits the sacred nature of this sovereignty, as that which stands over and against the total community, outside of all normal communal relationships, outside the common good and justice. A system of esteem upholds and validates particular commands (as well as setting the boundaries for true religion, as we have seen). There is no way to question the validation by that power, no way to separate the person from the office. By contrast, a commitment to the common good as preexisting the ruler enables us to separate the person from the office by which he acquires his special responsibility. Then instead of unconditional obedience, we have a responsibility to guide and advise the person on finding the best path towards promoting the common good.[114]

Luther offers us a choice between either complete obedience to constituted authority or revolutionary social upheaval. Christians must therefore always support their rulers, and rebels who disrupt the peace are always in the wrong, always a deviation from true Christianity. As a result, there is no justice to which we could appeal over and against the doctrines of esteem, the system of values, which buttresses our rulers in their authority. By contrast, for us, a commitment to the common good and justice as embodied in the harmony of our relationships, rather than as defined by a sacred sovereign, avoids fracturing the common order and enables us to make an integral appeal to justice. This could be defined by the transforming love of God that harmonizes our relationships with others, a "City of God" as St. Augustine puts it in the great eponymous work that has defined Christian political thought more than any other. The violence that is the result of sin—Augustine's "earthly city"—would need to be tempered as far as possible, rather than given a sacred justification.[115] Then we could speak of justice not as an external imputation, a matter of esteem, but as realized in human relationships. If justice were real, politics would definitely be obliged to pursue it—as would the Christian religion—or stand accused of siding with oppressors. If justice were an actual quality of human relationships, it would make no sense to say, "I am trying to be a good Christian, but I do not care that I am unjustly exploiting my neighbor," or "I am working for justice in the political realm, but that is independent of my Christian faith." The only way to keep these two realms distinct is to replace justice with esteem; *then* we could say, "I am trying to be a good Christian, and I do not care about the opinions of some people who disesteem my business practices," or "I am working to promote certain values in the political realm, values people from all faiths can accept, values independent of my particular Christian faith."

Turning Christianity into a religion means we look for the causes of violence in the wrong place—namely, in the content of a doctrine rather than in our relationships with others. This creates the disharmony it purports to solve.

If there is no justice but only esteem, then *we have to take sides* and strive for an ideological uniformity which distinguishes right from wrong in advance of our relationships with others. But in reality, our relationships subtend the content of our views, and we should strive for as much harmony with others as possible.

But in Luther's view, striving for harmony in our relationships is not a matter of justice, but rather outer works, which are inessential. The important thing is individual belief. Even though there is no spiritual authority which resides in the church, nevertheless, it is not the case that anything goes when it comes to the content of faith, and the boundaries of acceptable belief must be set by the worldly rulers. Spiritual and temporal power/authority is now concentrated in the ruler, who has no competitor. This unified central power/authority is sovereignty, and its preeminent theorist is Thomas Hobbes, to whom we now turn.

NOTES

1. D. C. Schindler, *The Politics of the Real* (Steubenville, Ohio: New Polity, 2021).
2. All translations from Luther's Latin will be modified to substitute forms of the word "justice" for *justitia* wherever it appears, instead of "righteousness."
3. WA 54, 186. LW 34, 337.
4. WA 54, 186. LW 34, 337.
5. Alister E. McGrath, *Iustitia Dei: A History of the Christian Doctrine of Justification*, 3rd ed. (Cambridge: Cambridge University Press, 2005), 220.
6. WA 54, 185. LW 34, 336.
7. WA 54, 186. LW 34, 337.
8. WA 54, 186. LW 34, 337.
9. "It is the same thing, whether we say, 'to whom God imputes justice,' or, 'to whom the Lord does not impute sin,' that is, injustice." WA 56, 284. LW 25, 272.
10. The just person, for Luther, "is always endeavoring to see his own evil works and to overlook those of others, likewise to see the good points in others and to overlook his own good points. The unjust, on the other hand, tries to look only for the good points in himself and for the bad points in others." WA 56, 17. LW 25, 15n1.
11. WA 56, 22. LW 25, 19n13.
12. Pierre Manent, *Natural Law and Human Rights*, trans. Ralph C. Hancock (Notre Dame: University of Notre Dame Press, 2020), 37.
13. WA 56, 448. LW 25, 440.
14. WA 56, 448. LW 25, 441.
15. For Luther, fulfilling the demands of our social roles does not factor into our striving for justice. WA 7, 37, 67. LW 31, 369.
16. WA 18, 614. LW 33, 35.
17. WA 18, 676. LW 33, 126.
18. WA 18, 678. LW 33, 128.

19. WA 18, 678. LW 33, 128.

20. "What, then, does Moses mean by these very plain and open words, except that he himself has fulfilled his office as a faithful lawgiver excellently? For he has removed every obstacle to their knowing and keeping clearly before them all the commandments, and left them no room for the excuse that they were unaware of or did not possess the commandments, or had to seek them from elsewhere. Hence if they do not keep them, the fault will lie neither with the law nor with the lawgiver, but with themselves." WA 18, 687–88. LW 33, 143.

21. WA 56, 269. LW 25, 258.

22. WA 18, 636. LW 33, 68. "God's foreknowledge and omnipotence are diametrically opposed to our free choice." WA 18, 718. LW 33, 189.

23. WA 18, 618. LW 33, 42.

24. WA 18, 786. LW 33, 294.

25. Martin Luther, *The Life of Luther Written by Himself*, ed. M. Michelet, trans. William Hazlitt (London: George Bell and Sons, 1904), 292.

26. God's love is therefore not an appeal to our freedom. Even when we are saved and the Spirit is working in us, we are not choosing God or the good freely, but rather necessarily, like a machine operates the way it is programmed: "[N]ot even here is there any free choice, or freedom to turn oneself in another direction or will something different, so long as the Spirit and grace of God remain in a man." WA 18, 635. LW 33, 65.

27. WA 18, 633. LW 33, 62.

28. WA 18, 712. LW 33, 180.

29. Even though human beings challenge and question God on many occasions in the Old Testament, for example, in Genesis 15:1–6; Genesis 18:16–33; and Psalms 10, 44, 74, and 77.

30. Cf. Jacques Maritain, "The Concept of Sovereignty," *The American Political Science Review* 44, no. 2 (1950): 343–57.

31. "Suppose that a people would rise up today or tomorrow and depose their lord or kill him. That certainly could happen if God decrees that it should, and the lords must expect it. But that does not mean that it is right and just for the people to do it. I have never known of a case in which this was a just action, and even now I cannot imagine any." WA 19, 634. LW 46, 104.

32. Love for Luther follows the same logic: it is a subjective perspective, a look that is blind to the bad, so to speak. "For all love is by nature blind. Who, then, is not blind? For who is without love—I am speaking of the sensual kind—except one who is not alive?" WA 56, 461 LW 25, 454. The addition of the "sensual" qualification does not mean that, for Luther, non-sensual love is not also blind. Ten years later Luther writes that charity "always thinks the best of everyone, and is not suspicious but believes and assumes the best about its neighbors." Translation modified. WA 18, 652. LW 33, 88.

33. WA 18, 743–44. LW 33, 227.

34. It could be the power that is so great that without it, there would not even be any power struggle at all. The power that is responsible for our very lives, the sine qua non of our existence, must always be right. The viewpoint that is not up for

contestation belongs to the overwhelming power that could destroy us but does not. This does not collapse truth into victory in a power struggle; it rather says that the basic truth responsible even for the conditions of any power struggle must be more powerful than any dependent viewpoints that only operate within its parameters. This necessary power is prior (*a priori*) to us acting and competing with each other, which comes later (*a posteriori*). It is the principle of our existence (transcendental), which is not up to our freedom and individual choice (empirical).

35. Luther writes, "Scripture uses the terms 'justice' and 'injustice' very differently from the philosophers and lawyers. This is obvious, because they consider these things as a quality of the soul. But the 'justice' of Scripture depends upon the imputation of God more than on the essence of a thing itself." WA 56, 287. LW 25, 274.

36. God's rule takes away our freedom: "For you would not call a slave free, who acts under the sovereign authority of his master; and still less rightly can we call a man or angel free, when they live under the absolute sovereignty [*imperio plenissimo*] of God (not to mention sin and death)." WA 18, 662. LW 33, 103.

37. WA 56, 172. LW 25, 152.

38. WA 56, 194. LW 25, 177.

39. WA 18, 627. LW 33, 54.

40. Luther writes that "confession and acknowledgment of sin humble the proud and just man who trusts in his own justice and for this reason downgrades the justice of God, who alone possesses justice along with virtue and wisdom and every good thing. Therefore he who humbly repudiates his own justice and confesses that he is a sinner before God truly glorifies God, proclaiming that He alone is just. Therefore it is not our injustice, which God forever hates as the enemy of His own glory, but it is the recognition and confession of our own injustice which glorifies God and commends us to Him." WA 56, 215. LW 25, 200.

41. Luther writes that "just, good, and holy works must not be understood as being disapproved in the sense that they are to be omitted, but only with respect to the meaning, esteem, and reputation we give them, that is, that we do not trust in them or esteem them or give them such honor as if we had the strength to be sufficiently just before God because of them (*quasi ex ipsis coram Deo sufficienter iusti esse valeamus*)." WA 56, 233 LW 25, 218.

42. WA 56, 416. LW 25, 408.

43. WA 18, 712. LW 33, 180.

44. "Philosophers habitually tend to shy away from analogous discourse, preferring the *terra firma* of univocity. Yet the quality of exchange among friends, which can allow for a common pursuit along different paths, requires the capacity inherent in analogous terms to let similarities retain their differences. Otherwise, communication will always presuppose agreement, requiring us to frame our convictions in a common language before we can be said to share them." David B. Burrell, *Friendship and Ways to Truth* (Notre Dame: University of Notre Dame Press, 2000), 61.

45. Luther thought believers would follow God's commands as a matter of course; the character of our works must be such that they flow from our already constituted goodness of soul, rather than change our soul. Humanitarianism is the ideal of good works. He writes that "a good tree cannot bear evil fruit and every good tree

bears good fruit. Therefore the will, which is the tree, or the root of the good tree, can do nothing but good and produces good fruit in its season." He continues in proto-Kantian fashion: "When a man's will is good, the whole man is good. Thus the tree is good when the root is good." WA 3, 25. LW 10, 25.

46. Cf., for example, WA 18, 606–9. LW 33, 24–28.

47. "If it were to happen that the pope and his cohorts were wicked and not true Christians, were not taught by God and were without understanding, why should the people not follow the obscure man? Has the pope not erred many times? Who would help Christendom when the pope erred if we did not have somebody we could trust more than him, somebody who had the Scriptures on his side?" WA 6, 411. LW 44, 134.

48. This justice "hates itself and loves its neighbor; it does not seek its own good, but that of another, and in this its whole way of living consists." WA 2, 147. LW 31, 300.

49. WA 2, 147. LW 31, 300. For Luther, the just works we pursue "are done only to serve others and to give them an example of good works." WA 7, 36, 67. LW 31, 369. Altruistically doing good to someone may serve them and set an example for them, but there is no measure of justice in them, viz. the status of the relationship between the parties.

50. He continues: "Here we see clearly that the Apostle has prescribed this rule for the life of Christians, namely, that we should devote all our works to the welfare of others, since each has such abundant riches in his faith that all his other works and his whole life are a surplus with which he can by voluntary benevolence serve and do good to his neighbor." WA 7, 35, 65. LW 31, 365–66.

51. Chad Engelland, *The Way of Philosophy: An Introduction* (Eugene, Oregon: Cascade Books, 2016), 56.

52. Thomas Heilke, "From Civic Friendship to Communities of Believers: Anabaptist Challenges to Lutheran and Calvinist Discourses," in *Discourses and Representations of Friendship in Early Modern Europe, 1500–1700*, ed. Daniel T. Lochman, Maritere López, and Lorna Huson (Burlington: Ashgate, 2011), 225–28.

53. WA 11, 274. LW 45, 121–22. Trust, of course, is the prerequisite for friendship and begins with loyalty. For Luther, loyalty is one-sided, with subjects owing their overlords total obedience. Cf. WA 19, 652–53. LW 46, 126–27.

54. WA 1, 606. LW 31, 213.

55. "Martin Luther and John Calvin had friends, and friendship was part of their lived experience; yet neither provided a theological or political account of human life that could make sense of friendship beyond a strictly utilitarian level. Neither their ecclesiology nor their political theology had a place for non-utilitarian friendship." Heilke, "From Civic Friendship to Communities of Believers: Anabaptist Challenges to Lutheran and Calvinist Discourses," 225.

56. WA 11, 261. LW 45, 103–4.

57. There is a "kingdom for the just," but "they themselves neither seek it nor think of it, for it has been prepared for them by the Father, not only before they themselves existed, but even before the foundation of the world." Luther continues, "What is more, if they did good works for the sake of obtaining the Kingdom, they would never

obtain it, but would rather belong among the ungodly who with an evil and mercenary eye 'seek their own' even in God. But the children of God do good with a will that is disinterested, not seeking any reward, but only the glory and will of God, and being ready to do good even if—an impossible supposition—there were neither a kingdom nor a hell." WA 18, 694. LW 33, 152–53.

58. "Behold, from faith thus flow forth love and joy in the Lord, and from love a joyful, willing, and free mind that serves one's neighbor willingly and takes no account of gratitude or ingratitude, or praise or blame, of gain or loss. For a man does not serve that he may put men under obligations. He does not distinguish between friends and enemies or anticipate their thankfulness or unthankfulness, but he most freely and most willingly spends himself and all that he has, whether he wastes all on the thankless or whether he gains a reward." WA 7, 36, 66. LW 31, 367.

59. Peter Blickle, *The Revolution of 1525: The German Peasants' War From A New Perspective*, trans. Thomas A. Brady Jr. and H. C. Erik Midelfort (Baltimore: The Johns Hopkins University Press, 1977), 188.

60. "Therefore let everyone who can," he exhorts, "smite, slay, and stab, secretly or openly, remembering that nothing can be more poisonous, hurtful, or devilish than a rebel." WA 18, 358. LW 46, 50.

61. It is noteworthy that Luther wrote *The Bondage of the Will* while he was preoccupied with the peasants' revolt.

62. John Bossy, *Christianity in the West 1400–1700* (Oxford: Oxford University Press, 1985), 171.

63. Francis Oakley, *Empty Bottles of Gentilism: Kingship and the Divine in Late Antiquity and the Early Middle Ages (to 1050)* (New Haven: Yale University Press, 2010), 8.

64. Cf. Thomas Aquinas, *Summa theologiae*, II-II, q. 81, a. 7, in *Summa Theologica: Complete English Edition in Five Volumes*, vol. 3, trans. Fathers of the English Dominican Province (Notre Dame, IN: Christian Classics, 1981), 1526–27.

65. Non-Western civilizations have different categorizations—hence the miscalculation of British policy in the Middle East during World War I, applying our post-Reformation categories to the institution of the caliph by thinking of him as a spiritual leader of an Islamic religion. Cf. David Fromkin, *A Peace to End All Peace: The Fall of the Ottoman Empire and the Creation of the Modern Middle East* (New York: Henry Holt & Co., 1989), 104–5. "Different people rarely mean the same thing when they say 'religion,' nor do they realize it." Nassim Nicholas Taleb, *Skin in the Game: Hidden Asymmetries in Daily Life* (New York: Allen Lane, 2018), 199.

66. By "reason," we understand the practice of science, which requires a high level of trust by scientists in each other, and when a scientist violates that trust—fabricating results, for instance—science fails to function. The character of other scientists is a very real concern; we have to know if we are being lied to, as this cuts to the core of whether an explanation built on their work is true. The credibility of others is itself something that can be questioned, investigated, and probed; determining someone's character is not a matter of blind belief. Since we rely on the testimony of others to assess a discrete instance of a scientist's character, science cannot do without faith.

Radical skepticism can never be answered except with committed belief, and faith in persons remains the bedrock for scientific discussions.

67. Cf. WA 18, 627. LW 33, 54.

68. Brad S. Gregory, *Rebel in the Ranks: Martin Luther, the Reformation, and the Conflicts That Continue to Shape Our World* (New York: HarperOne, 2017), 4.

69. "But if we are unwilling to let this term go altogether—though that would be the safest and most God-fearing thing to do—let us at least teach men to use it honestly, so that free choice is allowed to man only with respect to what is beneath him and not what is above him. That is to say, a man should know that with regard to his faculties and possessions he has the right to use, to do, or to leave undone, according to his own free choice, though even this is controlled by the free choice of God alone, who acts in whatever way he pleases. On the other hand in relation to God, or in matters pertaining to salvation or damnation, a man has no free choice, but is a captive, subject and slave either of the will of God or the will of Satan." WA 18, 638. LW 33, 70.

70. This is true even though Luther as a person pursued the "abstract question" of God with his whole being. Heiko A. Oberman, *Luther: Man Between God and the Devil*, trans. Eileen Walliser-Schwarzbart (New Haven: Yale University Press, 1989), 151.

71. Oberman, *Luther: Man Between God and the Devil*, 80.

72. Oberman, 256.

73. "But if this liberty is given again, that is, that fasts and prayers, obedience to ordinances, the services of churches, etc., should be committed to each of us on the basis of our own free will and conscience to do as much as he wishes, moved by his love for God, I believe that in one year all of the churches would fairly be closed and the altars deserted. And yet so it ought to be, and we should approach all of these things as people about to serve God freely and happily and not out of fear of conscience or punishment, nor in the hope of reward or honor." WA 56, 499. LW 25, 493.

74. Charles Taylor admits being confused by what the term "secular" means at the beginning of an eight-hundred-page tome on the topic, where he also fails to adequately define "religion." Charles Taylor, *A Secular Age* (Cambridge, Massachusetts: The Belknap Press, 2007), 14–15.

75. For example, Robert Markus's use of "sacred history" and "secular history" to explicate the thought of Augustine, which he admits the saint did not use. *Saeculum: History and Society in the Theology of St Augustine* (Cambridge: Cambridge University Press, 1988). Joseph Ratzinger points out that biblical monotheism accomplished a sober demythologization, getting rid of the numerous deities thought to have power over human life. Joseph Ratzinger, *Jesus of Nazareth: The Infancy Narratives*, trans. Philip J. Whitmore (New York: Image, 2012), 101.

76. The twentieth century alone had 65 percent of all the Christian martyrs in history. Antonio Socci, *I Nuovi Perseguitati: Indagine Sulla Intolleranza Anticristiana Nel Nuovo Secolo Del Martirio* (Milan: Piemme, 2002).

77. For example, WA 56, 172, 207, 215. LW 25, 152, 191–92, 200.

78. WA 11, 262. LW 45, 105.

79. In his *Temporal Authority*, which Luther ranked as one of his favorite works, he writes, "Among Christians there shall and can be no authority; rather all are alike subject to one another, as Paul says in Romans 12." He continues: "What, then, are the priests and bishops? Answer: Their government [*regiment*] is not a matter of authority or power [*uberkeyt odder gewallt*], but a service and an office, for they are neither higher nor better than other Christians. Therefore, they should impose no law or decree on others without their will and consent. Their ruling is rather nothing more than the inculcating of God's word, by which they guide Christians and overcome heresy." WA 11, 271. LW 45, 117.

80. "Because we are all priests of equal standing, no one must push himself forward and take it upon himself, without our consent and election, to do that for which we all have equal authority. For no one dare take upon himself what is common to all without the authority and consent of the community. And should it happen that a person chosen for such office were deposed for abuse of trust, he would then be exactly what he was before. Therefore, a priest in Christendom is nothing else but an officeholder. As long as he holds office he takes precedence; where he is deposed, he is a peasant or a townsman like anybody else. Indeed, a priest is never a priest when he is deposed." WA 6, 408. LW 44, 129.

81. "No one shall or can command the soul unless he is able to show it the way to heaven; but this no man can do, only God alone. Therefore, in matters which concern the salvation of souls nothing but God's word shall be taught and accepted." WA 11, 263. LW 45, 106.

82. "Even in the world, rebellion never stems from obedient service but from an ambitious desire to rule. But it is a confusion and a mingling of the secular and the spiritual realms when those sublime and meddlesome spirits want to change and correct the civil law in a dictatorial and dominating fashion, even though they have no directive or authority to do so, either from God or from men." WA 51, 240. LW 13, 196.

83. WA 51, 240. LW 13, 196.

84. Jarrett Carty notes this in his *God and Government: Martin Luther's Political Thought* (Montreal: McGill-Queen's University Press, 2017), 168.

85. "Temporal obedience and authority, you see, apply only externally to taxes, revenue, honor, and respect." WA 11, 266. LW 45, 110. "A human ordinance cannot possibly extend its authority into heaven and over souls; it is limited to the earth, to external dealings men have with one another, *where they can see, know, judge, evaluate, punish, and acquit*." Italics added. WA 11, 266. LW 45, 111.

86. "For the hand that wields this sword and kills with it is not man's hand, but God's," writes Luther, "and it is not man, but God, who hangs, tortures, beheads, kills, and fights. All these are God's works and judgments." WA 19, 626. LW 46, 96.

87. Christ "allows kings, lords, and princes to be rich and powerful [*reich und gewaltig sein*], and permits them the authority they have. He grants them all this without interference. Indeed, He confirms them in it by forbidding riots and rebellion and commanding people to be subject and obedient." WA 41, 107. LW 13, 251.

88. WA 6, 461. LW 44, 205.

89. "If it happens that in a parish, a city, or a principality, the papists and the Lutherans (as they are called) are crying out against one another because of certain matters of belief, and preaching against one another, and both parties claim that the Scriptures are on their side, I would not willingly tolerate such a division. . . . [I]f neither party is willing to yield or be silent, or if neither can do so because of official position, then let the rulers take a hand. Let them hear the case and command that party to keep silence which does not agree with the Scriptures." WA 31.1, 209. LW 13, 62–63.

90. WA 31.1, 210. LW 13, 63.

91. Luther writes in 1520 that "since the temporal power is ordained of God to punish the wicked and protect the good, it should be left free to perform its office in the whole body of Christendom without restriction and without respect to persons, whether it affects pope, bishops, priests, monks, nuns, or anyone else." WA 6, 409. LW 44, 130.

92. WA 6, 258. LW 44, 91.

93. WA 31.1, 208. LW 13, 61.

94. WA 31.1, 208. LW 13, 62.

95. Gregory, *Rebel in the Ranks*, 116.

96. Gregory, *Rebel in the Ranks*, 151.

97. John Witte, *Law and Protestantism: The Legal Teachings of the Lutheran Reformation* (Cambridge: Cambridge University Press, 2002), 53, 83–84.

98. Walter A. McDougall, *The Tragedy of U.S. Foreign Policy: How America's Civil Religion Betrayed the National Interest* (New Haven: Yale University Press, 2016), 356.

99. Matthew J. Tuininga, *Calvin's Political Theology and the Public Engagement of the Church* (Cambridge: Cambridge University Press, 2017), 39–41. Like Luther, Melanchthon also argued, as historian Peter Wilson puts it, "that, as sovereign, a ruler must be obeyed. Subjects must have faith in God and were to suffer princely transgressions in silence as further tests of their piety and convictions." Peter H. Wilson, *Absolutism in Central Europe* (London: Routledge, 2000), 56.

100. Not to mention a lot of wacky things that are in the bible. Cf. the series by Anthony Giambrone, "Is That in the Bible?" in *Magnificat* 2019–2022 (New York: Yonkers).

101. Gregory, *Rebel in the Ranks*, 166. "In its open-ended variety, the radical Reformation simply reflects the Reformation, period. It shows what 'scripture *alone*' led to when political authorities did not enforce the biblical interpretations of reformers such as Luther, Zwingli, or Calvin. It reveals what the freedom of Christians looked like when you actually left people free to believe what *they* believed was true. It's not easy to see that this was the nature of the Reformation all along." Gregory, *Rebel in the Ranks,* 161.

102. The Old Testament prophets and Christ's own actions belie any idea that doctrines which please political leaders are therefore truly inspired. For example, Mark 11:15–18.

103. Brad S. Gregory, *The Unintended Reformation: How a Religious Revolution Secularized Society* (Cambridge: Belknap Press, 2012), 150.

104. Alec Ryrie, *Protestants: The Faith That Made the Modern World* (New York: Viking, 2017), 51.

105. "Luther was not thereby sanctioning religious war, as he made clear in a letter to Linck, his old friend in Nuremberg. Rather, both the constitutional and political situation made it legitimate and prudent (and not un-Christian) for the princes to prepare to defend themselves, should war be forced on them. Yet Luther was still uneasy about what he had done. He sensed that he (and his great public authority) were being used by others for their own political purposes." James M. Kittelson and Hans H. Wiersma, *Luther The Reformer: The Story of the Man and His Career*, 2nd ed. (Minneapolis: Fortress Press, 2016), 186–87.

106. Diarmaid MacCulloch, *Reformation: Europe's House Divided* (London: Allen Lane, 2003), 157, 164.

107. James M. Estes, *Peace, Order and the Glory of God: Secular Authority and the Church in the Thought of Luther and Melanchthon 1518–1559* (Leiden: Brill, 2005), 52.

108. It is noteworthy in this connection that Luther views the Decalogue not as a revelation of God's love for a particular people, but as universally valid. WA 18, 80–81. LW 40, 97–98.

109. WA 51, 240. LW 13, 195–96.

110. WA 51, 240. LW 13, 196.

111. WA 31.1, 193. LW 13, 46.

112. WA 31.1, 191–92. LW 13, 44.

113. We could think of this as the secular realm. The word *secular* comes from the Latin *saeculum* or "century"—that is, the longest duration of a human life. The relationships a person has over the course of a life come into being and pass away, intertwine and affect each other, forming a grand symphony. These relationships form the context for our lives and choices. I cannot choose who my father is, my hometown, or how I was raised. The patterns of relationships in a society are found in a given time period—the *saeculum*. This landscape, with positive and negative features, built up allegiances and grievances, must be navigated but cannot be created *ex nihilo*. A society is not a *tabula rasa*, at least within any human lifespan. Any institution has its patterns of loyalties; these can be worked on and altered over the course of a lifetime but not refashioned all at once. Mundane, secular life brings us face to face with our interdependence and reliance on each other as well as the inescapable nature of our human situation of giving and receiving loyalty. This is where justice is found: in secular life, in our concrete relationships. These cannot be controlled by a central power.

114. Cf. The "theory of the regulated will" in Bertrand de Jouvenel, *Sovereignty: An Inquiry into the Political Good*, trans. J. F. Huntington (Indianapolis: Liberty Fund, 1997), 239–57.

115. Saint Augustine, *Concerning the City of God against the Pagans*, trans. Henry Bettenson (New York: Penguin, 2003), 593.

Chapter 3

Thomas Hobbes

Like many other good politicians, Martin Luther presented himself as no politician at all. In his telling, he was a preacher who had nothing but the Word: "I simply taught, preached, and wrote God's Word . . . I did nothing; the Word did everything."[1] Luther's reform differed from previous heretical movements, however, because he had significant segments of the German nation behind him. "Though no professional politician, Luther was an eminent political mind," writes Heiko Oberman. "Luther provided the legal foundations for [German] grievances by disqualifying canon law as foreign, papal law, and providing a scriptural basis for the temporal authorities' right to self-determination."[2] Due to the new technology of the printing press disseminating Luther's work far and wide, his writing in the vernacular and talent for appealing to common folk, and Lucas Cranach's woodcut portraits of him, Luther was popular to the point where he has been called the first "celebrity" in world history.[3] Tapping into German discontent with the Roman curia, Luther's tumultuous journey and reception at the Diet of Worms—the most important event of the Reformation, where he refused to recant his teachings—showed that he was a German hero.[4] The knights accompanying him into the city even swore to kill him if he did recant.[5] Luther's writings were used by the princes to justify their actions in the German Peasants' War, as was his pro-German propaganda in the conflicts that raged after his death.[6] After he died in 1546, destructive conflict engulfed Germany for a century, devastating the population and ending only at the conclusion of the Thirty Years' War (1618–1648) with the Peace of Westphalia. Political scientists often interpret that settlement as laying the groundwork for the sovereign nation-state as the fundamental political unit in Europe, though this is debatable.[7]

This chapter takes up the thought of the preeminent modern thinker, Thomas Hobbes, who worked through the problem of violent, ideological conflict and offered the sovereign state as the solution. Hobbes did so by extending and refining Luther's approach: the replacement of justice with esteem is his starting point, and when subsequently faced with the same problem of the competition for esteem causing violence, he endorses Luther's solution of imputed worth and sacred sovereignty, creating a logic of politics that derogates personal relationships in favor of a language of "values." The idea of value is, of course, contrasted with that of *fact*, and the being of values one of timeless *validity*—two additional concepts that this chapter will put into question.

As we have seen, the concept of religion must also be put into question. Interpreting the Thirty Years' War as part of the "wars of religion" that were only solved by the introduction of sovereign states validates the political theory of Luther and Hobbes. But we should hesitate to do so since, as we have seen, this was the period in which the categories of religion and politics were being created. As William Cavanaugh shows in *The Myth of Religious Violence*, our concept of religion not only enables the marginalization of impulses towards universal justice in the populace but it also supports the power of the state. For example, in our day, labelling Hinduism a religion while excluding nationalism from that category is illogical, but is politically advantageous.[8] The myth of religious violence aided the project of creating sovereign states, since "it would obviously benefit state-making elites," as Cavanaugh writes, "to present an increase in their power over that of the church as the salvation of Europe from doctrinal fanaticism."[9] Accepting the Reformation allowed rulers to expropriate church property in their lands, get rid of a competitor for the loyalty of the people, and resist the Emperor. The exclusivity of Christian sects also helped the princes in their project of consolidating power, as it fashioned an us-versus-them loyalty and cast the prince in the role of protector of the faith.[10] As a British historian was heard to quip, "'religion' is a sixteenth-century word for nationalism."[11]

The myth of religious violence is a "just so" story along the lines of "Hebrew Genesis or the Babylonian Enuma Elish."[12] It is propagated today by political theorists, who, as Cavanaugh documents, typically fail to cite work by historians of the period.[13] The Thirty Years' War was "not primarily a religious war," as Peter Wilson puts it in his authoritative history.[14] The "wars of religion" were actually "the birth pangs of the state, not simply the crisis which required the state to step in as savior."[15] The historical record shows that the creation of the modern state was a violent process, much less because of disputes over church doctrines than because this consolidation of power, particularly the attempt to collect taxes to fund wars, was inherently conflictual.[16] "The so-called wars of religion appear as wars fought by state-building elites for the purpose of consolidating their power over the church and other rivals."[17] Religion formed a pretext. "The Thirty Years' War was not fought by the German people, least of all was it fought for religious reasons. It was fought by and against the German princes," A. J. P. Taylor writes. "In every age rulers, fighting for their survival or for the extension of their power, have to talk the claptrap of the time: in the seventeenth century the claptrap happened to be religious."[18]

THE ORIGIN OF VIOLENCE

It is important prior to our discussion of Hobbes to consider the question of the cause of violence. For us, violence results from irreconcilable human desires. As the great theorist René Girard has shown, desire is mimetic, that is to say, it copies the desires of others. The increase of others' desires for an object increases our own desires for it, bringing us into conflict with them.

Violence stems from our lust to outdo others, to triumph over them. That desire, in turn, comes from wanting what they want, because they want it: this is blind imitation, or mimetic desire. This means that our desires are often not our own but are copied. What we desire is suggested to us by others—not, however, in an explicit suggestion out of a friendly relationship, but implicitly, by them showing off. All advertisements work this way, with beautiful, smiling, happy people shown using a product and the implied message: "If you buy the product, you will be like them." The invitation is to copy desire. The ads show *models*, people we are supposed to desire to be like.

The desire to show off is mimetic. When asked once about his most embarrassing moments on stage, Yo-Yo Ma answered, "When I forget why I am there, why I do what I do."[19] The desire for fame and fortune is not a desire for the object but a desire that other people see that I have the object. When we are both grasping for the same thing, this makes us similar to each other, not in the manner of the common ground of friendship or the fellowship of collaborators, but rather as rivals.[20] Something I can show off when I possess it is a good that we cannot both have at the same time, in the same way, and in the same respect. Mimetic desire pursues a competitive good, not a common good.[21]

Copying the desires of others brings us into conflict with them. We both want the same thing, but we cannot both have it. After we start competing for the desired object, we quickly forget about it in our passion to get the better of the other. We never really wanted the desired object anyway; our only desire now becomes triumphing over our opponent. When a child rips a toy away from his sibling, he lacks a fixed idea of what he is going to do with it. He does not want it for himself. When he has it, he eyeballs his sibling to make sure it is driving him nuts. Mimetic desire is childish: it is to want something without knowing why one really wants it. Mimetic desire hides its object from us. Mimeticism is unsatisfying even when successful, since we do not really want to possess it in the first place. "What makes the object valuable is not its true price but the desires that are already focused on it."[22] The point is not possessing some trophy, but rather taking it away from our hated enemy: to outstrip them, to get the better of them, to one-up them. There is a conflict without end, as there is no common good that can bring us together and negotiate our differences, if what we really want is just to triumph over the other person. It is also a conflict over nothing—over prestige—that is, something that is only the opinions of others.[23] I could decide to forgo my desire, and saying "you first" would dissolve the conflict. However, "if desire were wise, it would not be desire."[24]

Mimetic conflict is particularly acute when we have been hurt. It is difficult to think of our sufferings dispassionately. Someone must be responsible for my misery. Meaningless suffering is difficult to accept, and it makes eminent sense that the misfortunes that befall us would be someone else's fault. The desire for vengeance when we have been wounded is the mimetic desire to inflict on another what has been inflicted on us. It is not rational; it does not ask, "What is to be gained by this? What am I really after? Will my vengeance solve anything?"

This desire for violence is transferable. If I cannot lash out at the one who harmed me, I lash out at someone else who is close by. Anger does not pass just because I cannot harm my real enemy. Everyone has had the experience of picking a fight with someone close to them because they are having a bad day. They do not deserve it, but anger is irrational. Or better, it has reasons initially, but it is not tethered to them and willingly mistakes its object. When we cannot get back at the source of our suffering and make them pay, we turn to victimize somebody near at hand. It is a very difficult process to arrest; my anger does not automatically subside when I realize I cannot strike back, and that often just makes me angrier.

The mimetic desire for sheer power, the will to triumph, to be a model for others, the idolization of success, and the lust to use others sexually—all these bring us into conflict with others. The violence of this conflict is transferable to parties who are not involved. This is what scapegoating does. Scapegoating is ubiquitous; an anecdote from a big city mayor captures this commonplace occurrence: "He reacted to the pressures of the job the way he usually did, by going after those who were the most helpless and posed the least resistance."[25] The easiest way to deal with violence in society is always to force it into acceptable channels, towards scapegoats who are its weakest members and therefore cannot strike back and perpetuate a cycle of violence. The scapegoat thus provides an outlet for the appetite for violence. It is no wonder that "the use of scapegoats is as old as civilization itself."[26]

THOMAS HOBBES

Now to Hobbes. Hobbes was an innovator, a brilliant writer, and the first foundational political scientist.[27] His groundbreaking ideas, careful exposition, and airtight arguments easily place him as the foremost political thinker in the English language. He has also been called the "specter that haunts moral theory," as his thought sets the direction for much of what followed—not only political but also moral philosophy.[28] Hobbes was inspired when he read Euclid's *Elements of Geometry* for the first time when he was forty years old. A Greek mathematician from the third century BC, Euclid's *Elements* was the standard mathematical textbook until relatively recently, and Hobbes wanted to apply his strict method of geometry to the study of politics. In his great work, *Leviathan* (1651), Hobbes proceeds with a rigorous logic, defining basic axioms about human nature and drawing conclusions from them, forming an impressive, interrelated, architectonic structure. The Hobbesian form of thought defines not just modern political thought but modern thought itself.

The problem Hobbes faced was the justification of Luther's *Obrigkeit*, authority/power. For Luther, worldly *Obrigkeit* was just a given: our worldly superiors are the people who are de facto superior to us, and it was obvious who they were. This immediately started creating problems. For example, when his supporter Elector John wanted to resist the Emperor, Luther initially held that the Emperor was his superior and so should always be obeyed. The Elector had to wear him down on this point, eventually succeeding in getting him to agree, though Luther was uneasy about being used in this way.[29] Whom we are to obey is not always clear cut, but we have seen that for Luther it needs to be, or else we will constantly face revolutionary upheavals. Additionally, as we have seen, Luther accepted no superiority in the spiritual realm; but if all spiritual authority is suspect, it is unclear why worldly authority would not be. If anything, it would seem to be *more* suspect. Luther tied himself in knots to avoid this conundrum, saying that worldly authority is much less important (but then why not challenge it?), must be followed because scripture dictates absolute obedience (but what if the ruler is doing something unjust; that cannot be God's will . . .), and that the whole idea of justice does not exist anyway. The latter position takes away principled challenges to worldly authority, leaving only the tautology: you have to obey your superiors because they are superior. But what reasons could be given for this absolute obedience in the teeth of a challenge?

Hobbes steps in with a precise answer. His system justifies impersonal, sacred Sovereignty as solving the problem of violent anarchy. He names the situation without Sovereignty a "state of nature" in which man is a wolf to man; horrible, violent anarchy reigns; and, famously, "the life of man is solitary, poor, nasty, brutish, and short." It is not an original idea; if there were no law and government, "seeing that the whole world is evil and that among thousands there is scarcely a single true Christian," Martin Luther noted, "No one could support wife and child, feed himself, and serve God. The world would be reduced to chaos."[30]

This threat of violent anarchy is the key to the justification of Sovereignty; without it—if we were friends with each other—we would have no need for the concept. The threat of violent social upheaval and the justification for Sovereignty go together and require each other. Hobbes is therefore not interested in addressing the root cause of violence, but rather in fostering it as a constant danger. Success in eliminating violent competition and fostering friendship would do away with his whole theory. All human relationships therefore must be reinterpreted by him as a competition for esteem. It is this competition for esteem that inevitably turns violent: right before his famous passage about the state of nature being "solitary, poor, nasty, brutish, and short," Hobbes writes that

> every man looketh that his companion should value him, at the same rate he sets upon himselfe: And upon all signes of contempt, or undervaluing, naturally endeavours, as far as he dares (which amongst them that have no common power, to keep them in quiet, is far enough to make them destroy each other,) to extort a greater value from his contemners, by dommage; and from others, by the example.[31]

We want to be valued by each other to the point where we are willing to use violence to gain such esteem. Value and violence go together. Ultimately, the competition for esteem leads to a contagion of violence and the breakdown of society. Hobbes asks us to consider "what values men are naturally apt to set upon themselves; what respect they look for from others; and how little they value other men" and concludes that this is the origin from which "continually arise amongst them, Emulation, Quarrells, Factions, and at last Warre, to the destroying of one another, and diminution of their strength against a Common Enemy."[32]

Mimetic conflict is explosive when a cycle of revenge spreads through imitation, and it can threaten an entire society.[33] Rather than diagnosing the root of violence in mimetic desire, Hobbes insists instead on making the search for esteem the only possible interpretation of all human relations. As he writes, "for both to love, and to feare, is to value."[34] Relationships are reduced to power, which is competitive: "[T]o Honour is to value highly the Power of any person: and . . . such value is measured by our comparing him with others."[35] But this is to make the problem insoluble. There is no possibility of us finding a common good when it is defined as the object of esteem, so we must instead find a mutual accommodation based on what we devalue and want to avoid—devaluing the scapegoat in order to avoid violent death. When threatened by the outbreak of violence, the solution is a victim we can blame, an outlet for our violence that can reestablish an irenic relationship between us. This is the function of the Sovereign power, to identify the scapegoats who become the focus of our now-justified violence. The state is violent, but its violence is *legitimate*. It is also beyond critique, as we can never hold that scapegoating by the Sovereign is wrong. There is no higher justice to which we could appeal, as the will of the Sovereign replaces justice. There is no balance of contenting demands for esteem that is inherently just; any attempt to do so only results in yet another partial perspective. It is only by enshrining the will of the Sovereign that we can avoid war between us. We ought not aim at justice, therefore, but rather at "peaceable, sociable, and comfortable living."[36] Complete obedience to the Sovereign gives us a chance at this. Belief in and pursuit of justice and the common good, by contrast, threatens the basis of Sovereignty.

Sovereignty baptizes violence. The physical action of a violent criminal becomes something else entirely when the criminal wears a soldier's or police officer's uniform. This must be thought of as a magical transformation, as it is not possible for Hobbes to defend a qualitative distinction here: it is not that the actions of the soldier or police officer are for the benefit of all and promoting justice against the actions of those who would harm the common good, but rather that they are doing exactly the same thing as private persons would do in the absence of a Sovereign. Hobbesian Sovereignty recapitulates Luther's distinction between religion and politics. As we have seen, Luther argues for a "spiritual" realm, where religious leaders have no power/authority; it is thus political leaders who determine everything, including the correctness of religious doctrine. This distinction is arbitrary, however. It is not that it is better for a certain type of authority to hold sway in an area of life because it is tasked to pursue a certain common good, but rather, the same action that is done under one aegis is illegitimate but when performed under another is suddenly necessary. That rulers determine the correct religion is right, because they are rulers. That spiritual leaders determine the correct religion is wrong, because they are spiritual leaders.

For us, a ruler is entrusted with care for the common good, and because of that role—which he can exercise well or poorly—we owe loyalty to him and have a responsibility to help him to exercise that role well. But for Hobbes, there is no common good and therefore no civic virtue. One private viewpoint among others becomes the official viewpoint, and although one might say it is still essentially one-sided and biased, nevertheless, it must never be resisted. Otherwise, we slip into terrible violence with each other. We are still subjected to the violence of the Sovereign, however. The person who is Sovereign is unable to join our community of non-violence. Also, our following the Sovereign must not include concern for him, as this would imply that there would be reasons for obedience beyond the avoidance of civil war. If there were something that is good or bad for the Sovereign *himself*, as we were concerned about it, then there would be a common good that includes us and the Sovereign, a potential friendship between us, a basis for action that is apart from Sovereignty and would threaten it. The ground of our action must be solely avoiding violent conflict between us. The Sovereign himself is excluded from consideration; he may use violence and so is still in the state of nature vis-à-vis us, his subjects. The good that Sovereignty achieves excludes the person who is Sovereign; he must first be expelled from the community in order for us to have a community at all. There is no justification for this exclusion; the Sovereign is an innocent victim, the first scapegoat.

Only the common good allows us to separate the person from the office and, therefore, to include the person who holds the office in our network of loyalties. If there is no common good, what is being elevated to the level of official public doctrine is the viewpoint of a particular person, which does not become enlarged and refined, but it is simply enshrined as is. We either obey it or we do not; the obligation is unidirectional. This is not loyalty, but rather expanded self-interest and indifference to the person of the ruler. Hobbesian Sovereignty is the attempt to strip loyalty out of politics. There is no potential for the mutuality of friendship with the Sovereign; it is a relationship of utility in which the person who is Sovereign is used to facilitate the good of peace for all, while he himself is excluded from that good.

Sovereignty is political power/authority that is built up apart from loyalty. Hobbes begins with a *state of nature* without loyalty and order. He then postulates that a dramatic moment generates a political society, in which these individuals all agree to stop fighting each other and to obey a central authority on everything (a central authority which overpowers them), but without loyalty to anyone except their own individual person. It runs as follows:

> This is more than Consent, or Concord; it is a reall Unitie of them all, in one and the same Person, made by Covenant of every man with every man, in such manner, as if every man should say to every man, "I Authorise and give up my Right of Governing my selfe, to this Man, or to this Assembly of men, on this condition, that thou give up thy Right to him, and Authorise all his Actions in like manner."

Sovereignty involves "more than consent, or concord" and is a "real unity." Rather than a healthy, noncompetitive loyalty, this bond is exclusive. However, this is at the same time juxtaposed with the idea that it is *conditional*: "I authorize this Sovereign only on this condition, that you do too." But what if some people do not consent? The grumblers would be overruled by the greater part of the community; however, the hearts of the former would not be in it. They would be holding back their full unconditional consent. They would not give up their *entire* will, judgment, and strength to the Sovereign, which is necessary for the "real unity of them all."

The missing ingredient here is the *sacred* nature of the Sovereign. Hobbes continues:

> This done, the Multitude so united in one Person, is called a COMMON-WEALTH, in latine CIVITAS. This is the Generation of that great LEVIATHAN, or rather (to speake more reverently) of that Mortall God, to which wee owe under the Immortall God, our peace and defence. For by this Authoritie, given him by every particular man in the Common-Wealth, he hath the use of so much Power and Strength conferred on him, that by terror thereof, he is inabled to forme the wills of them all, to Peace at home, and mutuall ayd against their enemies abroad.[37]

The Sovereign is a god. To our god we owe everything we have, and our god can demand it from us. The mechanism through which this sacralization of political authority occurs is the Sovereign "forming our wills" through "terror." This is very different from bargaining, from "I'll consent if you consent, in order to achieve our mutual purposes." This is no negotiation, but rather a turning of the Sovereign into an idol, a "mortal god," an object of worship through sacrifice. The way we know that the god is real and effective is its power to demand sacrifice; exclusive loyalty—the sacred—can only be formed through sacrifice. A "real unity" is formed by sacrificing those who do not consent. Hobbes acknowledges above that the covenant that creates the sovereign is made by a "plurality of voices." This is different from his definition, in the previous book, of a multitude of men represented as one person, which occurs "with the consent of every one of that Multitude."[38] How can a great many voices, a plurality which is still short of everyone, be made into "the consent of everyone"? The answer is the elimination of those who do not consent. Hobbes writes that "because the major part hath by consenting voices declared a Soveraigne; he that dissented must now consent with the rest; that is, be contented to avow all the actions he shall do, or else justly be destroyed by the rest."[39] This sacrifice of those who do not consent creates the "real unity," as opposed to the "consent, or concord" that describes a political order which allows the malcontents to free-ride off of the protection afforded them by the Sovereign.

If I say I am loyal to you, nothing is stopping me from also being loyal to someone else. The only way to transform my loyalty into an exclusive bond is by sacrificing one loyalty to the other. Such an exclusive bond crowds out other loyalties, destroying their character by turning them into preferences. In so doing, the central loyalty is made sacred. Taken further, it can lose its character as a loyalty and become a transcendental necessity: it is the sacrifice I must make in order to get any chance at a peaceful, commodious existence. It is an expression of my self-love, a logical extension of my self-interest, rather than a loyalty at all. Far from secularizing human authority, building a society on self-interest radically sacralizes it. Hobbes removes any hint of the secular when it comes to ultimate political authority.[40] We cannot talk about the Sovereign in terms of our normal categories. We are beyond the contingency of "I'll consent only if you consent." We must always bow to the Sovereign's will, thinking of that will as our own will. We mystically participate in Sovereignty. The Sovereign is not a person like the rest of us, with a job to do (which can be done well or not so well), but he is the fount of justice, and whatever he touches turns just. He is the holder of the magical power that replaces the essence of justice itself. Just as everything I desire turns into that which is good, at least for me, everything the Sovereign wills becomes, for his subjects, that which is just and right. No matter how wrong the law of the Sovereign *seems*, this is just an appearance. Our logic tells us he can never be wrong.

This reasoning can only seem plausible to the degree that our mind dwells in abstractions. In reality, we cannot do without loyalty. Political, spiritual, and social questions all concern our loyalties on some level.[41] There is no political society when there are individuals who have desires but no loyalties to each other.[42] As we descend to concrete relationships with other real persons, it becomes harder and harder to believe the justification for Sovereignty, and ultimately, it seems ridiculous. Personal relationships are secular. Friends can laugh and be laughed at by each other; they can talk about anything and can see injuries as accidental. It is when our relationships fail, when our loyalties are lost, becoming twisted and competitive, that we become isolated individuals locked in mimetic conflict with each other, hopelessly at odds like the individuals in the state of nature, and we are primed to believe that social order is the product of a magical intervention that is renewed every time we witness the public sacrifice of a scapegoat. The justification of Sovereignty requires that we constantly keep the danger of violent anarchy before our minds. The power of Sovereignty derived from this fear is the ability to scapegoat, to determine who is to be sacrificed. Such power consists in a monopoly of meaning, not of violence. The essence of Sovereign power is to determine and to enforce our public morality.

A MONOPOLY OF MEANING, NOT VIOLENCE

In the Leviathan state, it is not that the ruler has all the guns and no one else has a right to use force. Hobbes knows this is impossible and does not advocate it. For him, by contrast, everyone has the right to use force against anyone who is coming after them to do them bodily harm, including against the state. "In the making of a Common-wealth, every man giveth away the right of defending another; but not of defending himselfe."[43] We also have the right to use violence against enemies of the state. A subject who is actually an enemy is one who would, Hobbes says, "deliberatly deny the Authority of the Representative of the Common-wealth."[44] If there are such people who are powerful enough to do damage to the state, then our relationship to them reverts back to a situation of war, in which we have the right to kill them. This is indeed how the state was founded to begin with, as those who did not consent to the Sovereign were "destroyed by any man whatsoever" without any injustice.[45]

The violence in the Hobbesian state which does not come from the Sovereign—but is still legitimate—is therefore either (a) the use of force for self-defense (even against the state), or (b) the use of force against the enemies of the state. It might be surprising that Hobbes allows violence against the state to be justified in cases of self-defense. However, the violent resistance of an isolated individual is easily overcome; it is simply not a threat. What is a threat is not the violence of a single person, but rather the *meaning* of such a conflict; namely, other people sympathizing with the targeted person and acting upon it. *This* is incompatible with Sovereignty. The right to assist the threatened person is given up in the social contract: "[E]very man giveth away the right of defending another."

The critical question is: "Who are to be considered enemies of the state?" The answer is: "Whomever the Sovereign says." Hobbes writes that "it is annexed to the Soveraignty, to be Judge of what Opinions and Doctrines are averse, and what conducing to Peace." This means determining what is true and false. "For Doctrine repugnant to Peace, can no more be True, than peace and Concord can be against the Law of Nature."[46] When the Sovereign declares someone to be an enemy, it means that person is stripped of his humanity—he becomes a wolf to his fellow men and vice versa.[47] Violence against him is therefore good; in reality, it is a limitation of violence, since properly considered, it is the protection of the whole society against collapse into violent disorder.

Sovereign power is the power of scapegoating, power to redefine the humanity of individuals such that violence against them is redefined to not be violence at all. It is not that the state has a monopoly on violence; rather, the state has a monopoly on the definition of what constitutes violence. If you are a threat to the state, then harming you can be redefined as a limitation of violence. The Sovereign holds not a science-fiction fantasy of a monopoly of actual violence, but rather a monopoly of defining what types of violence matter.[48] As long as everyone uses words in the way the Sovereign dictates, there can never be any basis to challenge the state. A commentator is right to note that "much of the quotidian work of the sovereignty consists precisely in defining and enforcing the meanings of such politically important terms," like "good" and "evil."[49] Half of *Leviathan* concerns Hobbes's interpretation of the Christian religion. Though often ignored, it is an essential part of his project to monopolize meaning. "To derive the modern doctrine of sovereignty and the 'science' of this construct, it was necessary for the new 'single' power to lay claim to the 'right' to interpret the Bible in all publicly significant respects and to neutralize all other acts of interpretation."[50]

In reality, action with others never involves a monopoly of meaning. The stalker thinks he is in a relationship, but it is only in his own mind. When we act in ways that hurt other people, it is not up to us to decide whether or not they are hurt. We have to ask them. We cannot determine it ourselves. We never have a monopoly on meaning. The Hobbesian state, however, thinks it does. It is the irresistible stalker.

Its mechanism of exercising a monopoly on meaning does not mean that there must be an *Académie française* with its own soldiers, determining the meaning of every word and then coercing everyone to speak in the approved way. It is rather a matter of inculcating a habit in the people of discounting their loyalties and remembering the transcendental nature of Sovereignty—without it, we have violent anarchy. On a prosaic level this is simply making the transcendental–empirical distinction. If I disagree, it is just my empirical preference. Unless I am the one actually making the law, my opinions are irrelevant.[51]

THE MYTH OF FACT

We might be tempted to think that Sovereignty is inherently limited by reality, that the Sovereign's power over meaning is restricted to settling conflicts over values, but not a matter of determining empirical facts. "Everyone is entitled to their own opinion, but not their own facts," as Daniel Patrick Moynihan's quip has it, or as Jean Louis de Lolme, the British political theorist wrote two hundred years earlier, "[I]t is a fundamental principle with the English Lawyers, that Parliament can do every thing, *except* making a Woman a Man, or a Man a Woman."[52]

Even in the realm of values, it is an affront to our intellectual pride that we must agree with whatever the Sovereign says. In the next chapter, we will examine precisely this reaction to Hobbes, and how it creates the concept of morality as an impersonal measure of right and wrong. Before turning to this idea and to Hobbes's attempt to turn social *mores* into a transcendental law of nature, we must emphasize how the distinction between "fact" and "value" itself is a narrow categorization that excludes and distorts the *personal*. The whole modern project itself makes political power/authority into an impersonal phenomenon. Hobbes's argument for Sovereignty is that it is the objectively true nature of human association. Without Sovereignty, there is violent anarchy—for him, that is a scientific fact.[53]

But persons and personal acts transcend the categories of fact and value, as the rest of this chapter hopes to show, by drawing on the resources of personalism, phenomenology, and Michael Polanyi's philosophy of science. The way persons transcend the categories of "transcendental" and "empirical"; the nature of truth as intentional and ecstatic; and the personal passion required for scientific discoveries, all show that our system of thought is not static but dynamic, not closed but open, not clear but tacit, not dogmatically absolute but probable, not a whole of disconnected parts but integral, and not known through an indifferent objectivity but only through a personal commitment.

We begin by briefly discussing the naïveté of the concept of a "fact," which forms the model of truth for the transcendental approach.

A hallmark of late modernity is the conception of facts as objective, that is to say, independent of human testimony.[54] However, there can never be a purely brute fact: the "facts" of anything depend on the context.[55] "All facts are discourse specific," as Stanley Fish has rightly insisted.[56] "Facts are made or fabricated; they are made within a structure, a network of persons and things."[57] Elizabeth Anscombe has shown that "brute facts" relate to a description of a situation that is contested, and which itself can only be understood in the context of conventional institutions.[58] Michael Oakeshott points out that facts stand in need of judgment if they are to constitute knowledge.[59]

Like "value," "fact" is a term of modern origin. David Weinberger writes that "only relatively recently have facts emerged as the general foundation of knowledge and the final resort of disagreements."[60] The term "fact" comes from the Latin *factum*, a thing done, which meant "an action, deed, course of conduct." The progression of meaning from "deed" to "known truth" comes from the sphere of law. As Barbara Shapiro has shown, while in the sixteenth century, English law distinguished between "matters of fact" and "matters of law," with "fact" referring to that which was to be proved—the issue at hand in a case—between the middle of the sixteenth century to the middle of the eighteenth, the term *facts* took on the meaning of "truth." What occurred was "the transformation of 'fact' from something that had to be sufficiently proved by appropriate evidence to be considered worthy of belief to something for which appropriate verification had already taken place."[61] With the introduction of multiple credible witnesses, along with an impartial judge and a jury giving a verdict according to their conscience, the judicial system had created a method of producing reliably true accounts.[62]

This genealogy exhibits the personal and agonal nature of truth; facts are not obvious givens but arise from contestation and can be reliable *when grounded in an informed judgment as to the trustworthiness of persons.*[63] "There is nothing more deceptive than an obvious fact."[64] It is false to think we can separate facts from personal testimony. Our use of technology encourages us to forget this, however; in medicine, for example, inventions like the stethoscope and the X-ray encouraged doctors to put less stock in "the traditional methods of questioning patients, taking their reports seriously, and making careful observations of exterior symptoms."[65] This does not automatically lead to better medicine, though, as it encourages medical aggressiveness that leads to treatment-induced illnesses.

As Donald Cowan writes, "The myth of fact so engulfs the present that reality itself often becomes obscured."[66] But there are no facts standing outside of my solidarity with others, and that are inherently neutral. All facts entail a personal witness. To think of truth as consisting in brute facts is plausible only to the degree we have a lack of loyalty to others and thus presuppose the primacy of potency over actuality.[67] Indifference to others is the very definition of *brute.* Isolated facts never make sense on their own but must be understood within a context that always involves the personal relationships at stake. Without them to give an orienting sense to the play of the factual, we are in a hall of mirrors; the same facts can take on very different meanings and we would not know which interpretation is correct.[68]

If I am going to relate to another person as a person—that is, not in a functional or exclusive manner, where I am only interested in one aspect of his existence, insofar as it affects me in a certain way—then I am interested in *everything* about him, including what he thinks is true. Treating someone "as a person" precisely means relating to him in a nonexclusive way; that is, not excluding certain aspects of his personality and existence but taking him as a whole, not just relating to him in a one-sided manner.

By contrast, why would I care about a brute fact? To be interesting to me, a thing would have to relate somehow to my interests, my desires. If I have no desires in a certain area, there is no need to reckon with the facts of that domain of truth. If I do have an interest, there are two manners in which a brute fact could be presented to me. First, it could be presented to me as something that could be changed, an *empirical* datum. That is to say, something that could in principle be overcome, overpowered. Or second, it could be something that I have to just accept, something written into the natural laws of the universe that cannot be changed by anyone, something in other words which overpowers me—a *transcendental* truth. We think here of the contrast between the divine and human systems of esteem in Luther and public law and private contracts for Hobbes.

The interpretation of truth as an impersonal fact gains credence the more we are alienated from others. The more we interpret facts as foreign to us, something neutral and independent, the less we recognize truth as resounding in a personal connection, always contextualized within our relationships. Truth is not the registration of facts, of being overpowered by them. It is a performance with others, which requires their contribution and their testimony. To see the witnessing to truth as extraneous to it—as if truths are there for individuals to just see, without affecting the relationship between individuals—only makes sense in a situation when our relationships with others are already conflictual. When I am lying and manipulating others, then the reality is a harsh truth that overpowers them when they discover it. When the relationship reflects mutual care for truth, then facts and testimony work in tandem. In this case, when we deal with each other as persons, the distinction between "transcendental" and "empirical" ceases to be an exclusive one. Overcoming the transcendental approach means turning our eyes to the realm of the personal.

THE PERSONAL

Persons are unique. The being of persons is not exhausted by categories. Knowledge of a person involves getting to know him, not merely the different identity categories he ticks off. Persons in their uniqueness transcend all supposed factual knowledge; they are centers of experience and of acting, not things known like objects. As the personalist philosopher Max Scheler puts it in his incomparable section "Person and Act" in his great work *Formalism in Ethics*, "[I]t is the person himself, living in each of his acts, who permeates every act with his peculiar character."[69]

In what follows, the insights of personalism, phenomenology, and the preeminent philosopher of science, Michael Polanyi, will be brought to bear on the question of personal knowledge.[70]

The breakthrough of phenomenology came with Edmund Husserl's (1859–1938) close description of conscious acts and their nature as "intentional," that is, filled with meaning insofar as they are always directed towards an object.[71] Intentionality is the being of consciousness, and this means that conscious acts are beyond the dichotomy of subject and object; objects are given in different ways, through different intentionalities or conscious acts.

These qualities of consciousness that reveal a thing *belong to the being of the thing itself* rather than being a subjective addition of another thing, the mind. There is no realm of appearances separate from being, such that we cannot know whether we are just knowing appearances and not the thing itself. The dilemma of how a self-enclosed subject somehow goes beyond itself to know objects is a phony problem generated by a fundamental misunderstanding: consciousness is not a box with contents in it that mirror the world; rather, it is already outside itself, directed to an object. The ideal and the real are not two realms that somehow need to be related to each other. When consciousness pays attention to the way that it is related to an object and recognizes that the object's manner of appearing itself belongs to the type of thing that it is, it takes on the phenomenological attitude. This does not separate the "object itself" and "its appearances," taking them to be two different things, but rather thinks their belonging together—the object correlated with the types of intentionalities that reveal it.

To play close attention to the being of consciousness is to go beyond the categories of inner and outer, ideal and real. Conscious being is not an entity in the world, because personal being is not limited to one type of being, one way of appearing. Rather, persons act. As Scheler puts it, "[T]he person is precisely that unity which exists for acts of all possible *essential differences* insofar as those acts are thought to be executed."[72] While other forms of being are delimited in their being, that is, their manner of appearing to consciousness—a material object can be understood according to its properties, or a tool understood according to its purpose—a person is not exhausted with these types of appearing. A person is not an entity but a site of disclosure for all types of being. A person can participate in the being of everything through his acts; a person is a correlate to world, as Scheler puts it.[73]

Husserl's student Martin Heidegger (1889–1976) elaborated on this breakthrough of phenomenology in his masterpiece *Being and Time*. Heidegger emphasized in that work how persons are implicated in what they know and how knowledge is only possible through its integration into our being. When we know something that is true, it is not disconnected from our lives but incorporated into our understanding of ourselves and our possibilities. If I understand something is bad, I will both avoid it and interpret myself as someone who avoids it. Truth is also not disconnected from our relationships with others. Our very being is one of *care*, a deep solidarity with each other and with our world such that thinking of it as a neutral facticity is hopelessly derivative, stemming from a narrow interpretation of ourselves in terms given by our environment—in other words, an interpretation that misses our personal uniqueness. Our individuality as persons is not, however, a property we possess, like the properties of present-at-hand objects; rather, it has to do with our existence in time, with our living our lives as a personal history. This fact that we have a life and death that are uniquely our own, not shared with others, is what enables us to understand anything at all. It is easy to forget this essential truth about what makes understanding possible, to take it for granted and be absorbed in what we think of as an objective world. Our mimetic desire, the communicable desires of the crowd (*das Man*), cause us to miss our incommunicable uniqueness and take the meaning of things for granted. A reflective, more comprehensive view reveals our remarkable difference, our personal uniqueness, which is incommunicable, not a thing that is fully present, and unfolds in time as related to the lack of presence, our death. Our unique personal being is this care or deep underlying solidarity with others and our world, which is refracted in our willingness to give our lives for something—and *that* is the ultimate possibility of our being, our ultimate meaning, and the necessary horizon for understanding the meaning of individual entities within the world. It is the being of consciousness, intentionality, which is seen more comprehensively and from the inside. Intentionality is not just the presence of objects but their presence against a horizon, a network of relationships, a personal world of meaning, which, insofar as it gives meaning, insofar as it is authentic care, is a type of absence; namely, giving up its life in its own death. We each live an individual life that is limited in duration; this gives our assent to truth meaning for the whole of our life. What we assent to is not an academic "right" or "wrong," according to truths of eternal validity, or logic games on a standardized test. Rather, truth is a pressing matter of living our life as an integral person, of living according to the determination or resoluteness that something is true, a posture which directly affects the meaning of our own being, the interpretation we give to our own life. We can always fail to live integrally, to attend reflectively to the interpretation of ourselves, and to live instead in the off-the-shelf interpretations that others give us. Such an attitude would be the mimeticism that causes us to be absorbed in our world, forgetful and narrow, thinking of "truth" as just assenting to expressions in a punctual present, rather than understanding things in their being, as making a claim on our manner of life and our relationships.

In the next chapter, we will refer to the work of Heidegger's disciple Jacques Derrida (1930–2004) to explicate the unique being of the common good and its symbolic supplement. For now, we will take an example from the fine arts in order to illustrate how a truth could be public but not "objective," something in which we personally participate but which is not "subjective" or merely conventional.

If we look at the sheet music of Modest Mussorgsky's *Pictures at an Exhibition*, we see the notes as Mussorgsky wrote them. To begin with, it requires a lot of proficiency to play this classic work; it is not something anyone can pick up. If we listen to a skilled pianist play the piece, he will inevitably interpret it in his performance. If we tell him, "We do not want to hear your interpretation; rather, play it exactly as Mussorgsky wrote it; just play the notes as they are written on the page, please," we are exhibiting a misunderstanding of what the nature of a piano composition is. Music is meant to be performed and, thereby, interpreted. Music is not supposed to be written but then lie fallow, sitting on the shelf collecting dust, remaining in a pristine state of black dots along horizontal lines on a white background. Its meaning is found in being played. A great work expands our musical horizons, altering the habits of our ears and our framework for analysis, but it can only do that if it is performed, and such a skillful performance requires learning it and interpreting it. To accomplish what a musical composition is meant to achieve involves the participation of the composer and the performer. They must work together for the work to be what it really is.

It would be nonsensical for a composer to create a great work and be content knowing it is sitting in a file folder forgotten, never to be played. The work may as well have never been written in that case, as it has no effect—it is a dud, it is not living up to its promise. The same is true for that shopworn paradigm of "timeless truth": mathematics. Knowing that two plus two is four "is true for all time always" and not a matter of mere convention does not relieve us of taking any responsibility for that truth. As with the musical work, the truth that two and two is four requires our participation. We have to learn it. Teaching and learning it requires interpreting it, in language or mathematical symbols. I can say "two and two is four" or "two plus two makes four" or use the numerals with plus and equals signs. The unity of this truth can only be communicated in a local language. This is not a diminution of it but its proper expression. An irreversible discovery adds to our knowledge and sets us up for future discoveries which expand our framework, the potentialities of our language; to do so, it needs to be diffused, expressed in that language. The advance and the diffusion are connected and work together, like the composition and the artist's interpretation. To separate them and play the two levels off against each other is to misunderstand the public yet personal nature of truth. Truth is meant to be diffused, and it is not attenuated but fulfilled by the activity of teaching and learning. Understanding the being of the advance, entails tacitly knowing the personal nature of truth. To light a lamp and immediately hide it under a bushel basket misunderstands the point of lighting the lamp in the first place. Accomplishing an irreversible advance in knowledge likewise demands its promulgation and acceptance by others.

Phenomenology helps us understand the connection of a work of art with its performance. In the phenomenological attitude, the being of the object is correlated with the intentionalities that reveal it, not artificially separated and treated as if we are dealing with two different things. Faith and works go together, as it were; our knowledge of the unity of the object is connected with its manifestations in time (its "works") to us, not artificially separated and opposed to each other. The connection of the object to consciousness is intentionality, which is not a thing but an experience. To understand the being of something is to understand, on some level, how it is given in experience.

Experience is not just a manner of encountering discrete objects, one after another, however. Experiences are connected and related together in a larger language. All our knowledge and our action operate within our world (as phenomenology puts it) within the whole of our language, or a framework of commitment (as Polanyi puts it).[74] Truths can be expressed only within this framework or language, which we accept at any given time. We understand our interpretive framework not as an object but by assimilating ourselves to it. A framework cannot be fully present to our mind, since it is known tacitly and involves a tradition of innumerable previous commitments that cannot be questioned all at once. A framework is not a viewpoint that can be dropped and replaced with another point of view, but it is more like a dwelling that we inhabit and accept implicitly, akin to living in our own skin. It is not given once and for all. Scientific progress is made by expanding or shifting a taken-for-granted framework towards something deeper, more rational, more comprehensive, and more real.

Science does not progress, in other words, by simply referring to a known, fixed, and objective framework that could presumably settle any dispute—this is the myth of the transcendental viewpoint. While an inference within a framework can be traced back to its premises, learning something new, by contrast, expands our framework and is irreversible. By contrast, thinking that one's framework is transcendental entails believing that there is nothing new under the sun to learn. This is disproven, however, every time we do acquire new knowledge.

While we can have complete commitment, we can never have complete certainty. The transcendental approach tries to replace the former with the latter. Hobbes's political theory strives to eliminate doubt and seeks to prove that the Sovereign must be obeyed on everything. "Hobbes's goal is to reach political conclusions which we find we *have* to agree to."[75] He does not do this solely with scripture but utilizes a transcendental argument. Hobbes "regards the *Leviathan* as presenting political principles that are correct for all time."[76] Previous political thinkers did not think this way.[77] It is an approach that has its roots in Luther, who, though he is identified as the thinker of *faith alone*, pursued what was really certainty, not faith. Luther was terrified when living as a monk, not because of his lack of faith but because of his lack of certainly about his salvation. His revelation that there is no such thing as justice and that we are saved *sola fide* gave him the conviction he craved. For Luther, if I accept Christ, I can be certain I am saved and that my works have value. If I do not sign on to Christianity, then my works are worthless.

Christianity becomes a transcendental viewpoint, God's viewpoint, expressed in the bible, which is clear. These assumptions of Luther's are important and foundational because they make us think about knowledge in terms of certainty—individually attainable, couched in a framework that makes them able to be clearly and, therefore, impersonally expressed.

For us, by contrast, the role of faith is considerable because as an individual, we can know only a small slice of the world. Science requires a community of researchers. It is not an individual enterprise. According to Charles Sanders Pierce it is "catholic consent" which constitutes the truth.[78] A scientist is always a member of a community of discussion, since expertise involves mastering the language of a domain, which cannot occur without "enculturation within a linguistic community."[79] This point tends to get downplayed in the modern era. In his essential *A Discourse On Method*, Hobbes's alter ego on the continent, René Descartes (1596–1650), limits himself to the fashioning of his own beliefs: "My project has never extended beyond wishing to reform my own thoughts and build on a foundation which is mine alone."[80] He says he resolved not to worry about the external consequences of his actions, since they are not under our domination.[81] While it is accepted today that trust plays a large role in social order, an understanding of the role of trust in constituting *knowledge* is lacking in the modern tradition, as Steven Shapin has shown. This is not because trust does not matter for knowledge in modernity; on the contrary, if anything, modern science is more trusting than ever: "Scientists know so much about the natural world by knowing so much about whom they can trust."[82] Yet as Michael Kochin writes, "It is hard to see this point in the glare of the reputation that impersonal reason has acquired from its supposed use in modern natural science and mathematics."[83] The problem lies in our interpretation of scientific truth as a product of a solitary skeptic. We need to reject the myth that "explicitly identified reliance upon trust and authority" is "a major source of epistemic error."[84]

Believing our framework to be transcendental gives us certainty that our knowledge and actions are correct, but this is an illusion: we can never have this certainty, and our relationship to our framework of knowledge is rather one of *committed belief*. The myth of the transcendental viewpoint is that this belief could be replaced by certain knowledge and that science could be methodically built on rational foundations. Were this to ever happen, however, it would be the death of science, as there would be nothing else to learn; a frozen framework deemed "scientific" would disbar discussion based on any other premises. This would be the end of science, the practice of which aims to make irreversible gains that expand our framework. The transcendental fallacy replaces the scientific community with a claim of superior power.

It also replaces the personal commitment of the scientist with an impersonal truth value. The transcendental fallacy thinks that it is *statements* that are true or false, rather than a personal witness, but this is mistaken; propositions by themselves can never be the main locus of truth. For one thing, they are always couched in a particular language. If you get someone who does not know German to repeat the sounds in the sentence *zwei plus zwei ergibt vier*, they are not saying something true but imitating meaningless sounds. For another thing, any given truth to which we are committed finds its place within a larger framework, which is unspecifiable as a whole—we live in it and can explicate only a portion of it. After all there are peoples, for instance the Pirahã of Brazil, who do not use numbers and have no names for them.[85] It is not unthinkable for a social order to revert to such a state, abandoning the public recognition of mathematical truth.[86] In our day we have seen our commitment to basic biological truths falter. Alasdair MacIntyre famously deployed a thought experiment in which the practice of science was destroyed while the language of science, as well as the judgment of scientific propositions as true or false, continued.[87]

The publicity of truth is not its dwelling among Platonic forms, for which all anyone has to do is look at them to know they are true. The participatory nature of truth is incompatible with an individualistic prejudice. It is not the case that if someone else fails to assent to a true proposition, it is simply because they are lacking the required human intelligence or will. Timeless truth is not just sitting there for anyone to discover by just looking at it; it requires the community of knowledge to critically certify it, as well as for teachers to teach it. It requires a language to be expressed, even as it expands that language. Contact with reality that increases our knowledge is a growth of the framework of our language—it can only exist in and through such a growth—and the advance that expands the framework needs the framework that it overcomes in order to express the new insight; it also needs the person advocating for it and the community of experts to critically confirm it. A new truth that is not critically authenticated or expressed does not have an impact. It fails to live up to its promise and expand our framework; it would be as if it were never discovered. An achievement demands to be confirmed and disseminated, that is, to be accepted and taught by the knowledge community.

We cannot skip over the dissemination and the teaching; they are as inherent to a discovery as performance is to a musical work. To fail to see this, to stick with the individualistic prejudice of the transcendental viewpoint, is as fallacious as thinking that science is based on the observation of experiments repeatable by anyone, missing both the long apprenticeship and training necessary to perform experiments, and likewise their nature as skillful performance. Theodore Porter relates how, in the 1930s, physicist Ernest Lawrence maintained someone trying to build a cyclotron if he had not worked with one in his lab was foolish, explaining, "It is rather ticklish in operation . . . and a certain amount of experience is necessary to get it to work properly." Porter concludes that "experimental regularities should perhaps be interpreted in terms of human skill rather than of stable underlying entities and the operation of general laws of nature."[88]

We cannot have complete certainty but only committed belief, because future advances could always potentially alter what we are committed to at present. This also means that what we are committed to is not fully known in all its implications. If what we hold to be true is an achievement, a positive advance, it will form the basis for further advances—even greater contact with reality, a more comprehensive sense of the whole. We never know exactly what our beliefs entail. To be completely certain of something, we would need to know all the implications, but this could happen only if we froze our framework, denied that it could ever be improved upon, made it comprehensive and coextensive with reality itself, obscured its reliance on other people and on tacit knowledge, and contended that it was fully explicated. *Then* the tautologies of our system would be eternal verities, truths of timeless validity, but only because we could not imagine ever expanding our knowledge. The truths of our system would be self-evident, the measure of rationality itself, insofar as all rational creatures should uphold them as proof of their rationality. In this case we would have nothing to learn from competing systems of thought, which could only be rejected. Our framework would spell out everything we would need to know, overlooking the tacit dimension, our pre-predicative contact with reality that is the source of new discoveries and insight. As static and self-evident, our truths would lose their quality of being *achievements*. They would become instead analytic statements, reversible implications from the premises of the system.

Take basic mathematical truths. Children need to be taught to count: to look at two fingers and say the word "two," to see two other fingers and collect them in the same way into a grouping, and then to focus out their attention on the whole of the two combined groups, resulting in a larger group of fingers that is then registered together as a whole as "four." Learning how to count and register groupings is an irreversible achievement, for which its symbolic representation is a shorthand expression. Taking that expression to be a timeless truth tends to obscure its nature as an achievement that is learned and taught. It makes us think that the "truth value" of the expression is somehow its property and possession, which elides not only how it is learned but also the subsidiary reasons for its truth. An achievement is foundational for further advances, and these confirm it. To go back to a society which further could not add two and two together would mean to go back to a starkly primitive way of life, as the primitive Pirahã demonstrate. There would be neither telecommunications, nor stock markets, nor internal combustion engines, nor architecture. We would live in huts and travel by foot. The superiority of our civilization to such a Paleolithic lifestyle is part of the subsidiary reasons that we are sure that two plus two is four.

The truth of basic, foundational achievements is overdetermined. We first believed them because our teachers taught them to us, then we registered the truth for ourselves, making it our own, and finally, we know tacitly that our whole network of relationships with others would have to be altered if we are wrong. Truth becomes embedded in those relationships as part of our heritage and the foundation for new achievements, just as Mussorgsky's *Pictures* anticipated musical styles in the twentieth century and opened up new horizons for composers both in Russia and the West.[89] If a work or discovery is not accepted as a great achievement—not performed and not taught—it fails to become a part of our tradition. When it does become a part of our tradition, it lays the foundation for future achievement. Those future accomplishments are not incidental to the work but part and parcel of it. That is what an advance does; it opens up new horizons. The future developments pay off the promise of the work and in so doing, validate it. If a work leads to a dead end, such that we have to do something different—go in a different direction or start over—then we can say that it falls short. Each work, each discovery of a truth, is a suggestion calling for a response, and persons responding are participating in the phenomenon of truth, a participation called for by its being; the confirmation process and the community doing the validating are not inessential, but necessary, equiprimordial moments of the phenomenon of truth.

To say that an achievement demands recognition is different from saying it is truth independent of culture and eternally valid. The latter is clearly false. The truth we discover is still couched in a language and tradition; even if it goes beyond it and overturns some of its assumptions, in so doing, it is expressing what is new in the discovery. The advance has contrasted itself with the *status quo ante* in order to be expressed. To insist that a truth and the expression of a truth are not in competition with each other is not to deny that a discovery is a real contact with reality. It is rather to insist that the unity of an ideal object cannot be opposed to the infinite manifold of its possible presentation. The two levels necessarily work together. Only an inordinate desire for certainty would make us downplay the presentations, in their temporality and open-endedness, in favor of the ideality, as if that were something that could be separately grasped, and capable of providing us indubitable knowledge exclusive to itself and apart from the vagaries of lived experience. The works of phenomenological philosophy provide us formal indications, a method which also describes how the ideal being of language must be enacted in order to have meaning, like a musical work.[90] A truth is access to the real, which is why it drags language along with it. Language can never fully express everything we know; the expression of a truth in a language is only a shorthand for our access to that truth in pre-predicative life. Our access to truth in our unreflective lived experience is not in competition with expressing it thematically; rather, the two work together as we come to terms with our surroundings. Faith and works are dance partners.

In denying that a proposition possesses eternal validity, we are not saying it is merely conventional and does not represent an irreversible advance. What we deny, rather, is an understanding of that validity as *impersonal*, disconnected from our commitment and responsibility. A discovery requires us to cash in on it; we have the winning lotto ticket, now we have to go to the authorized location to claim our prize. A discovery is a real contact with reality; nevertheless, it inevitably requires an advocate. *Pictures at an Exhibition* is a great piano work; nevertheless, it requires a performer. Truth is not an overwhelming power that forces anyone who considers it to assent to it—something that is true proposes itself, never imposes itself. The truth is defenseless, as it were.[91] We can always turn our focal attention elsewhere. If a truth is going to hold sway, it is because of us speaking it in our local language. We have to be committed to a truth and take personal responsibility for it, or else it will not become incarnate. The publicity of truth is no automatic mechanism. Something that is true at all times and in all places is so only as a result of particular proselytization, even if it took place in the immemorial past, the trace of which we experience now as self-evidence. To insist, contrariwise, that it is in the nature of a universal truth to be true apart from whether or not it is taught, misleadingly opposes two sides of the same coin that actually work in tandem: something that is a real advance *should* be taught, just as a great piano work should be played. To fail to think this is to either deny that it is an advance or to misunderstand the nature of an advance. When we imagine that a proposition is timelessly valid, we efface the timeliness of its reality; for example, the necessary teaching that led up to the performance of the achievement as well as the significance of our commitment to it. Falsely released of the duty of gratitude for being taught and the responsibility of teaching as a result, we congratulate ourselves in the present for our knowledge, while ignoring what made it possible and missing what our knowledge really means.

When I pretend that an expression of truth is self-evidently true, my commitment to it becomes a flat necessity rather than a passionate pursuit of something real. Truth loses its ecstatic, participatory, and evangelical character, leading me to think that if someone else does not see the self-evidence for himself that I see, there is no convincing him. When our framework is frozen and becomes transcendental, the world is mysteriously divided into the saved and the damned, those who accept it and those who do not.

Hobbes, of course, presents his system as a timeless truth, a transcendental rule setting the conditions for the possibility of life in society. Yet his description of authority as sovereignty only captures one manifestation of it; namely, the cases in which authority stems from fear of a society's imminent collapse, as when a city turns to a dictator when threatened by an invading army. However, not all authority is reducible to escaping violent death, and that is just one possible instance of following a suggestion. Political leadership is a complex phenomenon with a multiplicity of different manifestations. Hobbes's approach rules these other types out of order, focusing on just one of them—an ideality that is then declared to be the essence of all authority, while other manifestations that show authority to be much broader and more complicated are reinterpreted as neutral facts, the way that the subjective desires of this individual actor affect his responses.

This enables Hobbes to claim that we can have complete certainty in his formula, that the Sovereign must always be obeyed in everything. With this we have captured the essence of politics for Hobbes. It is not a matter of committed belief of thinkers and actors, which could turn out to be wrong, but rather, the source of absolute knowledge of the future: if we disobey the Sovereign, then our society will collapse. Talking about the functioning of a whole society cannot be a matter of tacit knowledge that can only be partially conceptualized, but rather, we *have* captured it in the doctrine of Sovereignty. Hobbes's transcendental truth is a narrow manifestation of political authority taken to be its eternal essence and then set over and against alternative manifestations, which now must be interpreted as empirical facts—that is to say, neutral data with no bearing on the meaning of the phenomenon. Like the realm of the "external" for Luther, which is indifferent to the inner, spiritual essence of Christianity, the manifestations of authority beyond its correct, eternal essence for Hobbes can be meaningful only to individuals privately, which is to say that they are in themselves meaningless. The Hobbesian system is awash in meaninglessness; the basis for public authority, the ultimate meaning that matters, is simply avoiding death. Beyond this, there is no point to our lives that could be publicly acknowledged. And since death cannot ultimately be avoided, that means our individual lives are futile.

It is not only individual, subjective meanings which must be interpreted as essentially meaningless, but also communal customs. The public meaning that local cultures give to life in and through their customs must be reinterpreted and made compatible with Sovereignty. Customs must be categorized as either transcendental or empirical: either as a logical implication of Sovereignty and therefore a custom with eternal validity, or as a local practice arising from the subjective vagaries of a group of people, their nonrational preferences. To that end Hobbes spells out as *laws of nature* the habits and customs appropriate in a state committed to Sovereignty. Just as one manifestation of authority is taken to be its eternal essence, only one set of customs is held to be valid and binding. From Sovereignty we deduce the only correct habits and customs that possess what today we would call moral force. These are the customs we ought to follow—Hobbes here moves in the direction of modern morality, with its impersonal imperatives and abstract standards of rightness.

THE LAW OF NATURE

Hobbes's term *laws of nature* is confusing, and no shortage of commentators have been befuddled by it. This is not surprising as they are badly misnamed: the laws of nature are not really laws, and they do not hold in nature. Hobbes tells us a better term for them is "dictates of Reason."[92]

They are not dictates of reason *tout court*, however. The law of nature in Hobbes is rather the habits of thought and action *appropriate to life in a regime with a Hobbesian sovereign*. If we are going to think about and justify political power in the way Hobbes wants us to, we need citizens to cultivate certain beliefs and habits in order to make the political arrangements work. Of course, in different regimes—certainly any with civic republican institutions—radically different habits and interpretations of those habits would be required. To think in these terms is incompatible with the transcendental approach, however, as it views itself alone as having eternal validity: there could not be different sets of *mores* which are appropriate for different sets of political institutions and the conditions and situations in which people find themselves, since Hobbesian Sovereignty is not one possible option among others, but rather the only correct option. This is why Hobbes calls the customs and interpretations of the customs for his regime "laws of nature": to present them as having unchanging, scientific validity (logical conclusions from his theory of transcendental Sovereignty).

To begin with, Hobbes's laws of nature are not all created equally. He writes in *Leviathan* that "to seek peace" is "the fundamentall Law of Nature."[93] The first law of nature we will name the "first table," while the rest of the laws of nature will be the "second table."[94] The difference between the two tables is the difference between the end and the means, Hobbes tells us in *De Cive*.[95]

There are a couple differences between these two tables. First, although according to Hobbes, both the end, peace, and the means to it are to be called "good," they are not evidently good in the same way. Hobbes writes that "all men agree on this that Peace is Good, and therefore also the way, or the means to Peace, which (as I have shewed before) are *Justice, Gratitude, Modesty, Equity, Mercy,* & the rest of the Laws of Nature, are good."[96] What Hobbes does *not* say, however, is that "all men agree" on these *means* to peace. This forms a big difference between the two tables: a case could be made that all men agree on the first natural law, but all men certainly do not agree on the rest, which are conclusions we have to tease out of the fundamental law. Hobbes calls the laws of nature "dictates of Reason" that are "but Conclusions, or Theoremes concerning what conduceth to the conservation and defence of themselves."[97] The latter phrase, "conservation and defence of themselves," describes the *first* table of the laws of nature, while the former, "Conclusions, or Theoremes," corresponds to the *second* table.

Second, the two tables are fulfilled in different ways. To begin with, the laws of nature do not have to be followed by me if no one else is following them. We name this characteristic the law of mimetic abrogation. If other people obey the laws of nature, we must do so too; but if they do not, we are relieved of our external obligation. "For he that should be modest, and tractable, and performe all he promises, in such time, and place, where no man els should do so, should but make himselfe a prey to others, and procure his own certain ruine, contrary to the ground of all Lawes of Nature, which tend to Natures preservation."[98] The loyalty we show to others must be reduced to a minimum—we only show them loyalty if they show us loyalty. We can wish that they would show us loyalty, but we cannot actually act out of loyalty to them in the absence of their loyalty.

The law of mimetic abrogation holds for all the laws of nature. For the second table, however, we do still have to follow them as a *wish* and before our own conscience, though not externally. Hobbes writes, "The Lawes of Nature oblige *in foro interno*; that is to say, they bind to a desire they should take place: but *in foro externo*; that is, to the putting them in act, not always."[99] This can *only* hold for the second table. The distinction between wishing the laws of nature be fulfilled, and actually following them in public, *cannot* hold for the first table of the laws of nature, which runs as follows: "That every man, ought to endeavor Peace, as farre as he has hope of obtaining it; and when he cannot obtain it, that he may seek, and use, all helps, and advantages of Warre."[100]

For the fundamental law of nature, the distinction between *in foro interno* and *in foro externo,* makes no sense. In this law, Hobbes is summing up the right of nature, "*By all means we can, to defend our selves*" and the law of nature, "*to seek Peace, and follow it*" in one "rule of reason"—however, these two parts cannot be followed at the same time. We cannot endeavor peace before our own conscience but total war in our external actions, and vice versa—and Hobbes makes clear it is not just war he is talking about but total war ("seek, and use, all helps, and advantages of Warre"). Simply put, if we were in a situation of war, we would not have to seek peace; we would be trying to survive and to kill our enemy. In this situation it is not possible to speak of *in foro interno* obligations.

These obligations only come after we have accepted a sovereign. The distinction between *interno* and *externo* makes sense only in the context of a commonwealth. Because they refer to discrete areas, the laws in the second table can be mimetically abrogated without a general declaration of war between parties. In a generally functioning and peaceful system, when a social subgroup within a state is not following laws of nature, those laws are abrogated when we are thrown into that group, with the *in foro interno* obligation remaining. This *interno/externo* distinction naturally cannot hold, though, when we are thrown into a situation of total war, as the war of all against all consumes the distinction.

The second table of the laws of nature are but conclusions of reason and not laws, at least until the commonwealth is established. If, in the state of war of all against all, we actually had a spare minute to think about the conditions for peaceful living, we might come up with some of the laws of nature. However, there is precious little time to think about such things when we are fighting for survival and everyone is our enemy. If such a thought did pop into our head, it might be interesting, but we would certainly not think of it as a law to which we must conform.

The laws of nature pass through the commonwealth. It is impossible, then, for someone to argue that Hobbes's arguments are just his own opinions and that separate conclusions of reason should be followed. First, Hobbes's laws of nature entail that we follow the commands of the Sovereign, which are clearly beyond the opinion of one person, since they form the will of the established institutional authority. Second, conclusions of reason proposed by someone other than the Sovereign may or may not be valid. If the Sovereign commands them, then they are automatically valid. If the Sovereign is silent, and these purported conclusions of reason do not violate any other commands, a proponent is free to convince other people to follow his lead. There is a *realm of freedom* left over to subjects where the laws are silent, a realm of acting with others, following their lead or attempting to get them to follow us. There are limits to this negative liberty, however. We cannot convince others to follow us in ways that would undercut Hobbesian Sovereignty. If ultimate authority is found in the Sovereign power, justified by a transcendental argument, and I am not the Sovereign, then I cannot claim any special rights or privileges vis-à-vis my fellows unless they explicitly grant them to me on a contractual basis. Even behaving in a way that contributes to peace does not give me any superiority, since no one is obliged to do this anyway—unless everyone else is already doing it. The law of mimetic abrogation therefore shows the laws of nature to be the *logical obverse of Sovereignty*.

If, for some reason, I think I am inherently better than others and should have special rights or privileges, the basis for my belief can only be a political theory that is incompatible with transcendental Sovereignty. The sphere of freedom to which the laws of nature apply can be summed up in the sentence, "There is a Sovereign, and we are not him." Only the Sovereign is special.

The rest of us are equal to one another. Others can follow me, but only if it is clear that they are doing so not out of an allegiance to me that would be a threat to the Sovereign. I must be seen as an equal. Equality, or as Hobbes calls it, "equity," is the sum of the laws of nature. Our comfort with this should not impede us from recognizing how revolutionary it is. "Because Europe's monarchies were supported by aristocratic families who were distinguished from the remainder of subjects by their social status, wealth, and education—if not by God's special grace—Hobbes's assertion of human equality challenged centuries of custom."[101]

The converse is also true. I cannot think someone or some others are inherently better, in terms of treating them qualitatively differently, giving them a loyalty that would not be mimetically abrogated. This would be to see them as special, as due conduct that is qualitatively different from that due to other people.

We are all equal under the Sovereign. The Sovereign is the magical oracle, the Midas whose pronouncements automatically turn into justice itself. The rest of us cannot claim that ability. Our views and pronouncements are not automatically just; they are only our own opinion, which is as good as anyone else's. If everyone agrees on a set of binding rules for competition, then those are the binding rules—binding because everyone agrees, not because a certain one of us came up with them—and the Sovereign is the mechanism through which this agreement of all is produced. In our realm of freedom under the Sovereign, other people can follow me of their own free will. They *cannot* follow me *because of* my virtue, historical loyalty, record of leadership, immemorial custom, or any other reason that would conflict with transcendental Sovereignty—the exercise of absolute power completely justified by an argument. This prohibition includes my record as a peaceful person, someone who contributes to the peace of society. Those laws are not to be followed unless everyone follows them, that is, unless everyone is equal. We are supposed to follow them internally when they are not followed at large; however, this is easy to do.

The laws of nature are the *mores* of a society committed to transcendental Sovereignty because they enshrine peace as the foremost public good without such good conflicting with the absolute initiative of the Sovereign. They are the habits, and the way of thinking about those habits, that we must cultivate in order to make a political order work in which there is a Sovereign whose will defines justice. We are to think of ourselves as inhabiting a sphere of social freedom in which we can interact with each other in a free market as equals, pursuing our own individual desires without coercing others. Hobbes sums up all the laws of nature in one maxim: "Do not that to another, which thou wouldest not have done to thy selfe."[102] In other words, he speaks of a negative sphere of freedom in which what we pursue is up to our own desire and thus differs radically from the positive, Christian formula which *directs* desire. We are to, on the one hand, follow certain *mores*, but on the other hand, refuse to give preference to any private person who follows those *mores* well in difficult circumstances, as this would conflict with transcendental Sovereignty. One could sum up the laws of nature for Hobbes as follows: "The only loyalty one must give another is one of minimum loyalty, one that is equal to all others." To make of loyalty a flat indifferent minimum is to destroy it. To enshrine Sovereignty is to eliminate loyalties.

Only because there is a Sovereign whose pronouncements are automatically just can we have such a realm of social freedom and equality. It is because the political problem has been solved through the creation of a Sovereign that we can have the *social question*—that is, "Whose lead should I follow?" in the context of "society," a situation of equality and negative freedom where I must not follow anyone, they must not follow me, and in which we are all equals pursuing our individual desires. If the political problem were not already solved through the creation of an absolute Sovereign, this idea of society would not make any sense. Following the suggestions of others and making suggestions to be followed by them would not be a matter of pursuing my individual desires with and among equals. Rather, it would involve questions of justice, the answers to which would inevitably have wider implications. Whom I decide to follow and why—this would not be just a matter of empirical preference, but decisions for which I would be answerable. My actions would not be declinable to my desire but to a complex set of considerations for which I can give a rational account. These considerations would not just concern me and my individual desire but would include my relationships with others as well. Ultimately, the account I would give of my action would be a public one, an account that includes other people and has implications for how we structure our behavior and institutions. The political question would not be solved but would remain very much alive and up in the air, and my personal decisions would be a microcosm of the whole. This is not to say that in such a situation it would be the case that "everything would be political," or that "there would be no private sphere"—these expressions indicate a horrible totalitarianism only in the context of Hobbesian liberalism where freedom is the negative liberty of pursuing desires in society—but rather that it is undeniable that my actions have wider repercussions beyond the fulfillment of my desire.

Hobbes's laws of nature govern a defined practice: namely, living in a state with a sovereign who is always right by keeping our loyalty to each other at a minimum. In other words, the laws of nature are not at all as Hobbes bills them, as a natural law valid for all time; but rather they are the rules and modes of thought appropriate to absolute Sovereignty, but not appropriate for other types of regimes. Hobbes hides their true character by calling them "laws of nature." In truth, for us, if we live in a liberal society which tries to promote individual freedom to pursue happiness, we will strive to accommodate ourselves to the *mores* appropriate to this regime *because* we are loyal to our fellow men. This is the reason to adopt any given moral code: through it we show our loyalty to other people and develop relationships of trust and friendship with them, not keep these at a minimum. Liberalism requires in practice, yet constantly undermines in interpretation, the strong relationships that are indispensable for its success, the depletion of which we are now seeing the bad effects of today.

For Hobbes, we are supposed to follow the laws of nature not out of loyalty to particular others but because they are conclusions of reason that get us the peace required for anyone to exist at all: they are not customs of a given people but transcendental conditions for peace. Like geometric proofs, we do not make them up: we discover them. Also like geometry, they are supposed to hold no matter what empirical details are involved—the color or exact shape of the triangle drawn on the chalkboard does not affect the Pythagorean theorem. For transcendental political theory, persons and the type of personal relationships are empirical details, that is to say, individual preferences. The laws of nature are the transcendental conclusions for how we can have peace in a society, abstracting from the actual persons involved and the quality of personal relationships. Considering this view, "natural" is a fitting word for Hobbes's purpose in the context of his own theory, since according to him, in our natural state we are all isolated individuals and there are no social groups—an aspect of the state of nature retained in transcendental argumentation.

Likewise, "laws" is a tactical word for Hobbes, as it short-circuits discussion not only of the quality of loyalty to persons but also to excellences and customs. Excellences involve more than effort, expertise, and tradition; as not every person can pursue every excellence, talking about virtue necessarily involves a discussion of which person is best to pursue which excellence, and such discussions can never rise to the transcendental level. Hobbes does not wish to talk about excellence, and he summarily reduces moral virtue to law. In *Leviathan* Hobbes writes that "the way, or means of Peace . . . and the rest of the Laws of Nature, are good; that is to say, *Morall Vertues*." The true moral philosophy is the "true Doctrine of the Lawes of Nature."[103] The term *laws* takes attention away from the practice of political excellence—that which can bring about actual peace in a concrete situation—and, likewise, forestalls discussions of customs. Instead of *mores* arising organically from the common life of a people, they are put under the control of the state, as it is up to the Sovereign to legislate new customs and enshrine the laws of nature, making them externally binding when they otherwise are not. By thinking in terms of laws of nature rather than the patterns of behavior shaped by individual interactions and politics in the wide sense of suggestion-response, agency is taken away from the people and given to the Sovereign.

Finally, the laws of nature indicate a direction to take in order to overcome a problem with Hobbes's theory of Sovereignty that stems from the anarchic origin of *mores*. If the Sovereign decrees something that is utterly opposed to the history, traditions, and customs of the people, resistance and intractable conflict will inevitably result. In practice, the Sovereign must respect *mores*, but Hobbes cannot acknowledge this and still claim transcendental status for his theory, as for him, it cannot be the case that we must follow the will of the Sovereign only when the person who is Sovereign exercises prudence. As a result, however, belief in the Hobbesian thesis *causes* the intractable conflict and division it is supposed to save us from, in the degree to which the person who is Sovereign takes it literally and is lured into reckless imprudence. The only solution is an alignment of the *mores* of the people with the idea of Sovereignty. Hobbes does not reach this solution himself; it only comes with the identification of morality with the substance of Sovereignty by his followers.

NOTES

1. "In short, I will preach it, teach it, write it, but I will constrain no one by force, for faith must come freely without compulsion. Take myself as an example. I opposed indulgences and all the papists, but never with force. I simply taught, preached, and wrote God's Word; otherwise I did nothing. And while I slept, or drank Wittenberg beer with my friends Philip and Amsdorf, the Word so greatly weakened the papacy that no prince or emperor ever inflicted such losses upon it. I did nothing; the Word did everything." Martin Luther, "The Second Sermon, March 10, 1522, Monday after Invocavit," Accessed September 2, 2022, https://www.theologie.uzh.ch/predigten/archiv-6/eight-sermons-wittenberg.pdf.

2. Heiko A. Oberman, *Luther: Man Between God and the Devil*, trans. Eileen Walliser-Schwarzbart (New Haven: Yale University Press, 1989), 205.

3. Eric Metaxas, *Martin Luther: The Man Who Rediscovered God and Changed the World* (New York: Penguin, 2017), 203–4.

4. Metaxas, *Martin Luther*, 207.

5. William Manchester, *A World Lit Only by Fire: The Medieval Mind and the Renaissance* (New York: Back Bay Books, 1993), 178.

6. James M. Kittelson and Hans H. Wiersma, *Luther The Reformer: The Story of the Man and His Career*, 2nd ed. (Minneapolis: Fortress Press, 2016), 193–94.

7. Cf. Andreas Osiander, "Sovereignty, International Relations, and the Westphalian Myth," *International Organization* 55, no. 2 (2001): 251–87.

8. William T. Cavanaugh, *The Myth of Religious Violence: Secular Ideology and the Roots of Modern Conflict* (Oxford: Oxford University Press, 2009), 84–101, 181–83.

9. Cavanaugh, *The Myth of Religious Violence*, 140–41.

10. Cavanaugh, 166–67.

11. Quote of the British historian Lewis Namier, in Immanuel Wallerstein, *The Modern World-System I: Capitalist Agriculture and the Origins of the European World-Economy in the Sixteenth Century* (Berkeley: University of California Press, 2011), 207. For Brad Gregory, the state formed the religious identity of the populace, writing that "the net result in the early modern period is that European countries forge the dominant, state-supported religious identities of their subjects and carry them into the modern world: Lutheranism in Denmark, Sweden, and much of Germany; Reformed Protestantism in Scotland, England (in some respects), the Netherlands, and parts of Germany and Switzerland; and Catholicism in Spain, Portugal, Italy, France, Austria, Bohemia, Poland, Ireland, Belgium, and the remaining parts of Germany and Switzerland." Brad S. Gregory, *Rebel in the Ranks: Martin Luther, the Reformation, and the Conflicts That Continue to Shape Our World* (New York: HarperOne, 2017), 145. Carlton Hayes has brought out the nature of nationalism as a civil religion. "Nationalists do not take kindly to the divided allegiance of fellow citizens who sometimes obey the state and sometimes obey a 'foreign' church, and who reserve to themselves the right of private judgement whenever it is a question of reconciling the two." Carlton J. H. Hayes, *Essays on Nationalism* (New York: Russell & Russell, 1954), 201. The more nationalism takes on the character of a religion, the more it demands exclusive loyalty. "There are degrees of nationalism, as of any emotion. Our loyalty to nationality and national state may be conditioned by other loyalties—to family, to church, to humanity, to internationalism—and hence restricted in corresponding degree. On the other hand, nationalism may be a paramount, a supreme loyalty, commanding all others. This usually occurs when national emotion is fused with religious emotion, and nationalism itself becomes a religion or a substitute for religion." Carlton J. H. Hayes, *Nationalism: A Religion* (New York: The Macmillan Company, 1960), 10.

12. Cavanaugh, *The Myth of Religious Violence*, 123.

13. Cavanaugh, 142.

14. Peter H. Wilson, *The Thirty Years War: Europe's Tragedy* (Cambridge, Massachusetts: Belknap Press, 2009), 9.

15. Cavanaugh, *The Myth of Religious Violence*, 166.

16. Cavanaugh, 162–63.

17. Cavanaugh, 162. "Although many liberal political theorists and moral philosophers point to Reformation-era violence to justify the exclusion of religion from present-day politics, they almost always ignore other historical realities that were intertwined with the emergence of an ethics of rights—including the state-building processes that antedated the Reformation, through which nonecclesiastical authorities increased their control of the churches after the Reformation began, and by means of which these authorities were the most important agents in the 'wars of religion.'"

Brad S. Gregory, *The Unintended Reformation: How a Religious Revolution Secularized Society* (Cambridge: Belknap Press, 2012), 185–86.

18. A. J. P. Taylor, *The Course of German History: A Survey Of The Development Of German History Since 1815* (London: Routledge, 2005), 13–14. "Regardless of the form it took, political power was central to the Reformation era. Religion in the period can't be understood apart from politics, and neither can politics be understood apart from religion. Without the support of political authorities, no form of Christianity could shape the hearts and minds and practices of large numbers of men and women in a sustained way." Gregory, *Rebel in the Ranks*, 209.

19. Story related by Saleem Ghubril, "Commencement Address," The 87th Annual Commencement of Robert Morris University, May 5, 2012, Moon Township, Pennsylvania.

20. As Sandra Lynch concludes, friendship must be modelled on difference, not similarity. "The recognition of difference encourages a view of the other as separate from ourselves; it alerts us to the possibility that the friend's desires, motives and concerns might conflict with our own and that we might need to tolerate some friction, or accept difference and perhaps some disappointment." Sandra Lynch, *Philosophy and Friendship* (Edinburgh: Edinburgh University Press, 2005), 191.

21. It is noteworthy that for Nietzsche, the term "common good" contradicts itself. Nietzsche, *Beyond Good and Evil*, §43. KGW 6.2, 52.

22. René Girard, *The Scapegoat* (Baltimore: Johns Hopkins University Press, 1986), 142.

23. Even the desire for money is relative in this way—what we want is not the green bills but our success relative to others, the possession of a scare commodity. It may be that "what we care most about is not material comforts, but one-upsmanship," as Arthur Brooks writes. Arthur C. Brooks, *Gross National Happiness: Why Happiness Matters for American—and How We Can Get More of It* (New York: Basic Books, 2008), 120–21.

24. Girard, *The Scapegoat*, 133.

25. Buzz Bissinger, *A Prayer for the City* (New York: Random House, 1997), 140.

26. Robert Greene, *The 48 Laws of Power* (New York: Penguin, 1998), 203.

27. As Paul W. Kahn puts it, "Hobbes is the first modern theoretician of the constitutional moment; that is, of a point from which political order is to be constructed anew on the basis of the insights of 'political science.'" Paul W. Kahn, *Putting Liberalism in Its Place* (Princeton: Princeton University Press, 2005), 64.

28. Abraham Edel, "Right and Good," in *Dictionary of the History of Ideas*, ed. Philip Wiener, vol. 4 (New York: Charles Scribner's Sons, 1973), 177.

29. Kittelson and Wiersma, *Luther The Reformer: The Story of the Man and His Career*, 192–93.

30. WA 11, 251. LW 45, 91. And again, "What would become of the world if everyone who was in the right punished everyone who did wrong? The servant would strike his master, the maid her mistress, the children the parents, the pupils the teacher. That would be a fine state of affairs!" WA 19, 641–42. LW 46, 114. The unmediated relationship with God in the religious sphere does not translate into the human sphere because of original sin. "Luther's position," Luigino Bruni writes, "is among the great

sources of the argument of *bellum omnium contra omnes* and of its remedy (the social contract and the Leviathan)." Luigino Bruni, *The Genesis and Ethos of the Market* (New York: Palgrave Macmillan, 2012), 81.

31. Thomas Hobbes, *Leviathan*, 13.5. CE 4, 190.

32. Hobbes, *Leviathan*, 18.15. CE 4, 276.

33. As scientists of social networks have noted, "violence—in both its minor and extreme forms—can spread . . . either in a directed fashion (retaliating against the perpetrators) or in a generalized fashion (harming nondisputants nearby)." Nicholas A. Christakis and James H. Fowler, *Connected: The Surprising Power of Our Social Networks and How They Shape Our Lives* (New York: Little, Brown and Company, 2009), 4.

34. Hobbes, *Leviathan*, 10.25. CE 4, 136.

35. Hobbes, *Leviathan*, 45.12. CE 5, 1028.

36. Hobbes, *Leviathan*, 16.40. CE 4, 242. It is not correct, therefore, to say that Hobbes's ethics has "two faces," since Hobbes is obliterating the good in favor of the right. Cf. Arash Abizadeh, *Hobbes and the Two Faces of Ethics* (Cambridge: Cambridge University Press, 2018).

37. Hobbes, *Leviathan*, 17.13. CE 4, 260.

38. Hobbes, *Leviathan*, 16.13. CE 4, 248.

39. Hobbes, *Leviathan*, 18.5. CE 4, 268.

40. The two parts of *Leviathan* therefore must be read as a coherent whole. Cf. Eric Brandon, *The Coherence of Hobbes's Leviathan: Civil and Religious Authority Combined* (New York: Continuum, 2007).

41. *Leviathan* itself was occasioned by the question of loyalty. The pressing political issue of the day was the question of switching loyalties from Charles I to the Interregnum republican government. Quentin Skinner, *Visions of Politics III: Hobbes and Civil Science* (Cambridge: Cambridge University Press, 2002), 19–20. The assumption that Hobbes was a staunch defender of the monarchy is complicated by the fact that two men who knew him personally and were royalists, Edward Hyde and Bishop Bramhall, wrote attacks on *Leviathan* and accused Hobbes of supporting Cromwell and even the radicals. Eleanor Curran, *Reclaiming the Rights of the Hobbesian Subject* (Houndmills: Palgrave Macmillan, 2007), 1–2.

42. Michael Oakeshott calls this "politics without a policy." Michael Oakeshott, *The Voice of Liberal Learning* (Indianapolis: Liberty Fund, 1989), 162.

43. Hobbes, *Leviathan*, 28.2. CE 4, 482.

44. Hobbes, *Leviathan*, 28.23. CE 4, 486.

45. Hobbes, *Leviathan*, 18.5. CE 4, 268.

46. Hobbes, *Leviathan*, 18.9. CE 4, 272.

47. What if the person is no enemy, and the Sovereign has made a mistake? It cannot be called an injustice, and we cannot come to the defense of the innocent person. It is an "iniquity" for which the person who is Sovereign has to answer for to God. It is not injustice but simply the opposite of equity, of treating everyone equally. It is not even an injury, because according to Hobbes, we cannot injure ourselves, and as everything the Sovereign does is authorized by us, it is us doing it to ourselves. Hobbes, *Leviathan*, 21.7. CE 4, 330.

48. Present-day America offers plenty of examples of defining away violence against the powerless. What is more violent than abortion? Short of actually killing children, what is more violent for them than their parents getting divorced? Or compare inner-city violence in Chicago to the terrorist bombing of white, affluent schoolchildren or marathon runners. Violence against those who are marginalized and therefore unable to organize and pose a real threat to the regime can be acceptable; violence against those able to mobilize less so.

49. S. A. Lloyd, ed., *The Bloomsbury Companion to Hobbes* (London: Bloomsbury, 2013), 102.

50. John Milbank, *Theology and Social Theory: Beyond Secular Reason*, 2nd ed. (Malden, MA: Blackwell, 2006), 21.

51. As we saw with Luther, rule over spiritual matters is necessary for the prince because he is a prince, but it is impossible for churchmen because they are churchmen. It is also interesting to listen to John Calvin in this connection. "It would be utterly pointless," Calvin writes, "for private men, who have no right to decide how any commonwealth whatever is to be ordered, to debate what would be the best state of the commonwealth in the place where they live." Harro Höpfl, ed., *Luther and Calvin on Secular Authority*, trans. Harro Höpfl (Cambridge: Cambridge University Press, 1991), 56.

52. Jean Louis de Lolme, *The Constitution of England, or An Account of the English Government* (Indianapolis: Liberty Fund, 2007), 101n.

53. The justification for sovereignty is a science, and science is finding the connection of facts. "And whereas Sense and Memory are but knowledge of Fact, which is a thing past, and irrevocable; *Science* is the knowledge of Consequences, and dependance of one fact upon another." Hobbes, *Leviathan*, 5.17. CE 4, 72.

54. Neil Postman names late modernity "Technopoly," and writes how it has no use for classic images or metaphors but rather "facts—hard facts, scientific facts. We might even say that in Technopoly precise knowledge is preferred to truthful knowledge but that in any case Technopoly wishes to solve, once and for all, the dilemma of subjectivity." Neil Postman, *Technopoly: The Surrender of Culture to Technology* (New York: Vintage, 1992), 158.

55. As Jordan Peterson writes, "Our hopes, desires and wishes—which are always conditional—define the context within which the things and situations we encounter take on determinate significance; define even the context within which we understand 'thing' or 'situation.' We presume that things have a more or less fixed meaning, because we share a more or less fixed 'condition' with others—at least with those others who are familiar to us, who share our presumptions and worldviews. . . . We assume that such things are permanent attributes of the world; but they are not." Peterson ends this passage with a reference to what we can recognize as the Hobbesian state of nature: "Our situations—and, therefore, our 'contexts of interpretation'—can change dramatically, at any moment. We are indeed fortunate (and, generally, oblivious of that fortune) when they do not." Jordan B. Peterson, *Maps of Meaning: The Architecture of Belief* (New York: Routledge, 1999), 34.

56. Stanley Fish, *Is There a Text in This Class?: The Authority of Interpretive Communities* (Cambridge: Harvard University Press, 1980), 199.

57. Michael S. Kochin, *Five Chapters on Rhetoric: Character, Action, Things, Nothing, and Art* (University Park, Pennsylvania: The Pennsylvania State University Press, 2009), 19.

58. G. E. M. Anscombe, "On Brute Facts," *Analysis* 18, no. 3 (1958): 69–72.

59. Oakeshott, *The Voice of Liberal Learning*, 54.

60. David Weinberger, *Too Big to Know* (New York: Basic Books, 2011), 24.

61. Barbara J. Shapiro, *A Culture of Fact: England, 1550–1720* (Ithaca: Cornell University Press, 2000), 31.

62. Ludwig Wittgenstein, when trying to sketch the boundary between the empirical and the transcendental in *On Certainty*, refers again and again to the example of a court of law. Ludwig Wittgenstein, *Major Works: Selected Philosophical Writings* (New York: HarperCollins, 2009), 320, 375, 395, 406–7, 426.

63. Which itself is not as easy as it seems. There are not merely two sides to every story; as any experienced investigator will say, if an incident happened two weeks ago and there are seven people recounting it, there will be seven sides to the story.

64. Arthur Conan Doyle, *The Adventures of Sherlock Holmes* (Minneapolis: Lerner Publishing Group, 2007), 64.

65. Postman, *Technopoly: The Surrender of Culture to Technology*, 99.

66. Donald Cowan, *Unbinding Prometheus: Education for the Coming Age* (Dallas: Dallas Institute Publications, 1988), 195.

67. D. C. Schindler points to the coinciding of nominalism and rationalism, both of which "posit pure logical possibility over the actuality of any given instance, which thus becomes nothing more than a contingent, relatively arbitrary, empirical 'fact.'" D. C. Schindler, *The Politics of the Real: The Church Between Liberalism and Integralism* (Steubenville, Ohio: New Polity, 2021), 50.

68. Emmanuel Levinas, "Meaning and Sense," in *Basic Philosophical Writings*, trans. Adriaan T. Peperzak, Simon Critchley, and Robert Bernasconi (Bloomington: Indiana University Press, 1996), 33–64. "The human body is beautiful: it is also repulsive and ridiculous, a fact which can be verified at any swimming pool. The sexual organs are objects of desire and also of loathing, so much so that in many languages, if not in all languages, their names are used as words of abuse. Meat is delicious, but a butcher's shop makes one feel sick: and indeed all our food springs ultimately from dung and dead bodies, the two things which of all others seem to us the most horrible." George Orwell, *All Art Is Propaganda*, ed. George Packer (Boston: Mariner Books, 2008), 314. The world is not an unfolding logical presence, but "it takes all sorts to make a world." Orwell, *All Art Is Propaganda*, 335.

69. Max Scheler, *Formalism in Ethics and Non-Formal Ethics of Values*, trans. Manfred S. Frings and Roger L. Funk (Evanston: Northwestern University Press, 1973), 386.

70. Michael Polanyi, *Personal Knowledge: Towards a Post-Critical Philosophy* (Chicago: University of Chicago Press, 1958).

71. For the best introductions to phenomenology, cf. Emmanuel Levinas, *The Theory of Intuition in Husserl's Phenomenology*, trans. André Orianne (Evanston: Northwestern University Press, 1973); Robert Sokolowski, *Introduction to Phenomenology*

(Cambridge: Cambridge University Press, 2000); and Chad Engelland, *Phenomenology* (Cambridge: The MIT Press, 2020).

72. Scheler, *Formalism in Ethics and Non-Formal Ethics of Values*, 382–83.

73. Scheler, *Formalism in Ethics and Non-Formal Ethics of Values*, 393.

74. Michael Polanyi, *Personal Knowledge*, 266–67.

75. Glen Newey, *The Routledge Guidebook to Hobbes' Leviathan* (London: Routledge, 2014), 8.

76. Howard Williams, *Kant's Critique of Hobbes: Sovereignty and Cosmopolitanism* (Cardiff: University of Wales Press, 2003), 224.

77. For Aristotle, the educated person knows not to expect a high level of precision (as in geometry) to subject matter where it is not appropriate (like political science). Cf. Aristotle, *Nicomachean Ethics*, in *The Basic Works of Aristotle*, ed. Richard McKeon, trans. W. D. Ross (New York: Random House, 1941) 1094b11–27, 1095a30–1095b14, and 1098a20–1098b8. There is an echo of transcendental morality in the ancient Stoics, but the extent to which Stoic ethics could be described this way is disputed. "[T]here is a debate within the Stoicism literature about whether the Stoics thought that 'natural laws' were general, universal, and exceptionless (as Julia Annas, Phillip Mitsis, and Gisela Striker contend) or whether they are better understood as heuristics, which the Stoic sage would have set aside when it was appropriate so to do (which is the view of A. A. Long and Brad Inwood)." Christopher Brooke, *Philosophic Pride: Stoicism and Political Thought from Lipsius to Rousseau* (Princeton: Princeton University Press, 2012), 45.

78. Charles S. Peirce, *Selected Writings: Values in a Universe of Change* (New York: Dover, 1958), 83. Peirce also defines reality with reference to community: "The real, then, is that which, sooner or later, information and reasoning would finally result in, and which is therefore independent of the vagaries of me and you. Thus, the very origin of the conception of reality shows that this conception essentially involves the notion of a COMMUNITY, without definite limits, and capable of a definite increase of knowledge." Charles Sanders Peirce, *Collected Papers of Charles Sanders Peirce, Volume V: Pragmatism and Pragmaticism*, ed. Charles Hartshorne and Paul Weiss (Cambridge, Massachusetts: Belknap Press, 1960), para. 311.

79. Harry Collins and Robert Evans, *Rethinking Expertise* (Chicago: University of Chicago Press, 2007), 30.

80. René Descartes, *A Discourse on the Method*, ed. Ian Maclean (Oxford: Oxford University Press, 2006), 15. Though he portrays himself as a solitary thinker, that was not the case for Descartes in his life: half of the volumes of his collected works are letters. Anthony Kenny, *The Rise of Modern Philosophy* (Oxford: Clarendon Press, 2006), 34.

81. Descartes, *A Discourse on the Method*, 23.

82. Steven Shapin, *A Social History of Truth: Civility and Science in Seventeenth-Century England* (Chicago: University of Chicago Press, 1994), 417.

83. Kochin, *Five Chapters on Rhetoric*, 23–24.

84. Shapin, *A Social History of Truth*, 416.

85. Daniel L. Everett, *Don't Sleep, There Are Snakes: Life and Language in the Amazonian Jungle* (New York: Vintage, 2008).

86. George Orwell, *1984* (New York: Signet Classics, 1977), 249–52.

87. Alasdair C. MacIntyre, *After Virtue: A Study in Moral Theory* (Notre Dame: University of Notre Dame Press, 1984), 1–2.

88. Theodore M. Porter, *Trust in Numbers: The Pursuit of Objectivity in Science and Public Life* (Princeton: Princeton University Press, 1995), 13.

89. Svetlana Nagachevskaya, *Pictures at an Exhibition: A Reconciliation of Divergent Perceptions About Mussorgsky's Renowned Cycle* (The University of Arizona, 2009), 55–57.

90. The term comes from Heidegger. Chad Engelland explains that "[O]rdinary terms can serve as *formal indications* for philosophical analyses. He calls them 'indications,' because they cannot be understood in a straightforward way; their very meaning can be fixed only thanks to the successful completion of an investigation that must be undertaken individually. And he calls them 'formal,' because these indications direct us not to the content of experience but instead to the relational structure of experience." Engelland, *Phenomenology*, 168.

91. This phrase is taken from the title of the last chapter of D. C. Schindler's *Plato's Critique of Pure Reason.*

92. Hobbes, *Leviathan*, 15.41. CE 4, 242.

93. Hobbes, *Leviathan*, 15.17. CE 4, 230.

94. The content of the second table of the laws of nature can be paraphrased as follows: (2) be contented with as much liberty vis-à-vis others as you would like them to have with you; (3) do whatever the Sovereign says, as that is what justice consists in; (4) if someone gives you a gift, be grateful; (5) strive to be agreeable and accommodate yourself to others; (6) forgive people who ask for forgiveness and desire to live in peace in the future; (7) do not seek revenge for its own sake but only for the benefit it can bring in the future; (8) do not declare contempt for others, which would make them want to get revenge on you; (9) see every other person as your equal; (10) do not claim any special rights that others do not have; (11) when judging between two parties, judge equally between them; (12) indivisible goods should be enjoyed in common with everyone, or else proportionately to those who have the right to enjoy them; (13) an entire right to an indivisible good should be distributed at random; (14) *at random* means whatever the competitors agree upon, or family inheritance; (15) mediators of peace should be allowed safe conduct; (16) controversies should go to arbitration; (17) no one can be an arbitrator for his own cause; (18) arbitrators should not have an interest in the case they are deciding; and (19) in controversies over fact, the testimony of each person should be given equal weight.

95. "But the first dictate of Reason is *Peace*; All the rest are means to obtain it, and without which *Peace* cannot be had." Thomas Hobbes, *De Cive: The English Version*, ed. Howard Warrender, vol. 2, Clarendon Edition of the Works of Thomas Hobbes (Oxford: Oxford University Press, 1983), 3.19. CE 2, 70.

96. Hobbes, *Leviathan*, 15.40. CE 4, 242.

97. Hobbes, *Leviathan*, 15.41. CE 4, 242.

98. Hobbes, *Leviathan*, 15.36. CE 4, 240.

99. Hobbes, *Leviathan*, 15.36. CE 4, 240.

100. Hobbes, *Leviathan*, 14.4. CE 4, 200. Italics removed.

101. Vickie B. Sullivan, *Machiavelli, Hobbes, and the Formation of a Liberal Republicanism in England* (Cambridge: Cambridge University Press, 2004), 98.

102. Hobbes, *Leviathan*, 15.35. CE 4, 240.

103. Hobbes, *Leviathan*, 15.40. CE 4, 242.

Chapter 4

The Origins of Morality

Values language begins with Hobbes, and we are now in a position to object to it with precision. Values are that for which individuals compete. The concept cannot accommodate a truly common good, a good that we participate in as parts of a more comprehensive whole. A common good corresponds to a form, an integrated whole, in which the individual parts participate noncompetitively because it is more than the sum of its parts.

This simple idea can be difficult for us moderns to grasp. Nevertheless, any human communal form involves a noncompetitive working together towards a good that benefits everyone. Take an orchestra performing Leo Funtek's orchestration of *Pictures at an Exhibition*. There are many elements involved: Mussorgsky's original composition, Funtek's orchestration, and the conductor's interpretation. Then, of course, there are over a hundred musicians playing their parts and the audience listening in the concert hall and over the radio. Understanding of the being of a phenomenon requires, as we have seen, viewing it as a comprehensive, noncompetitive whole; to juxtapose the ideality of the music on the page over and against the performance of the musician who brings it to life is to misunderstand the type of thing that it is. In this example of the orchestration, everyone is participating in the performance of the work and understands the good that is at stake, a good that corresponds to the type of thing that it is and which requires all the parts working together to achieve it. This whole is greater than the sum of its parts. It is a good irreducible to individuals seeking esteem from each other. If the attempt to win as much value for themselves as possible were actually, in a particular instance, an accurate explanation of the participation of the musicians, the conductor, or the audience in a work, then we would not be describing a successful performance, but an embarrassment. If I am a performer and I try to extract a recognition of my value to the performance from everyone else, I am only revealing how I do not understand what I am doing. Because the whole is more than the sum of its parts, my insistence on my partial contribution is destructive of the good at stake. My partial contribution *cannot be measured*, cannot be given a value.

A competitive good always involves a higher and a lower, a greater and a less, which exclude each other in a zero-sum way. A comprehensive good, by contrast, involves a unity which involves participation in a whole greater than me, which I do not fully control, and which all the participants share. Such goods are public, not private, as they are not restricted to something—my pleasure, for instance—which is mine alone. The stock of the good available for others is not depleted by my enjoyment of the good. We have focused here on the comprehensive whole of friendship. Friends share mutually in their friendship, and we have argued that properly understood, one friendship does not compete with others the parties have. Likewise, a political order is a comprehensive whole, a form, or a type of thing with its own goodness at stake and in which we participate. Properly understood, the good of a political order is not in competition with other forms that exist elsewhere.[1]

This chapter will reflect on the common good and its symbolic mode of expression, as contrasted with the self-undermining nature of a political order founded on the competition for value. Such a political order ostensibly pursues peace but actually sows division, as we shall see occurs in Thomas Hobbes. But even the thinkers who oppose Hobbes fail to do so by pointing to the reality of the common good. Instead, they participate in its destruction by developing the modern concept of *morality*. An abstract morality that does not correspond to the concrete common good of a real community involves instead a competition for esteem, for *moral value*. This situation only recapitulates the Hobbesian system: we ultimately cannot agree on what constitutes morality and require a Sovereign to end our squabbling by making an official determination.

VALUE OR THE COMMON GOOD

At the root of both Hobbesianism and modern morality is the search for value. "Values" form liberalism's conception of the good. Seemingly open and inclusive, "values" form the symbol for private, unreal, disputable, competitive goods.[2] What is excluded by values language is the common good, the good of the functioning of a whole in which we can participate in concert and collaboration with others. The common good is evidently real. No one wants to live where there is a breakdown of trust between neighbors to the point of violence; everyone would prefer, rather, to live where the inhabitants are good friends with each other. The *effects* of the common good are undeniable. However, the common good is not "objective"; it does not have the being of an object. While it can be reflected to some degree in states of affairs—for example, property values—these cannot exhaustively capture the common good.

The common good forms the symbolic backstop for all striving and all suggestions in general, and it is unavoidable as soon as we reflect deeply enough on the end of our endeavors. With a long enough chain of questioning as to the justification of our strivings—asking why that to which our action contributes is good—we will ultimately reach the overarching symbol of the common good. Even diametrically opposed suggestions when questioned in this manner will ultimately arrive at the same answer; namely, *everyone and each one will be better off in the end.* If by contrast, I am asked why I pursue a certain action, what I hope to get out of it, and why it is good, but I answer that it will sow destruction and discord for its own sake, this would be the sign of a degenerate mind. Or better, one that is simply confused: to aim at perpetual war for its own sake is to undo the very social order that makes our desires and our questioning possible. It contradicts itself in practice. Such an idea is simply not our symbolic order: we do not *say* this. Hobbes does his best to try not to say this, even though, as we shall see, the state of war is never fully escaped in his thought. We do not fundamentally desire war against each other and destruction of one another as a permanent condition of our life; we do not live under the symbol of permanent war but under the symbol of the common good.

This macro symbolism is the answer to the question why we should want to be just at all. I am not obtaining an object of desire by trying to be a just person. Rather, I am ordering the micro level under my control to harmonize with the macro level in a chiasmic, participatory symbolism. An object can be desired and have a value, and we can order our practical action to attain it, but that structure does not adequately describe how persons pursue the common good. Persons and the community of persons can never be an object, can never be directly the target we aim at without remainder. They can never be exhausted or achieved like objects. Subject to all possible relationships and not defined by only one relation or set of functional relationships, persons and community transcend objective being. They are free: persons experience the world and act; they form and order relationships, and their acting is refracted through the reactions of other people. Our relation to the common good of the social order is one of participation and not control, an oblique, symbolic linkage, not occurring directly or predictably, not a simple means–ends calculation, but rather one of the microcosm reflecting the macrocosm and vice versa.

If I do not harmonize my actual and potential relationships within my circle, I can hardly expect peace and harmony within the wider social order in which I am a part. The consequences of my actions may be indirect and unpredictable, but they are no less real. My ordering of loyalties, such that I am an integral person, bears good fruit for others now and in the future and for the wider social group. The personal task of bringing one's relationships into harmony with each other has real, observable significance over time for other people and for the whole. To care about those people and for the whole society of which I am a part entails trying to be just. My very being consists of this care, as Heidegger saw. A lack of care means we miss what a person is, that we mistake him for an object, something external, without the personal core that relates him to the whole of the common good, a center which can be the subject of all possible relationships.

The common good plays on the level of symbolism and is not dispositive on the level of concrete habits and customs, of suggestions. An orientation towards the common good does determine the way we think about our *mores*—our practices and our interpretation of our practices—and in particular, whether we see them as a participatory reality implicating us, or whether we view them as an impartial spectator or a stranger would, as "objective." Political theories attempt to explicate the common good, but can never capture it.[3] It is not an empirical reality, but neither is it ever a universal principle.[4] The common good is a relationship not an object. It is not something we can possess. It is not a first principle. In short, it is never a *value*.

The common good forms the backdrop of all our political disputes; that we are related together in a wider whole which we both care about enables us to come together in the first place, and only then can we agree or to disagree about the best policy, rather than just ignoring or fighting each other. It is not just politics in the narrow sense, however; the unique personal task of bringing our relationships into harmony with each other is accomplished politically, in the wider sense of suggestions and responses. While "value" symbolizes a first principle which is the cause of irreconcilable conflict, the "common good" is the symbol for the bringing together of people that enables them to both to agree *and* to disagree. Conflict is not irreconcilable in principle precisely because friendship is more primordial than agreement. "To be free of conflict you need to have no friends."[5] Dissention between people does not necessarily mean that one of them is failing to seek the common good, or that there is no such thing as the common good. Rather, it is *because* there is a common good that there are disagreements between those who are not apathetic or ignorant. One of the most stressful trials for the Renaissance ecclesiastical reformer Philip Neri occurred when he was persecuted by Pope Pius V . . . who was, like Neri, also a saint.[6] When it comes to fundamental human goods or the comprehensive common good, what we actually want is not harmony at all, but rather *more* of the right kind of conflict along with the effective leadership that can manage and direct it.[7] Even in mathematical logic, it takes time and study to be convinced by a proof, and even trained logicians do not immediately agree.[8] This time lag means that some people are opposing the right answer. The more complicated the subject matter, however, the longer this time lag takes before consensus, even among wise and knowledgeable people of good will. Political decisions involve the most variables of any type of decision, so a lack of immediate agreement is completely unsurprising. Not only that: we can say that the vast majority of the time, it is undesirable.[9] Just as it would be foolish to conclude that the practice of medicine is not knowledge because you can get a second opinion from another doctor, likewise in politics, which has a much greater causal density, we should expect that there are going to be different opinions even among a group of informed and dedicated political actors.[10]

Politics is not primarily conflict, however, because it is not primarily about exclusive good, "who gets what, when, and how."[11] The intensity of the disagreements about what best serves the common good also presupposes the comprehensive integrity of our social order, as various opinions differ about the same reality.[12] There must be a basis for the conflict and an underlying speaking of the same language in order for us to even know that we have a conflict. This basis comes to expression in symbolic and inspirational rhetoric, a mode of speaking that is, crucially, outside of competitive rivalry. Symbols have no specific content, and nothing immediately follows from them, differing in this way from statements with which we could agree or disagree, and which are therefore divisive and exclusive.[13] Symbols are therefore able to express the basis for a social order, the quality of relationship that a people share. Pure political action involves the creation and maintenance of loyalties and the symbols corresponding to them. Two and a half centuries ago, the symbols "George Washington," "Bill of Rights," "Bald Eagle," "Stars and Stripes," and "Fourth of July" did not exist—and neither did the United States of America. Inspirational rhetoric goes beyond definitions and logic in expressing the common good. Any claim in the form of "the common good *is* xyz," if taken too seriously, that is, as excluding those who think differently, is *prima facie* false. The common good is not a matter of objective propositions and demonstrations but is akin to a dance or a ritual, expressing and evoking noncompetitive solidarity, viz. friendship and social trust.[14]

The French post-phenomenologist Jacques Derrida has brought out how the chiasmic, symbolic order cannot be made present like an object. Symbolic or indicative language is responsible for our subjectivity, our presence to ourselves, and we cannot bring everything to presence, to make everything available, without losing the unique being of the person and the common good in the process. Phenomenology is praiseworthy for paying close attention to the type of being of the person and how consciousness is not an object;

nevertheless, it can fall prey to the logical prejudice, of taking *bringing to presence* as the ultimate telos of meaning.[15] Derrida's post-phenomenology, elegantly expressed in his book on Husserl, *Speech and Phenomena*, exposes this narrowness.[16] He coins a term, *différance*, as a symbol for the unique and dynamic process of what we here name the common good. The term *différance* is unable to be brought to presence as a thing because it means two different things: to differ and to defer. It is also a homonym with "difference" in French, so one must consult the spelling to distinguish the two words, slowing us down in our quick identification of words with things that happens in speech and drawing our attention to the nature of *différance* as a symbol. A symbol, or indicative sign, has no logical meaning. It therefore cannot be effaced before a present object, kicked away like a ladder we do not need any longer after we have reached the desired height, but it remains as an evocative point of reference. Because it means two different things, *différance* points to a reality that transcends thingness, to the constitution of subjectivity itself, our ability to mean anything at all, the giving of language in the first place, to that which we call the common good.

Like *différance*, the "common good" is a symbol for that which both differs and defers presence. Any given desire that can form the basis for a discrete suggestion cannot be identified with the common good. In order that different suggestions be brought together in discourse, there must be a common order that we share; we might disagree, but in order to disagree at all—to understand our disagreement as a disagreement about our common order—we have to have a basis for it. We must be united in our disagreement, rather than simply trying to destroy each other: the common good is the *origin of differences*. Likewise, any given desire that can form the basis for a discrete suggestion is justified by its good effects, its positive impact which benefits everyone, but because that impact occurs on persons, it is always circuitous, never immediate; we have to wait and to trust in order to realize the good of following it: its effects are *deferred*. The common good symbolizes a future that is not immediate gratification but a sharing in the life of others. Without this, we would be reduced to seeking immediate gratification, either in addiction or in mimetic conflict, and the self would be lost in each punctual moment, lacking the time to consider the bigger picture of what exactly it wants and how it can get there: the common good is the *origin of temporality*.

Derrida, as Heidegger before him, brings out a relationship with language that is not merely functional, not merely a means to getting at a discrete object of desire—namely, the logical meaning, a "wanting to say" ("to mean" in French is *vouloir dire*)—but which rather is symbolical, a use of language that does not express a discrete meaning but reflects our relationship to the whole of language or giving of language itself, which evokes wonder and directs desire. The symbolical relation is more primordial than the functional.

The presuppositions of such a view tack against our traditional philosophical prejudices, however, when it comes to our understanding of our own being. As Derrida shows, a person cannot be thought of as a fullness of subjectivity, as a completed being, who knows what he desires, in a symbolical relation to language. Rather, a person is a radical lack of completeness who does not know what he wants. Symbols come to shape desire, to gesture towards the common good as that which is most eligible, to teach us what we should desire. Derrida and Heidegger's discussion of a person's relationship with death is relevant here. If the subject is seen as having a fullness of being, an object without a relationship to its own death, it could not have a relation to the whole of language, a relation which allows for things to be presented to it as such in the first place. If I were a completed object (if I could not die), then I could only relate to things on the basis of my desire. I could go after the object to satisfy my desire, but the object could not teach me anything about what I should desire. To admit that I need to learn about myself, to admit that I do not know what I desire, is to admit that I am unfinished, that I do not know everything, that I do not control the strings of my own subjectivity, and that I do not give myself my own subjectivity—to concede all this is to admit that I will die. If I am the fullness of being, if I cannot die, then I do not need other people. I would know what I want and what I have to do to get it; there would not be any part of the world that I do not know and for which I would need the testimony of others. Another person would be reducible to his function in my life. In actuality, I must admit that I am an incomplete subjectivity and am related to something else—the whole of language—that gives me my subjectivity. This giving is not an object, not a thing. If it were, then I would dominate it through knowledge, include the basis for my own subjectivity within myself, and I would, as a result, lack a relationship with my own death. This giving is language itself as a gift, and what we name here as the *common good*. I am related to it in my being, but not in the manner in which I am related to an object. The giving of language itself cannot be given in the present like an object.

A functional relation to language forgets the whole of language, the giving of language in the first place. When we take it for granted, we think of language itself only in terms of its effects; namely, the use it can be put to and its ability to make objects present to us. The gift of language itself—the common good—is not merely a collation of its effects, an assemblage of objective uses or goods, however; it is the origin of differences and of temporality and is not reducible to either. The transcendence of the common good with its effects is mirrored in the way a person transcends the functions he performs. A person is not just the labor or pleasure that we can extract from him, like a replaceable thing. Rather, a person is someone we can talk to; someone to whom the world manifests itself; someone with a view, a perspective, and a voice to tell us about the parts of the world that we do not know; and someone with whom my desires must be compatible for us to share a language and a future together. Likewise, the gift of language itself should therefore not be treated just as a collection of effects, but as manifesting something to us that transcends what can be present to our consciousness—namely, that we are in need of learning, that as a subjectivity, we are not complete. In principle we could not know all language; we could not give ourselves language. We do not have the totality of language at our command, nor could we ever, because we have a relationship with our own death. Thus, our relation to the whole of language can never become functionalized but must always remain symbolic, a gift. Gifts are not just something we enjoy and are happy to have, they also refer back to the giver of the gift and that personal relationship—to reduce the item to its function is to miss it as a gift.

Derrida's reflections help us to understand how our relationship to language is embedded in our relationships with others. Through a personal relationship the world achieves objectivity, as objects become known as present not only to me, like a hallucination, but also to another person. Through a personal relationship language is given to us, as this is how we learn language in the first place, as children. In the relationship of trust that is required in order to initially learn a language—where a child must accept everything the adult says in order to make progress—we find the noncompetitive loyalty that is not only directed to the other person but reflects all possible personal relationships. The parent is giving the child the ability to communicate with all others (not just in a particular language, though that is its effect, but the faculty of language to begin with, as children deprived of language during the critical period of life are unable to acquire it later on). Further, our relationships are properly personal—involving the whole person, not just his effects—when it is noncompetitive with other possible personal relationships. The other person to whom we are related has other potential and actual relationships with third parties. When a relationship can only endure when third parties are sacrificed—whether it be a common enemy or a whipping boy that is necessary to keep the two parties from turning on each other—there is a partial, functional relationship, a depersonalization, not only of the third person but also of the original pair. A full personal relationship with another is at the same time a relationship with the whole of all possible personal relationships: the common good. The common good can only be pursued symbolically; it is not *present*, though, standing like an available presence that could be brought to mind and understood thoroughly, but rather it is "present" as absent in its traces, in the personal relationships where the parties respect each other's transcendence, or potentiality for all possible relationships.

To speak the language of the common good is inseparable from actually maintaining noncompetitive personal relationships. This is the intentionality proper to the common good, so to speak: an intentionality that is flipped; instead of relating to an object through the use of a word, I relate to a symbol and live up to it. To speak of the common good is an objective, not a subjective, genitive; it is not an object of our thought, but rather, our thoughts and deeds should belong to it. There is here a mutual intertwining: a sign is a relation between persons, and the positive relation between persons can itself be expressed in symbolic signs. This expression does not efface the sign; we are not after the intelligible, logical essence of an automobile, for example, such that it does not matter whether it is called a "car," or an "*auto*," or a "*voiture*." A symbol, by contrast, is not effaced before the meaning brought to presence. To signify this, Derrida crosses out a word so that it can still be read, indicating that it is not to be taken as simply referring to a present object. While the symbols come *after* the common good is already operational, arising in discourse as the ultimate backstop for discussion concerning suggestions, the common good must have *already* been effective for us to be brought together in discussion in the first place. The symbol comes afterwards, manifesting the type of relationship that we already share with each other, but that relationship is not a fulfilled but an unfulfilled intention; it points outwards to the whole of all possible relationships, a future that is nonexclusive. The symbols are not merely signs of a preexisting reality but are, in turn, necessary for that reality to continue, as a necessary supplement. A symbol is not simply effaced before a presence, because it calls to mind at the same time the non-presence of the greater whole.

By contrast, speaking of "values" expresses competitive relationships with others. A "value" is always what it is in comparison with other values.[17] Hobbes has already said as much. For him, the object of our striving is describable in terms of value and never personal uniqueness: "Vertue generally, in all sorts of subjects," he writes, "is somewhat that is valued for eminence; and consisteth in comparison."[18] We are placed in the field of desire, and there is no escape, for "[L]et a man (as most men do,) rate themselves as the highest Value they can; yet their true Value is no more than it is esteemed by others."[19] As Joel Backström writes, "values" express an attempt at self-definition that plays within an "existentially speaking shallow dimension of the soul."[20] There is a name for this type of communicable covetousness: mimetic desire. Within a field of desire, and without any unique personal task of our own, we copy the desires of others. It seems logical to think that what other people want must have value for me, too. I look to others as models and think that if I possess what my model possesses, then I will be satisfied like them. Lust for money is paradigmatic; if I get what other people want, I will possess something I can use over and against them. In falling prey to mimetic desire, I do not exercise my own capacity for judgment about what qualitatively will make me happy; rather, I only evaluate quantitatively to try to get the most possible of the desired commodity, that is, money. The words "value" and "evaluate" are used in their most proper sense when they refer to a comparison according to a common measure. The term after all comes from the classical Latin verb *valere*, "to be worth," which forms the origin of "valuta," the European term for the value of a currency. The great nineteenth century linguist Niccolò Tommaseo writes of the Italian *valutare* (to value, to evaluate) that it "is not figurative, except in corrupt and barbaric use: in its proper use, it indicates the determination of a value that can or must be paid in money. We evaluate in order to pay, to sell, to calculate, to compare the value of something to a sum of money."[21] To *evaluate*—"value" plus the exclusionary "e-" prefix—is to measure something in the context of a mimetic struggle where everyone rates "themselves as the highest value they can." The political task of *judging*, by contrast, takes place in the context of personal relationships rather than a mimetic struggle. Ivo de Gennaro and Gino Zaccaria write that "real judging has nothing to do with evaluating, and there is an abyss between the two."[22]

If our strivings for value are for ourselves in competition with others, then our relation with them can only be one of minimum loyalty. We have already encountered this in Luther's account of altruism. At the moment we wish to point out how, to the extent that it refracts goodness through the prism of the minimum-loyalty relationship, values language is diabolical.

The account of modern liberty as "diabolical" comes from D.C. Schindler's magisterial *Freedom from Reality*.[23] Values language is part and parcel of the modern understanding of liberty, and thus our analysis dovetails with Schindler's. When we talk about values, we are no longer talking about real things. We are talking, rather, about a certain idealization—or perhaps an idolization—of things. To talk about the value of something is to make it a little too perfect, to consider it as stripped of a relational or personal core, making a relationship with it impossible. Values are *not real*. The expression "Could we get real?" captures the sense of reality that is lost with values; namely, the down-to-earth communication of one person to another. Values are parasitic on the real; they are the real considered in a certain light, as finding a place in the economy of mimetic desire. In that necessarily impersonal economy, things are not considered in their complexity but economized, taken as the price of their power, as Hobbes puts it. The Nietzschean morality of strength disaggregates; for him, it is only the weak who are brought into communion with each other.[24]

This is "diabolical" insofar as it makes personal relationships impossible. The word διαβάλλω means malicious slander, the bringing of false charges; in other words, that which destroys a relationship. The temporal reality of a thing—the personal core of connections that make something unique, incommunicable, impervious to mimetic desire, and that which also forms the basis for a relationship—cannot be measured by any value and must be both presupposed and also driven out of consideration when thinking in value terms. The more we take values seriously, the more it disrupts our relationships for the simple fact that we cannot be friends with someone who opposes our values.[25] Rather than being a rhetorical, symbolic reflection of our relationships, values determine their possibility. Symbols, as Schindler has shown, arise out of friendship and bring terms together, without destroying their individuality. We can use values language with pure intentions, that is, symbolically; however, we do not end up saying what we really mean, particularly when we split reality between the transcendental and the empirical, conceptualizing both on the model of the "fact." Friendship cannot be understood in this way. Personal relationships are rendered superfluous and idiosyncratic when understood as empirical facts, things which must be overcome to get to universal value.

Another problem with supposedly universal values is that people do not agree on them.

THE PUBLIC PURSUIT OF "VALUE" IS DIVISIVE

The common good is already operative when we are already related in a fundamental will to live together in peace. This makes it possible to engage in politics as suggestion-response. By contrast, when we try to take the common good as a piece of knowledge, inspirational rhetoric becomes superfluous, and the only thing that matters is following or not following a concrete suggestion in the present, rather than the quality of our loyalties, the relationships that transcend transitory accommodations. The form of our political order and our *mores* rely on a prior peacefulness of our relationships in which we have included, and not excluded, each other. This is not an agreement on a proposition. Propositions are an abridgment of the reality, not its substance.

Peace is good, according to Hobbes. On his own terms, though, would this not just be his own opinion? He writes that "all men agree on this, that Peace is Good." However, perhaps he should have written instead, "All men are of the opinion that peace, only insofar as it fulfills their designs, is good"? After all, what do I care if there is war disrupting the lives of other people wholly unconnected with me? It is not really war itself as such that is bad for me, but rather war that affects me. Even within my own state, maybe peace is good for me, but maybe it isn't. Maybe I could profit from war, even civil war. Revolutions feed on those who have nothing to lose from an upheaval. War might be the worst evil to those with something to lose, those interested in carrying out their projects for which a lack of conflict is a prerequisite, but this is not everyone, and *war there is*, so it is demonstrably true that any order is *not* always preferable to the status quo peace. Peace is just as subjective and disputable as any other "good." Some people want peace, others do not.

This lack of agreement on what is good and evil is that from which arise "Disputes, Controversies, and at last War." The state of nature occurs when there is no other measure of good and evil than private appetite. Note what follows, however: "And therefore so long as man is in the condition of meer Nature, (which is a condition of War,) as private Appetite is the measure of Good, and Evill: and consequently all men agree on this, that Peace is Good."[26] We fall into the state of nature when private appetite is the measure of good and evil. When we are in a commonwealth together, there is of course such a measure, viz. the will of Sovereign. Likewise, it is only in the state of war that all men agree that peace is the highest value. In the wretched war of all against all, everyone can agree that peace is preferable, but if they forget this wretchedness, given human nature, they may understandably tend to rank their own ideas of goodness higher. The peace that takes hold under a Sovereign in practice undercuts the immediate, obvious nature of the transcendental argument.

Let's take a closer look at the nature of this peace to see how the Hobbesian project is "not the elimination, but rather, potentially, the very *institutionalization* and *manufacture* of chaos."[27]

First, escaping the state of nature grants peace, but only for those inside the state. Those outside are enemies, still in the state of nature vis-à-vis us. Protection from them is the essential reason for us covenanting together.[28] The whole point of the modern state is war.[29]

Second, the default condition of the state is war against other states. According to Hobbes, war is not actual fighting, but the time in which there is a known hostility, and as far as one state among other states is concerned, that time is always.[30] The state is a state only so long as it is in perpetual war with other states. The state is dissolved by losing a war with its enemies,[31] and the only possibility of not being at war with other states is if a state would combine with other states into one Sovereign power, which under Hobbesian premises it could only do in response to the threat of total destruction from a greater empire. Hobbes at one point even admits that the state of nature is an imaginary construction, but he proves its probability by referring to the hostility of foreign relations.[32] When it comes to international affairs, the "state of nature" is never actually escaped.

Third, the Sovereign wages perpetual war against internal enemies as well. As we have already seen, this is true right from the start; not everyone is eager to have peace in the state of nature. At the beginning, the covenant is created by the plurality, which destroys anyone who does not consent. This founding violence persists. When someone breaks the covenant, he puts himself back in the state of nature. One is either a member of the state or an enemy, categories that are mutually exclusive.[33] To deny the Sovereign is to ask for one's own destruction.[34] Enemies of the Sovereign have it coming to them: "[I]n declared Hostility, all infliction of evill is lawfull," writes Hobbes.[35] If someone refuses to acknowledge the Sovereign's power, all hell will be unleashed upon that poor soul's head, all the other citizens will be deputized to kill him on sight, and no one is to show mercy or tolerance.[36]

The "peace" the Hobbesian Sovereign provides is actually continuous war. What the Sovereign protects us against is not war but the destruction of the market economy, the society of minimum loyalty.

This is Hobbes's real position. The catastrophe of civil war is the worst of all evils because we cannot enjoy the fruits of our labor, we have no chance for commodious living, and the economy is devastated. Ultimately it is *industry*, not peace, that is desirable for Hobbes. It forms the basis for the only critique of the passions he indulges in: what is lamentable for Hobbes is not our passions but their irregularity, since this is what interferes with industry.[37]

The market economy under the Sovereign enables us to utilize the power of other people for our benefit and to fulfill our desires, at least to some to some degree. There are inconveniences, but life cannot be without some inconveniences.[38] We cannot focus on the undesirable aspects, but rather on what we are being saved from: it is only by comparison that the desirability of market economy becomes clear. If the only alternative is our total destruction, then it becomes apparent that we are massively benefitting from our organizing together for war and trade under the Sovereign. If the alternative is to be an isolated individual, the enemy of everyone else—what happens if we deny the Sovereign—then it is clear that our life would be incomparably impoverished and, indeed, quickly ended, as compared to what we now enjoy. Therefore, we should just be happy to avoid the state of nature.

The collective purpose of the market economy under a Sovereign is to wage war. The Leviathan state needs the threat of war, since without it, there would be no convincing people that a market economy under a Sovereign is the best we can do. If we were not convinced that we had an external enemy and that we were not the enemies to each other, then our Sovereign itself would be unmasked as a tyrant, the source of our misery.[39] For Sovereignty to have a purpose for existing, the state must always be fighting against enemies. Therefore, for good reason, Hobbes is content with many sovereigns coexisting in a state of war.[40] Indeed, the foundation of his theory presupposes continual war: God's will is the cause of all the passions in men, he says, yet as these passions are the direct cause of war—if there is war, then, ultimately, the blame must lie with God.[41]

It cannot be true, therefore, even in Hobbes that all men agree on peace. Even in the state of nature, there are some who do not accept the Sovereign for the sake of peace and must be destroyed, and after the covenant is created, there are still some who oppose the Sovereign, both internally and externally. It is not "peace" that "all men" agree on. Rather, it is only some men—those who covenant under a Sovereign—who agree to organize and work together for the sake of war with the rest. If anything, Hobbesian theory requires us to believe that all men agree that war is the inescapable human condition and that the best we can do is band together and join the fight.

For those who prioritize the minimum-loyalty society, that is, a market economy under a sovereign, this is indeed an argument that they all accept. They will submit to the Sovereign, who protects this economy against enemies through war, for the reason that the alternative is worse. However, those who disagree with this presupposition, argumentation, and conclusion are violently excluded. The transcendental argument, then, turns out to be highly tautological. It tells us only that all men who in fact agree, do agree. Everyone in community X, which defines itself as being constituted by agreement on X, believes X—and everyone else is either destroyed or worthy of destruction, such that their views do not matter. This is the Procrustean bed of politics and a far cry from the promise of the transcendental foundation—namely, of a simple and compelling argument that it can clear up any doubts as to the origin of authority and power.

It also involves a rhetorical contradiction. Hobbes demands perpetual war *in the name of peace*. He proposes the primacy of market economy under the Sovereign, and not the primacy of peace. The two things are very different, as life in Leviathan is an arrangement of war such that it can coexist with industry.

It is a sleight of hand to name this "peace." Hobbes's thought assuredly does not aim at peace; nevertheless, he uses this rhetoric. We should not be taken in—transcendental theory requires that all times be times of war and that persons are fundamentally at odds with each other. The war of all against all is the actual overarching symbol for transcendental theory. Is our basic relationship with each other one of conflict? This is, of course, highly questionable, and we do not have to accept it as fundamental.[42]

It is telling, though, that Hobbes clothes his theory in the rhetoric of peace. A straightforward description of his thought—the establishment and maintenance of industry for some people only, with war on everyone else—is *prima facie* unappealing. Human beings do indeed prefer peace to war.[43] The common good orients us towards peace. In presenting his system rather as the search for peace and the good for all, Hobbes attempts to align his system with the deeper truth of the common good. This is in appearances only, however.

In its substance, transcendental theory diabolically undermines the deeper relationships responsible for peace and the common good by reducing everything to relationships shrunken to the point of being grasped by our thought, viz. minimum-loyalty relationship. This is the self-contradiction at the heart of transcendental theory. It promises hardheaded scientific truths but, inevitably, must use inspirational rhetoric to make itself appealing. As soon as we take seriously the rhetoric, however, the content of the theory contradicts it. Transcendental politics is self-undermining, promising to do away with myths and symbolism, replacing ambiguity with clear terms and demonstrations; in the end it is left with a symbolism so repellant—the war of all against all as the fundamental human condition—that this must be concealed under the old rhetoric in order to gain a hearing at all. Wherever it does gain adherents, it dashes all hope of its initial promise by replacing it with a very different system and symbolism.

To recognize the fraudulent nature of transcendental theory is to recognize the symbolic, rhetorical nature of the common good. The common good is not an object; it cannot be grasped by the intellect, distinctly identified, and form the basis for the indubitable discrimination between policy stands taken seriatim and placed on separate ledgers. While the common good is the ultimate backstop for judgments, it has the nature of an end—the harmonizing of relationships—that appeals to our freedom, rather than taking it away by substituting a right answer for it.

The early critiques of Hobbes failed to grasp this. Instead, they appropriate his thought on exactly this point. "The continuous dialogue with Hobbes," for Amos Funkenstein, forms "the distinguishing mark of modern political theories." He continues:

> The most important political thinkers since the seventeenth century did not reject him outright even if they were profoundly irritated by his claims. Instead, they absorbed the full force of his arguments before transforming them into a different, sometimes even a contrary, theory.[44]

The rest of this chapter will take its bearings from this observation. The thinkers who followed Hobbes, whether they followed or opposed him, adopted his transcendental manner of argumentation. For those who opposed his conclusions, their arguments created what we know today as "morality."

THE BIRTH OF MORALITY

The search for the common good is a search for happiness and peace of a real social group. By contrast, modern "morality" does not seek the common good or happiness but rather the justified use of power. The early commentators on Hobbes played on his home turf. Opposing his scandalous conclusion that the will of the Sovereign is the common good, their solution is universal "morality."[45] But this only begs the Hobbesian response: this is why we need a Sovereign to mediate between us, because we do not agree on the content of morality and would be otherwise tearing each other apart.

We examine here the two main early commentators on Hobbes, Samuel Pufendorf (1632–1694) and Richard Cumberland (1631–1718). Both of them thought in terms of a morality that would go beyond probable reasoning to demonstrative certainty, as in mathematics, with clear definitions of terms for the sake of drawing necessary conclusions. A new genre emerged in their wake: "[T]he History of Morality, which was to be eminently characteristic of the early Enlightenment."[46] Pufendorf was a Lutheran and follower of Hobbes and Grotius who had an outsized influence on political thought up until the early nineteenth century. A German, Pufendorf read Hobbes in English.[47] His first book, *Two Books of the Elements of Universal Jurisprudence* (1660), contains the basic elements of his thought, which came to full expression in his massive work *De Jure Naturae et Gentium* (1672). The latter was turned into a textbook called *De Officio Hominis et Civis*, which was translated into multiple languages and used in universities throughout Europe. The Anglican cleric Richard Cumberland, who also published his great work *A Treatise of the Laws of Nature (De Legibus Naturae)* in 1672, assembled a number of different arguments into a "mosaic" with the overriding purpose of combating Hobbes.[48] His contemporaries took him very seriously, and although after his death he fell into obscurity, his thought is indelibly burned into the development of modern liberalism.[49] He has rightly been called the "most successful"[50] opponent of Hobbes, "one of the three or four most powerful influences in the history of British ethics,"[51] and even the "founder of English ethics."[52]

Modern morality thinks of itself as a demonstrable theory of the law of nature. This can be traced back to Pufendorf. For him, it is wrong to think that "in matters of morality, by their very nature, there is no firm and infallible certainty, and that all knowledge of such matters rests upon probable opinion only."[53] Law can be a true and certain science based on demonstration.[54] This means separating the investigation of natural law from theology and from nature. For Pufendorf, there are norms that reason can discern without any grace or revelation. A new realm of "moral entities" opens up above nature, which is subject to rational demonstration. There is morality that is binding prior to enforcement by the Sovereign, so Hobbes's idea that all justice comes from the Sovereign is wrong.[55] However, "Pufendorf aimed to provide foundations for political and social order which do not depend on contested (moral)theological doctrines."[56] This means that natural reason considers only the state of corrupted man—in other words, it is built on a Hobbesian foundation. For Pufendorf, "[M]an is an animal which is not only intensely interested in its own preservation but also possesses a native and delicate sense of its own value."[57] Different people hold different things to be pleasant and useful; this is also because the good as "fitting" differs from person to person, due to the value each person puts on himself.[58] In sum, everyone has different opinions about the good. As with Hobbes, for Pufendorf, the natural state of man is at war of all against all, and the solution is absolute sovereignty.[59] As Pufendorf puts it in *De Officio Hominis et Civis*, natural law regards man as "an animal seething with evil desires."[60] In a state, by contrast, people have subjected their wills to the will of the rulers and are "willing to do whatever the rulers wish."[61]

Though it contests the Hobbesian conclusion that the Sovereign is the source of all justice, modern morality is built on Hobbesian premises and value language. For Pufendorf, our natural state with each other is equality; however, in social life we attain different statuses. Similar to how our bodies inhabit space and time, as persons we inhabit a *moral* space, our social status vis-à-vis others. For Pufendorf, "[T]he desire for esteem 1) provides people with the content of central moral norms 2) and can move people to act in accordance with moral norms."[62] The esteem we get from others is our value. Pufendorf calls it a quantitative incorporeal thing, "*value* [*Valor*], which is sometimes of persons, and is then called *esteem* [*existimatio*]."[63] Esteem is thus "the value of persons in communal life [*Existimatio est valor personarum in vita communi*] in accordance with which they are fit to be placed upon an equality with other persons, or to be compared with them, and to be rated either above or below them."[64] The effect of acting well is the enjoyment of esteem, both internally, "the approbation of conscience which follows, and gives itself sweet joy in the recollection of that act," and externally, gaining "the approbation of it on the part of good men, and principally on the part of him who commanded that action."[65] People will think well of us, analogous to valuing highly a piece of property.[66] We compete with each other for property and, similarly, for value or moral status, as it involves excluding other people from what is ours. Morality orders what is mine and what is not mine. Elemental goods—like wind, air, and light—can enter into our moral space, when we value them differently. They cannot be transferred, "as things inherent in space," but they can "also come under an estimate of value, and therefore, as far as proprietorship is concerned, they participate in the nature of space. Thence it follows in due consequence that the man whom I can exclude from my space I can also prevent from enjoying the air, the wind, the warmth and light of the sun existing in my space."[67]

Given these presuppositions, what is the correct valuation of ourselves? It can only stem from how we use the power of our free will.[68] Insofar as we exercise this power, actions can be imputed to us and therefore "by the figure of synecdoche, are called moral."[69] "Synecdoche" is a figure of speech in which the name of a part is given to the whole. The term "moral" takes a part of human experience—having power over something—to be the whole. Pufendorf even says at one point that someone who does not have voluntary action, for example, a slave, is not a person but a thing.[70]

Richard Cumberland also sees the science universal morality as taking the precision of mathematics as a model.[71] For Cumberland, this is the reason that Hobbes cannot be correct to say that the will of the Sovereign is the essence of justice. Even the Sovereign must follow natural laws, which are eternal, unchanging truths, similar to mathematical equations. Cumberland writes that "human Nature suggests certain Rules of Life, in the same manner that it suggests the Skill of Numbering." In these matters, "The Sentiments of all Nations are *necessarily* the *same*."[72] Correct moral action is not a matter of healthy relationships but of following correct moral principles. Cumberland uses a language of value to express this.[73] What is an example of a correct moral principle? Cumberland's foremost example is the necessity to value the common good over our own private good. It is a simple quantitative measurement: since our good is smaller than the common good of the whole public, the latter should give way to the former. This principle of preferring the common good over one's private good is the wellspring of all good action.[74] "All the Virtues prefer the Publick Good before the Private Advantages of any one,"[75] Cumberland writes. All virtue and vice are reducible to this principle of correct preference.[76]

Crucially, this principle is not symbolic. It dictates *both* ends and means. It makes it *clear* what should be done. Cumberland writes that "it is most *certain*, 'That no Method of Action can be propos'd according to right Reason, in which all cannot agree.'"[77] It is the litmus test of rationality everywhere. There is no room for disagreement anywhere.[78]

On the surface this directly contradicts Hobbesianism, as the Sovereign would not control what is considered just and in the common good. Nevertheless, in Cumberland as in Pufendorf, modern morality turns out to be Hobbes redux.

If we cannot get everyone to agree on something, this only shows that it is a matter of preference rather than of natural law. Either something is universally valid or it is a matter of indifference.[79] In the morally neutral realm, it does not ultimately matter whose particular preference is adopted. In these matters it is simply not worth fighting about, so rulers are free to decide on them authoritatively. "For it evidently *conduces more* to the *publick Good*," says Cumberland, "That the Opinion of the Magistrates should prevail; in things indifferent and doubtful, and that the Subjects should take that for Good, which seems such to the supreme Power, rather than eternal Broils should continue among them, whence may reasonably be expected Wars and Murders, which are, without all question, Evil."[80] Conversely, for the universally valid moral law, Cumberland has already told us that there is *already* general agreement, so there is no problem of conflict to speak of. The absolute authority of the sovereign therefore remains intact as much for Cumberland as for Hobbes. "The will of the Sovereign is absolute in all things," for Hobbes, is exactly the same in practice as "the will of the Sovereign is not absolute on those things where everyone already completely agrees, but it is absolute on any disputed matters," for Cumberland.

Indeed, at the end of *De Legibus*, Cumberland actually accuses Hobbes of *undermining* the Sovereign's authority.[81] It is striking to think that there might be someone more concerned to uphold the basis for the Sovereign's power than Hobbes himself. But consider. The Sovereign cannot make poison be healthy through a decree, and to fail to see this not only makes one subject to ridicule but also, more importantly, affects how we view Sovereignty. If people think that the Sovereign makes fundamentally irrational decisions, they are going to think less of him. Cementing the Sovereign as an object of popular esteem requires them seeing his decrees as true for reasons beyond his whim. It is a heightened respect for the Sovereign to view him as a conduit for a higher truth. Opposition to such a Sovereign would then be more than opposition to a man and his opinions but a wicked attack on the order of the universe itself.

Any doctrine of clear morality must embrace Hobbesian Sovereignty as its logical consequence. Just as Luther admitted the prince into the church by the back door while ostentatiously denying him entry through the front door, Cumberland's achievement was to take away the Hobbesian stigma by sticking with his methods and retaining his conclusion, while making a great show of opposing him.[82]

The presuppositions of morality arise from and reinforce absolute Sovereignty. Nothing is more mimetic than the search for esteem. Nothing is more exclusive and zero sum, and nothing confirms Hobbes's fundamental anthropology more. Our desires conflict and lead to chaotic violence; order must be imposed through official valuations given by the Sovereign. Any appeal to universal values should entail their automatic acceptance; however, in practice they are inevitably hotly contested, and thus, we are always led back to Hobbesian Sovereignty. As Glen Newey writes,

> Some of Hobbes's insights have been lost by modern theorists. Modern academic political philosophy, at least in the English-speaking world, usually tries to infer political arrangements from moral considerations. . . . But such arguments tend to undermine themselves. It starts off with the political problems posed by disputes over morality or "values," and then tries to resolve the disputes by coming up with a moral solution. The risk is that the solution is open to disputes similar to those which caused the political problem in the first place. If so, the agreement is no longer "universal," and theorists find themselves

> reduced to saying, in effect, that people who do not agree with the suggested principles, at any rate *ought* to do so. This is a journey up the hill and then back down again.[83]

It is also a journey away from Hobbes and then back to him.

MORALITY AND SOVEREIGNTY UNITED

Belief in Sovereignty has its own naïveté, however. When the Sovereign decrees something that is utterly opposed to the history, traditions, and *mores* of the people, it inevitably provokes intransigent conflict and resistance, and simply as a practical matter, we cannot possibly expect everyone easily to switch habits and the way they think about those habits. The Sovereign must therefore show great respect to the customs and belief system of the people. This cannot be admitted, however, as it reveals that Sovereignty depends on the prudence of the person who is Sovereign, and this is at odds with the theory of Sovereignty, which bypasses the need to address the nature of human virtues, to provide for their cultivation, and to explain their relation to authority. All of these things require reflection on how desire ought to be checked and shaped by personal relationships and the integral forms of human community. This gives us a "moral space" very different than that of modern political and moral theory, wherein individuals compete for status.

Modern moral and political theory fails. People will not spontaneously agree on a universal morality, nor will they automatically accept it when a sudden shift in their *mores* is demanded of them. The answer to this conundrum is given by John Locke (1632–1704), the inventor of popular sovereignty. If we identify Sovereignty and morality, the problem can be solved.

For Locke, before the codification of laws, we determine our morality together; social esteem forms the bedrock for political arrangements and laws. *Sovereignty is morality*, the popular system of esteem that forms the meaning presupposed by any lawgiving.

In his *An Essay Concerning Human Understanding*, which first appeared in 1690 and is easily one of the most important works of philosophy ever published, Locke points to the strong coercive power of social esteem: anyone "who imagines Commendation and Disgrace, not to be strong Motives on Men, to accommodate themselves to the Opinions and Rules of those, with whom they converse," he writes, "seems little skill'd in the Nature, or History of Mankind."[84] For Locke, people will disobey the laws of God and of the State, but no man escapes "the Punishment of their Censure and Dislike, who offends against the Fashion and Opinion of the Company he keeps, and would recommend himself to. Nor is there one of ten thousand, who is stiff and insensible enough, to bear up under the constant Dislike, and Condemnation of his own Club. . . . This is a Burthen too heavy for humane Sufferance."[85]

We cannot, in our day, but admit that public opinion can indeed enforce what it believes to be virtuous more swiftly and with more severity than a political chief could ever dream.[86] However, cannot public opinion err? Could it perhaps be the case that "what is of human esteem is an abomination in the sight of God"?[87] Locke, on the contrary, closely identifies public opinion and God's esteem. Virtue is visible to all; God has "joined *Virtue* and publick Happiness together; and made the Practice thereof, necessary to the preservation of Society, and visibly *beneficial* to all, with whom the Virtuous Man has to do."[88] At bottom, "every-where that, which is thought Praise-worthy; and nothing else but that, which has the allowance of publick Esteem, is called *Vertue*. *Vertue* and Praise are so united that they are called often by the same Name."[89] For Locke, the essence of human excellence is to obey the system of public esteem. A popular political pamphlet that transmitted Locke's theory in plagiarized form shortly after his death was entitled *Vox Populi Vox Dei.*[90]

Locke's interlocutors were befuddled on this point, thinking that Locke was simply identifying universal morality with the customs of the community. But Locke refers to "the unchangeable Rule of Right and Wrong"[91] and the "eternal Law and Nature of things,"[92] endorsing the project of making morality demonstrable like mathematics. In the second edition, Locke addresses this misreading, saying that he is "not laying down moral Rules, but shewing the original and nature of moral *Ideas*, and enumerating the Rules Men make use of in moral Relations, whether those Rules were true or false . . . I only report as matter of fact, what others call *Vertue* and *Vice*."[93] Morality is *enforced* by group praise and censure, "Esteem and Discredit."[94] That is what it is: without enforcement, it would not be a moral law but merely a suggestion. Morality must be exclusive, i.e., understand itself as transcendental, in order to be morality at all. It cannot understand itself as changeable *mores* united under the banner of a symbolic common good, but rather as a general, impersonal, and clear standard that is identified with the law of God himself. As with Cumberland, for we are talking about ends *and* means: concrete suggestions, and not inspirational rhetoric.

It is for this reason that Locke must reject the doctrine of "innate ideas" at the beginning of *An Essay*. He does not want us to think in terms of rhetorical indications, for example, "all men desire peace" as an evocative expression. He simply points out that it is broken in practice and therefore cannot be considered innate. The search towards practical principles should be directed to the level of clear and distinct ideas, such that what matters are the precise ways our desires our checked through the moral law, and not the types of relationships we want to have with others.

Locke solves the problem of the person who is Sovereign going against popular *mores*. Sovereignty is not a leader's whim but the system of taken-for-granted esteem that we share. Our absolute moral system is up to our collective will. When someone violates it, no matter how high a position he occupies, the sovereign system of esteem takes precedence. Our system of values is always right; it is that which we can never rebel against. For Locke, "[T]he citizens themselves do what Hobbes reserved for the sovereign," writes Reinhart Koselleck. "They set 'the mark of the value' of all acts" and determine what is to be esteemed (which they call virtue) and what is to be blameworthy (vice).[95]

This is *modern freedom*: leeway to pursue one's desires except when checked by the Sovereign power, which one is able to participate in by helping to determine what is collectively esteemed. It presupposes that our loyalties be kept to a minimum; these are reinterpreted as subjective preferences and cannot form the foundation of any legitimate, general system of esteem. As Karl Jaspers identified nearly a century ago, ours is "the age of anonymous responsibility."[96] By giving up deeper loyalty to others, we gain the freedom to pursue any desire, subject only to the collective restrictions imposed by the Sovereign power. Such an approach is deeply opposed to loyalty to communities as integral forms, which would require us to check and direct our desire for the sake of our relationships and for the common good. Modern freedom, the freedom to pursue our desires subject only to external, collective restrictions, is freedom from loyalty. Loyalty is slavery because it is the source of restrictions and prescriptions about our desire which are not universalizable—not a source of collective law of esteem in a Leviathan state—and for Modernity that can be the only legitimate check on desire. We moderns are individual units of autonomous freedom. This is a contradiction in terms if freedom is instead participation in a community of friends.

We can see this clearly in the preeminent moralist of the modern tradition, Jean-Jacques Rousseau (1712–1778). Mankind's problems and guilt are laid by Rousseau at the feet of loyalty relationships. Our original state of nature was one of innocence, as individual self-sufficiency held sway.[97] This state existed in a kind of timelessness, a perfection sufficient to itself.[98] The relationship of one individual to another, when it tangentially took place, consisted of pity—or altruism—a sentiment that wishes someone be happy and not suffer but apart from any relationship with them.[99] Because individuals did not need each other, slavery could not exist.[100] The story of the corruption of this natural state, leading to horrible, mass enslavement is the story of the loss of natural self-sufficiency and the effects that personal relationships have on the human psyche.[101] Human relationships give birth to mimeticism.[102] People trying to get others to value them leads to violence.[103] For Rousseau, the problem with such mimetic conflict is not a problem with desire, but rather a problem with relationships as such. Men's natural desires are always good; it is the relation he enters into with others that cause the innocence of autonomy to be lost.

To restore that original Eden of nature, our institutions must relentlessly undermine loyalty relationships. We can recover our lost autonomy by membership in a state that would be "a form of association that defends and protects the person and goods of each associate with all the common force, and by means of which each one, uniting with all, nevertheless obeys only himself and remains as free as before."[104] Only our general, abstract relationship to the whole society is legitimate. Personal loyalties are suspect and to be discouraged: relationships between citizens should be "as small as possible" and the relationship of each individual to the whole should be "as large as possible" in order that "each Citizen is in a position of perfect independence from all the others and of excessive dependence upon the City."[105]

Rousseau supports absolute Sovereignty as much as Hobbes.[106] Sovereignty is a "total alienation . . . without reservation."[107] It is perfect.[108] It is also *apolitical*, and here we see the paradoxical hostility of modern political theory to the real activity of politics, viz. suggestion-response.[109] Rousseau builds on Locke's identification of the sovereign with the pre-political community.[110] Government is a straightforward implementation of the will of the people as to what is good and bad—a will that might be misled here or there as an empirical matter, but which is, in principle, fundamentally good.[111] The problem is not our desires but the corrupted institutions that frustrate them. It is possible for free citizens not to follow the general will but this would not happen "unless the people is seduced by private interests that some wily men have been able to substitute for its own by influence and eloquence."[112] The latter is as clear as scripture is for Luther. Problems arise only when particular interests triumph over the general will, which is always correct: "[T]he voice of the people is in fact the voice of God."[113]

Modern political thought is a war on loyalty, and values language is an essential weapon in this war. It makes no difference how value is interpreted, whether as a universal truth or a useful empirical construct. For David Hume (1711–1776), morality is an empirical adaptation to our needs and circumstances. Nevertheless, for him the "general system of morals" is clear and impersonal.[114] It is revealed in clear language—not ambiguous rhetoric—to which there must be common assent.[115] The connection between microcosm and macrocosm is broken.[116] Esteem is the substance of morality,[117] and is given priority over personal relationships, which are considered to be suspect.[118]

Hume's innovation, which enables him to reinterpret morality as empirical, is the concept of "intrinsic value."[119] Intrinsic value is an objective view, where we detach ourselves from the emotions stemming from personal relationships.[120] To be moral, we must learn to see our circumstances from a distance. "There is no quality in human nature, which causes more fatal errors in our conduct, than that which leads us to prefer whatever is present to the distant and remote, and makes us desire objects more according to their situation than their intrinsic value."[121] When we strip away our particular attachments, we can see what is really valuable.[122] Correcting our sentiments according to intrinsic value is the basis for language itself.[123] We can communicate with others—and can judge others—only because we can reach a general point of view. While our narrow sphere of benevolence causes us to fight with other groups, attaining a common point of reference can settle our differences without hostilities.[124] To refuse to leave our narrow sphere of personal attachments risks our expulsion from humanity.[125] We need help to do this though; the solution is for our interests to be dispassionately adjudicated by a disinterested party, namely "civil magistrates, kings and their ministers, our governors and rulers," who, because of their disinterest, are unlikely to be unjust.[126] For Hume, the state is the neutral organ that can determine things rationally from a distance.

As for Hobbes, for the moralists there is no daylight between official state morality and the judgments of God. At least, there can be no contradiction between the two; whether we can really know the mind of God depends on the degree of our religious faith. For Hume, modern morality is separate from the dogmatism of religion, and it is entirely possible to credit our morality to empirical sources. We get our morality from the type of society we live in and the type of beings we are. We do not need to claim to know things outside our experience, such as the judgments of God concerning individuals. Here Hume does not oppose but develops the modern tradition as we have been following it: Luther himself believed God predestined people to heaven and hell for inscrutable reasons, and he rejected the doctrine of works that would see a connection between moral behavior and winning eternal salvation. God's decision is inaccessible to our rationality. Dropping our dogmatic belief that we have knowledge as to what pleases God in no way affects the use of our rationality.

Hume's promotion of empirical morality is what awoke Immanuel Kant (1724–1804) from his dogmatic slumber and led him towards transcendental idealism, the view that we know appearances rather than things in themselves. For Kant, the moral worth we get from following the law is completely unconditioned, not relative to culture or human nature. "Kant's ultimate concerns were moral," writes Manfred Kuehn; Kant "wanted to save morality from becoming too naturalistic and too relativistic."[127] However, Kant does not oppose but develops Hume's insight.[128] For Hume, intrinsic value brackets our personal relationships to see them at a distance—a general point of view taken by the state which can mediate objectively between competing interests. For Kant, our personal worth comes from following the moral law independent of any empirical interests, and it makes us worthy of happiness from the point of view of an impartial spectator.[129] The state works out conflicts of views for Kant as well. The substance of morality is the categorical imperative: act such that the motive of your action could become a universal law. Legislating for everyone is just what the state does, of course, so as long as the laws do not conflict with each other, following the laws of the state is always the moral thing to do.[130] There can be no personal motives for acting. You cannot do something because *this* person asked you, since that is not generalizable.

To the question about why we should follow morality, Hume has a ready answer: it is useful. This is problematic because it ultimately destroys individual motivation to be moral: if violating moral norms and getting away with it is possible and, undoubtedly, eminently useful, then there would be no reason not to do so. Kant addresses this by making morality unconditional. A person "can expect no satisfaction of his desires and hence no condition that would satisfy any of his actual or otherwise imaginable inclinations." Instead, what a person gets in return is *value*: "[H]e can expect only a greater inner worth of his person [*einen größeren inneren Wert seiner Person*]."[131] But why should we care about this value? In the last section of the *Groundwork of the Metaphysics of Morals*, Kant says that we do take an interest in this unconditional esteem, but it is impossible to say why: "[I]f someone asked why the universal validity of our maxim as a law must be the limiting condition of our actions," he writes, "and on what we base the worth we assign to this way of acting—a worth so great that there can be no higher interest anywhere—and asked us how it happens that a human being believes that only through this does he feel his personal worth [*persönlichen Wert*], in comparison with which that of an agreeable or disagreeable condition is to be held as nothing, we could give him no satisfactory answer."[132] We do take an interest in moral laws, but for Kant, it is inexplicable why we do so. The term value indicates the breakdown of Kant's theory. It cannot be an empirical benefit, yet it is supposed to attract everyone, even the "most hardened scoundrel."[133]

THE LABOR THEORY OF VALUE

Hume has no answer to the free-rider problem of morality. If morality should be followed only because it is useful, we have nothing convincing to say to a "sensible knave" who is intent on violating moral norms for his own benefit.[134] While Kant solved this problem by making morality unconditional, this in turn has created its own difficulties, not the least of which is that it makes the practice of politics impossible. Politics is suggestion-response between persons. Responses inevitably involve assessments of the trustworthiness of the authors of the suggestions, and as a result, we cannot evaluate much of anything on the merits alone. In practice, politics is not universalizable. For modern morality, by contrast, it is the very definition of immorality to choose a subjective preference over objective value. Since personal relationships which are the foundation of trust are reduced to something "subjective," it therefore cannot be moral to base our collective resolutions on them. We must therefore pretend—and it is always a pretense—that our decisions follow moral principles or objective values, that they are logical conclusions from the content of the suggestion alone. This leads us, however, to misidentify and misjudge what is happening in public life. It makes the necessary and good activity of politics seem corrupt, replacing it with morality, which does not do justice to the necessary and difficult work of discussion and building trust with those who have different points of view. Morality encourages bigotry, since our formulation of moral principles seem self-evident to us and can justify treating poorly those who disagree. In our day the most tangential acquaintance with political discussions on social media demonstrates this. Turning politics into morality fulfills the misanthropic anthropology at the origin of modernity. We cannot agree, and we treat each other terribly, so we are not up to the task of self-governance; we need political decision making to be taken out of our hands and given to someone else. In practice, in North America, this has meant taking political decisions out of the hands of democratic institutions and giving them to the courts.[135]

The free-rider problem is also a problem in the economic sphere. For us, human labor is more than the accomplishment of tasks, as it is always embedded in a network of relationships and engaged in the work of building trust. We labor not only to accomplish a discrete result that we desire, but for the sake of the common good of the social wholes of which we are a part; that is, for the sake of our relationships with our coworkers and those depending on us. If labor is taken out of this social context, it becomes an individual calculation of incentives. Such a view cannot explain a sustained personal commitment to the well-being of an organization. That, however, seems to be necessary for the flourishing of a social group, as without it, we have the tragedy of the commons.

The modern political thinkers follow Hobbes in desiring a society that is rich and strong. But does Hobbes have a realistic path towards this result? If labor is a matter solely of individual calculation apart from all loyalty, then we can only look to generalizable laws or moral principles for why people choose to work hard rather than be free-riders, and not to their personal commitments to the good of the social wholes in which they participate. This explanation can never fit reality, however. Consider that immediately after concluding that the Leviathan state will be a welfare state, Hobbes addresses the obvious next question, how to prevent idleness, and writes, "But for such as have strong bodies, the case is otherwise: they are to be forced to work; and to avoyd the excuse of not finding employment, there ought to be such Lawes, as may encourage all manner of Arts; as Navigation, Agriculture, Fishing, and all manner of Manifacture that requires labour."[136] External laws to coerce people to work is tall order, and it is safe to say that a state that turns to it as a remedy has already forfeited the chance of becoming rich and strong. What is needed instead is to turn moral value into an economic incentive, such that the more you work, the more moral value you have. This is what is achieved by the labor theory of value.

The labor theory of value goes back to some suggestions Hobbes makes in *Leviathan* that were picked by Sir William Petty (1623–1687), his student and lifelong friend.[137] Petty, the "father of English Political Economy," wrote that "all things ought to be valued by two natural Denominations, which is Land and Labour."[138] Locke gave the classical expression of it in the chapter on property in his *Second Treatise*, writing that whatever a man "removes out of the State that Nature hath provided . . . he hath mixes his *Labour* with, and joined to it something that is his own, and thereby makes it his *Property*."[139] Adam Smith (1723–1790) wrote in *The Wealth of Nations*, "Labour . . . is the real measure of the exchangeable value of all commodities,"[140] and he is echoed by David Ricardo (1772–1832) in his famous *On the Principles of Political Economy and Taxation*: labor is "the foundation of all value," the relative quantity of which determines "almost exclusively . . . the relative value of commodities."[141] Rousseau also accepted the idea as well.[142]

Money as something earned through labor explains how there can be suggestion-response when everyone is showing each other only minimum loyalty. This happens on the side of instigator as well on the side of the respondent. For the latter, when we are working at the behest of another person, the labor theory of value allows us to see ourselves as actually working for ourselves, since we are working for a wage and not for a person. Work is not an expression of loyalty between persons, but rather of individual self-sufficiency. To the question, "Why does A do the work which B commands?" the answer is that B owns the productive capital in order to pay A a wage. Wealth as capital, as the vehicle to carry on fresh production, is the principle of social leadership. It provides the ability to get people to comply with suggestions by paying them. It is "earned" social leadership, as the capital was acquired, according to the dogma, through individual labor, and it is therefore another expression of individual self-sufficiency rather than loyalty. Capital, and the leadership role that stems from owning it, is therefore not a trust or a social responsibility. It is not embedded in wider social structures of loyalty. And crucially, it is impersonal, owned by someone who earned it independent of any bonds of obligation to other persons and groups to whom, through proximity and facilitation of the labor, loyalty could be due. Instead of seeing the whole process of production as creating a durable work for others, it is rather interpreted as laboring for oneself.[143]

Now the pursuit of value overlaps with the aim of greedily amassing wealth. Our commitment to our work would be the same thing as loving money; the piling up of wealth would simply be producing a lot. For Locke, because we have money, which does not spoil, we must be content with economic inequality and actually have agreed to the "disproportionate and unequal Possession of the Earth"[144] Those who own capital can employ others; they are our worldly betters, they hold *Obrigkeit* so to speak, not because of any bonds of loyalty but because they are in a position to pay a wage.

The modern idea of equality does not produce actual equality. Far from being a formula to make people independent and free, it requires and justifies inequality and dependence. It does this by first reducing loyalty relationships to altruism, and then mocking the idea that altruism could be a viable alternative to self-interest.[145] In practice, this has predictable results. In the wake of the industrial revolution, workers worked long days for low wages.[146] Young children were paid a fraction of a man's wage to do dangerous work for long hours, and orphans and abandoned children were slaves.[147] Thirty percent of people in the late nineteenth century in London, where Karl Marx (1818–1883) lived, were living beneath the level of subsistence.[148] The exploitation of workers was justified by laissez-faire liberalism. Thomas Malthus (1766–1834) had written the *Essay on Population* (1798), a widely read and influential tract that held that population growth would outrun the available resources, causing rising food prices, until the mortality rate rose and the birth rate fell. Though his argument ignored the possibility of technological progress, Malthus presented it as a natural economic law; his aim was to "assert the uselessness of any attempt at improving the situation of the great mass of workers."[149] The economist David Ricardo referred to it in support of the "iron law of wages," a proof that wages will tend to remain at subsistence level, which was brought up again and again in debates over policy.[150] Thus, the exploitation of workers was given a scientific justification, reaching a fever pitch with Herbert Spencer's (1820–1903) "survival of the fittest" and the doctrine of social Darwinism.[151]

This tradition was ripe for reexamination. Economic exploitation tended to be justified by the moral and political theories of liberalism, rather than labelled the abomination that it was. Karl Marx was determined to so label it, but instead of questioning the modern tradition, he doubled down on morality and the labor theory of value, going so far now as to replace economics with morality. For Marx, the labor theory of value marks a new epoch in world history. Accordingly, he maintains that his account of value in the first part of volume 1 of *Capital* is fundamental for the rest of his work—an account wherein he advocates for the simple banning of economic exchange.

Marx claims that for millennia, the human mind has failed to get to the bottom of the idea of value.[152] Concrete *use value*—when something fills a need of ours, when something is useful to us, when something pleases us—is the real, primary phenomena. But *exchange value* is very different from this. Exchange value (or just "value" for short) is, for Marx, the critical concept that is responsible for harmful illusions about society. Exchange value is the amount of social labor contained in a product. Social labor is the total amount of labor in a social order; the value of a commodity stems from the amount of labor it took to make it, on average and under normal conditions, as a fraction of the total amount of labor exercised in a society. This qualitative similarity allows dissimilar items to be compared. Exchange value only comes about when commodities are put in relation to each other. This is responsible for the central illusion of capitalism, which makes it seem that individuals are free, rather than being exploited by the ruling class. This happens because labor itself becomes a commodity. For Marx's moral view of the world, however, labor cannot be bought or sold. It is inalienable—like life is for Locke or life and liberty for Rousseau. This means it essentially degrades a person's being to give it up. Even of our own free will, writes Locke, we cannot enslave ourselves completely to another person.[153] No temporal goods can compensate for giving up our life or our liberty, writes Rousseau. "It would offend both Nature and reason to renounce them whatever the price."[154] The same holds true with labor for Marx; he calls what is actually bought and sold "labor-power," to distinguish it from that which is the real source of all value and is inalienable: labor itself.[155] This makes sense within the tradition. The whole point of Locke's labor theory of value is that our labor takes what is common and removes it into the sphere of our private property, making it rightfully ours without the consent of anyone.[156] It does not make sense that we would be able to alienate this essential capability of being human, our labor. After all, we are not able, according to Locke, to put ourselves "under the Absolute, Arbitrary Power of another, to take away his Life, when he pleases"?[157] Why would we ever then be able to put ourselves under the absolute, arbitrary power of another, to take away our labor, when he pleases?

Our social form enables this exploitation to happen. That social form is the market economy, which makes things comparable on a common measure. "Labor does not, in itself, give value to the product," notes an influential interpreter of Marx's theory of value, "but only that labor which is organized in a determined social form (in the form of a commodity economy)."[158] But we do not have to have this type of social form, which reduces the value of all things to their exchange value. We do not have to turn things into commodities. We do not have to see social labor as properly put into the hands of private individuals. We can simply eliminate the market. It is social labor that allows things to be compared and to take on exchange value, and what is properly social should be controlled by the whole society, not by a part. Under communism, Marx explains in the *Critique of the Gotha Program*, we would get what we need. In the initial stage of communism, instead of having to sell our labor, its products would go into a common stock, and we would take out what we need based on the labor we put in and not what we could reap in exchange.[159] Ultimately even this would be overcome, as communism advances and wealth increases, and the principle becomes "From each according to his ability, to each according to his needs."[160]

Marx follows Rousseau and the tradition of progressive liberalism. Lower-level loyalties must be sacrificed to the general loyalty to the collective, as this is what gives real individual freedom. Rousseau banned politics—suggestion-response—from the city, replacing it with a central administration that would keep individuals isolated from each other and excessively dependent upon the state. Individual autonomy is a sham, however, if individuals are subject to economic exploitation: Marx, therefore, bans not only politics but also economics. As for Rousseau, we cannot engage in meaningful suggestion-response, and for Marx, we cannot engage in meaningful trade; just as the practice of politics taints the purity of the general will, the practice of trade taints the purity of labor. Economics must be remade to be moral. Instead of personal preferences winning out (economic exchange), there has to be true value. That must be determined objectively, universally—that is, by the state. If the state determines who gets what, then it is not immoral. As with all modern political thought, if the sovereign state does it, it is automatically right.

NOTES

1. In international relations, for example, a state has a certain role to play, a contribution it can make to other states and to the whole.

2. To talk about values is deceptively open and inclusive. Everything can have a value, even evil—an interpretation given by René Descartes that Rémi Brague sees as inaugurating a new epoch. "The good no longer is directly worthwhile, as good, but rather as what has value," writes Brague. "It no longer derives its goodness from itself, but from the value assigned to it." Rémi Brague, *The Kingdom of Man: Genesis and Failure of the Modern Project*, trans. Paul Seaton (Notre Dame: University of Notre Dame Press, 2018), 100.

3. "Old establishments are tried by their effects," writes Edmund Burke. "They are not often constructed after any theory; theories are rather drawn from them." Edmund

Burke, *Reflections on the Revolution in France*, ed. L. G. Mitchell (Oxford: Oxford University Press, 1993), 173.

4. "Modernity put it in our heads that there are two units: the individual and the universal collective," writes Nassim Nicholas Taleb. Actually my "skin in the game" is to be found "in a broader set of people, one that includes a family, a community, a tribe, a fraternity. But it cannot possibly be the universal." Nassim Nicholas Taleb, *Skin in the Game: Hidden Asymmetries in Daily Life* (New York: Allen Lane, 2018), 60.

5. Taleb, *Skin in the Game*, 113.

6. Paul Türks, *Philip Neri: The Fire of Joy*, trans. Daniel Utrecht (New York: Alba House, 1995), 65.

7. The management of good conflict—the art of political leadership—is not easy. Leymah Gbowee, a peace activist in Liberia, offers poignant recollections of her struggle to lead: "If you were looking from the outside, our unity was effortless. But almost everything we did required endless work. The women's movement politics were exhausting. . . . There were constant personality clashes to resolve. Women came to the nightly organizers' meeting with endless complaints and accusations. . . . For me the worst confrontations were those that got personal, [like] whispers that I pretended to be working for good, but I was evil and immoral. It was hard to ignore them. . . . 'Maybe I should resign,' I said after one of these attacks on my character." Leymah Gbowee with Carol Mithers, *Mighty Be Our Powers: How Sisterhood, Prayer, and Sex Changed a Nation at War* (New York: Beast Books, 2011), 144–45.

8. The wait for publishing in mathematics journals is notoriously slow.

9. "Consensus is horrible. I mean, if everyone really agrees on something and consensus comes about quickly and naturally, well that's terrific. But that isn't how it usually works, and so consensus becomes an attempt to please everyone. Which usually turns into displeasing everyone equally." Patrick Lencioni, *The Five Dysfunctions of a Team* (San Francisco: Jossey-Bass, 2002), 95.

10. Cf. Jim Manzi, *Uncontrolled: The Surprising Payoff of Trial-and-Error for Business, Politics, and Society* (New York: Basic Books, 2012). This causal density and corresponding lack of precision is why taking "values" too seriously means vacating the possibility of a science of practical life, as for example, Rudolf Carnap does. Cf. Thomas Mormann, "Carnap's Logical Empiricism, Values, and American Pragmatism," *Journal for General Philosophy of Science* 38, no. 1 (April 21, 2007): 127–46.

11. Harold D. Lasswell, *Politics: Who Gets What, When, How* (Cleveland: Meridian, 1958). The best response to this definition is that of A. James Reichley: "Viewed in one light, no doubt. But if that is politics, then what is economics? Is not economics also who gets what, when, and how? Are politics and economics then identical? Hardly, since there are clearly economic activities—like selling automobiles and buying cucumbers—that are not political activities. Is politics, then, a division within the general class of economics? One thinks not. . . . In short, is not politics the 'art of government'? And if this is true, is not the question of why human beings should 'love politics' similar to the question of why men should love women? Is not the answer to both, that is, that it is the nature of the beast?" A. James Reichley, *The Art*

of Government: Reform and Organization Politics in Philadelphia (New York: Fund for the Republic, 1959), 124.

"Because virtue presupposes justice, and justice involves a real peace," writes John Milbank, "the ontological priority of peace to conflict (peace is what is most real, most secure, most guarantees human life) is an issue of yet more importance than that of virtue." John Milbank, *Theology and Social Theory: Beyond Secular Reason*, 2nd ed. (Malden, MA: Blackwell, 2006), 367.

12. Tolerance based on an unscientific attitude—a lack of curiosity in the face of conflicting accounts—is based on narrow self-interest or a lethargic and unreflective preference for the status quo. By contrast, a scientific attitude does not rest content with seemingly irreconcilable accounts of the same reality, no matter how pleasant present circumstances seem. Plato includes perceptions that seem to contradict each other as a category that can be used in education to awaken thought: the "provocatives." Plato, *Republic*, 523a-524d. Satisfaction with contradictions is unscientific; being able to give an account of them is far better. If everyone's opinion is as good as everyone else's, then we are a lover of opinion and fail to take the time to think about anything more deeply. The unscientific attitude is essentially superficial. The "lover of spectacles" according to Plato, "cannot endure to hear anybody say that the beautiful is one and the just one, and so of other things," to which the scientist responds, "My good fellow, is there any one of these many fair and honorable things that will not sometimes appear ugly and base? And of the just things, that will not seem unjust? And of the pious things, though not seem in pious?" For Plato, it is inevitable "that they would appear to be both beautiful in a way and ugly, and so with all the other things you have asked about." Plato, *Republic*, 479a-b.

13. Michael Walzer expresses this difference well in terms of thin, universal principles (which can never form their own point of view) and the thickness of a morality shaped by historical circumstances. Michael Walzer, *Thick and Thin: Moral Argument at Home and Abroad* (Notre Dame: University of Notre Dame Press, 2019).

14. This view of the common good and its expression is nothing new. It was held by Thomas Aquinas when he spoke of the first principles of natural law. Cf. Philip J. Harold, "Economics, Politics, and Natural Law," in *Human Rights and Natural Law: An Intercultural Philosophical Perspective*, ed. Walter Schweidler (Sankt Augustin: Academia, 2012), 153–54. J.G.A. Pocock also points to ancient Chinese political thought, which saw society as properly governed by a code of rituals. J. G. A. Pocock, *Politics, Language, and Time: Essays on Political Thought and History* (Chicago: Chicago University Press, 1971), 42–79.

15. Max Scheler writes that "*phenomenological* philosophy is a continual *desymbolization of the world*." Max Scheler, *Selected Philosophical Essays*, trans. David R. Lachterman (Evanston: Northwestern University Press, 1973), 143.

16. Jacques Derrida, *Speech and Phenomena*, trans. David B. Allison (Evanston: Northwestern University Press, 1973).

17. Value is always value in exchange. Cf. Hannah Arendt, *The Human Condition*, 2nd ed. (Chicago: University of Chicago Press, 1958), 163.

18. Hobbes, *Leviathan*, 8.1. CE 4, 104.

19. Hobbes, *Leviathan*, 10.16. CE 4, 134.

20. Joel Backström, "Of Dictators and Greengrocers: On the Repressive Grammar of Values-Discourse," *Ethical Perspectives* 22, no. 1 (2015): 45.

21. Quoted in Ivo De Gennaro and Gino Zaccaria, *The Dictatorship of Value: Teaching and Research in the Planetary University* (Milan: McGraw-Hill, 2011), 85.

22. De Gennaro and Zaccaria, *The Dictatorship of Value*, 84–85. Eliding this difference leads to what they call the "dictatorship of value."

23. D.C. Schindler, *Freedom from Reality: The Diabolical Character of Modern Liberty* (Notre Dame: University of Notre Dame Press, 2017).

24. Nietzsche, *Genealogy of Morals*, III:18. KGW 6.2, 402.

25. One study of sacred rhetoric in politics rightly emphasizes how strident, absolutist appeals to unquestionable values treats opponents as enemies, rather than as fellow citizens to be won over by persuasion. Morgan Marietta, *The Politics of Sacred Rhetoric: Absolutist Appeals and Political Persuasion* (Waco, TX: Baylor University Press, 2012), 59.

26. Hobbes, *Leviathan*, 15.40. CE 4, 242.

27. John P. McCormick, "Fear, Technology, and the State: Carl Schmitt, Leo Strauss, and the Revival of Hobbes in Weimar and National Socialist Germany," *Political Theory* 22, no. 4 (1994): 645.

28. Hobbes introduces the paragraph on the "Generation of the Commonwealth" as the need for a "Common Power" as that which can "defend them from the invasion of Forraigners, and the injuries of one another." Hobbes, *Leviathan*, 17.13. CE 4, 260. "And Law was brought into the world for nothing else," writes Hobbes elsewhere, "but to limit the naturall liberty of particular men, in such manner, as they might not hurt, but assist one another, and joyn together against a common Enemy." Hobbes, *Leviathan*, 26.8. CE 4, 418. The ability to defend oneself in a war is, for Hobbes, what distinguishes a big family from a commonwealth. Hobbes, *Leviathan*, 20.15. CE 4, 314. "And be there never so great a Multitude; yet if their actions be directed according to their particular judgements, and particular appetites, they can expect thereby no defence, nor protection, neither against a Common enemy, nor against the injuries of one another. For being distracted in opinions concerning the best use and application of their strength, they do not help, but hinder one another; and reduce their strength by mutuall opposition to nothing: whereby they are easily, not onely subdued by a very few that agree together; but also when there is no common enemy, they make warre upon each other, for their particular interests." Hobbes, *Leviathan*, 17.4. CE 4, 256.

29. This is true both in its theory and its history: "War made the state, and the state made war" (Charles Tilly), and "war is essentially the health of the State" (Randolph Bourne).

30. "Hereby it is manifest, that during the time men live without a common Power to keep them all in awe, they are in that condition which is called Warre; and such a warre, as is of every man, against every man. For WARRE, consisteth not in Battell onely, or the act of fighting; but in a tract of time, wherein the Will to contend by Battell is sufficiently known: and therefore the notion of Time, is to be considered in the nature of Warre; as it is in the nature of Weather. For as the nature of Foule weather, lyeth not in a showre or two of rain; but in an inclination thereto of many dayes together: So the nature of War, consisteth not in actuall fighting; but in the known

disposition thereto, during all the time there is no assurance to the contrary. All other time is peace." Hobbes, *Leviathan*, 13.7. CE 4, 192.

31. Hobbes, *Leviathan*, 29.20. CE 4, 518.

32. Hobbes, *Leviathan*, 13.13. CE 4, 196.

33. Hobbes, *Leviathan*, 28.13. CE 4, 492.

34. "For the Punishments set down in the Law, are to Subjects, not to Enemies; such as are they, that having been by their own act Subjects, deliberately revolting, deny the Soveraign Power." Hobbes, *Leviathan*, 28.13. CE 4, 486.

35. Hobbes, *Leviathan*, 28.13. CE 4, 486.

36. Hobbes, *Leviathan*, 18.5. CE 4, 268. "He therefore that breaketh his Covenant, and consequently declareth that he thinks he may with reason do so, cannot be received into any Society, that unite themselves for Peace and defence, but by the errour of them that receive him; nor when he is received, be retayned in it, without seeing the danger of their errour; which errours a man cannot reasonably reckon upon as the means of his security; and therefore if he be left, or cast out of Society, he perisheth." Hobbes, *Leviathan*, 15.5. CE 4, 224.

37. Cf. Hobbes, *Leviathan*, 15.41. CE 4, 242; and Hobbes, *Leviathan*, 27.33. CE 4, 474.

38. For example, we have to work. As we will see at the end of this chapter, the tying of the production of things other people want to the value we gain for ourselves is what enables the functioning of an economy based on minimum loyalty.

39. A world sovereign who successfully eliminated war would find himself becoming the next target, as sovereignty itself would have to be dismantled. This is exactly the logical conclusion later drawn by Karl Marx.

40. Hobbes does not consider the solution of world government, even though the "problem of universal war inherent to the state of nature requires a universal, or global, solution." Trevor Shelley, *Globalization and Liberalism: Montesquieu, Tocqueville, and Manent* (Notre Dame: University of Notre Dame Press, 2020), 9.

41. Hobbes, *Leviathan*, 21.4. CE 4, 326. Hobbes, *Leviathan*, 17.1. CE 4, 254.

42. Take Hugo Grotius (1583–1645), for example. A hugely influential political thinker until the late eighteenth century and often seen as a precursor to Hobbes, Grotius seems to offer us a universal political theory of individual rights secured by clear, calculative reason. However, as Jeremy Seth Gedder has shown, this proto-Hobbesianism is only half of the story; Grotius also aimed at positive justice and the need for prudence to attain friendship. Jeremy Seth Gedder, *Hugo Grotius and the Modern Theology of Freedom* (New York: Routledge, 2017). His great work was entitled *The Rights of War and Peace* (1625). Unlike Hobbes, he did not just focus on the first (war) and drop the second (peace).

43. Cf. Alex J. Bellamy, *World Peace (And How We Can Achieve It)* (Oxford: Oxford University Press, 2019), 10–11.

44. Amos Funkenstein, *Theology and the Scientific Imagination* (Princeton: Princeton University Press, 1986), 327.

45. This is the common tack of those opposed to Hobbes, starting in his lifetime; for example, Ralph Cudworth (1617–1688) and Samuel Clarke (1675–1729). Cf.

Perez Zagorin, *Hobbes and the Law of Nature* (Princeton: Princeton University Press, 2009), 114–15.

46. Richard Tuck, *Natural Rights Theories: Their Origin and Development* (Cambridge: Cambridge University Press, 1979), 174.

47. Most European scholars relied on the Latin texts of *Leviathan* and *De Cive*. Glen Newey, *The Routledge Guidebook to Hobbes' Leviathan* (London: Routledge, 2014), 318.

48. Linda Kirk, "The Political Thought of Richard Cumberland: Sovereignty and the Escape From the Search For Origins," *Political Studies* vol. 25, no. 4 (December 1977) 547. *De Legibus Naturae* was paraphrased in English by Samuel Parker in 1681 and James Tyrrell in 1692; a full translation in English appeared in 1727.

49. The fact that interest in Cumberland has only recently started to be revived after a long period of neglect is not an accurate testimony of his importance. Cumberland is one of those thinkers whose achievement is so thorough that, afterwards, everyone accepts what he says as obvious, and as a result, he falls into obscurity. This is often an affliction of great thinkers: their triumph is too complete. Henri Bergson (1859–1941) overcame mechanism, an achievement everyone takes for granted, though his thought is neglected. There are no Freudians today, yet everyone knows that maltreating a child has consequences for them in adulthood. We will encounter another example in Hermann Lotze, a thinker whose influence is so total that he lacks partisans.

50. Ernest Albee, "The Ethical System of Richard Cumberland. I.," *The Philosophical Review* 4, no. 3 (1895): 265.

51. Frank Chapman Sharp, "The Ethical System of Richard Cumberland and Its Place in the History of British Ethics," *Mind* vol. 21, no. 83 (July 1912), 371.

52. Frank Spaulding, *Richard Cumberland als Begründer der englischen Ethik* (Leipzig: G. Fock, 1894).

53. Samuel von Pufendorf, *Two Books of the Elements of Universal Jurisprudence*, ed. Thomas Behme, trans. William Abbott Oldfather (Indianapolis: Liberty Fund, 2009), 7. GW 3, 5. Citations to Pufendorf will give the English translation first, followed by the Latin version in the Collected Works, with the volume and page number. In this, Pufendorf breaks with the approach of Grotius. Cf. Hugo Grotius, *The Rights of War and Peace, Book II*, ed. Richard Tuck (Indianapolis: Liberty Fund, 2005), 1115.

54. Pufendorf, *Two Books of the Elements of Universal Jurisprudence*, 8, GW 3, 5.

55. As Heikki Haara summarizes it, for Pufendorf, "The dictates of right reason offer substantial and binding moral norms already prior to the founding of political society." Heikki Haara, *Pufendorf's Theory of Sociability: Passions, Habits and Social Order* (Cham, Switzerland: Springer Nature, 2018), 28.

56. Heikki Haara, *Pufendorf's Theory of Sociability*, 21.

57. Samuel Pufendorf, *On the Duty of Man and Citizen According to Natural Law*, ed. James Tully, trans. Michael Silverthorne (Cambridge: Cambridge University Press, 1991), 61, GW 2, 35.

58. Pufendorf, *On the Duty of Man and Citizen According to Natural Law*, 20, GW 2, 14–15.

59. Pufendorf, *Two Books of the Elements of Universal Jurisprudence*, 10–11, 391–97, GW 3, 6, 163–65. Pufendorf follows Hobbes even in allowing rebellion by subjects whose Sovereign has turned into their enemy, since Hobbes allows that we can disobey the Sovereign when we are pursued, since the situation reverts back to the state of nature. What is not allowed for both Hobbes and Pufendorf is abandoning my self-interest and coming to the aid of my fellow citizens who are unjustly pursued. "It will not be permissible," Pufendorf writes of the Sovereign seeking the destruction of one's fellow citizens, "for the rest of his subjects on this account to put off obedience, or to defend the innocent by violence, whether the prince present some pretext or not." Pufendorf, 394, GW 3, 164.

60. Pufendorf, *On the Duty of Man and Citizen According to Natural Law*, 10. GW 2, 7. Cf. Pufendorf, pp. 35, 43, 115, 119, GW 2, 22–23, 26, 61, 63.

61. Pufendorf, *On the Duty of Man and Citizen According to Natural Law,* 139, GW 2, 73. Of the people's relation to the sovereign authority, Pufendorf writes that "even when it has threatened them with the most atrocious injuries, individuals will protect themselves by flight or endure any injury or damage rather than draw their swords against one who remains the father of their country, however harsh he may be." Pufendorf, *On the Duty of Man and Citizen According to Natural Law*, 146–47, GW 2, 76.

62. Heikki Haara and Aino Lahdenranta, "Smithian Sentimentalism Anticipated: Pufendorf on the Desire of Esteem and Moral Conduct," *The Journal of Scottish Philosophy* 16.1 (2018), 20.

63. Pufendorf, *Two Books of the Elements of Universal Jurisprudence*, 85, GW 3, 34.

64. Pufendorf, *Elements*, 94, GW 3, 38.

65. Pufendorf, *Elements*, 266, GW 3, 111.

66. These are two types of value for Pufendorf: price (*pretium*) for things, and esteem (*existimatio*) for people. Pufendorf, *Elements*, 98–102, GW 3, 40–41. For Grotius, scarcity and common estimation determines the value of things. Grotius, *The Rights of War and Peace, Book II*, 14. We have seen Hobbes apply this to persons as well. Cf. Hobbes, *Leviathan*, 10.16. CE 4, 134.

67. Pufendorf, *Elements*, 81, GW 3, 33.

68. Pufendorf, *On the Duty of Man and Citizen According to Natural Law*, 63, GW 2, 36.

69. Pufendorf, *Two Books of the Elements of Universal Jurisprudence*, 20, GW 3, 7.

70. Pufendorf, *Elements*, 39, GW 3, 15. He walks this back in *De Officio Hominis et Civis*: "For the liberty of the subjected person is not abolished by the subjection of one person to another; he may still resist the other's control and go his own way." Pufendorf, *On the Duty of Man and Citizen According to Natural Law*, 23, GW 2, 16. For us, persons are, of course, more than centers of power or seekers of value. We do not just compete for esteem but participate and contribute to an ethos. We can take responsibility for things that were not our decisions, and indeed, just this is required for the success of any political leadership of a real social aggregate, which is inevitably historically constituted; this is where the decisions of the past can have

bad effects for the present, which must be dealt with by those who take responsibility for them, even though they are not responsible. We can only understand the common good in this way—as a matter of relationships—where our task is to include others in networks of loyalty, rather than the struggle for esteem, which is competitive and thereby exclusive.

71. Cumberland writes that "the science of *Morality* and *Politicks*, both can, and ought to, *imitate* the *Analytick Art*, (in which I comprehend, not only the Extraction of Roots, but also the whole doctrine of specious Arithmetick or Algebra,) as the noblest Pattern of Science." Richard Cumberland, *A Treatise of the Laws of Nature*, trans. John Maxwell (Indianapolis: Liberty Fund, 2005), 489; *De Legibus Naturae* (London: E. Flesher for Nathanael Hooke, 1672), 179–80.

72. Cumberland, *A Treatise of the Laws of Nature, 369*; *De Legibus Naturae*, 74.

73. For example: "It is sufficient, in few Words, to *affirm*, 'That in *all Affairs*, whether *private* or *publick*, Mathematicks is the principal *Instrument* of *Certainty* and *Justice* in Action, wheresoever *Exactness* is requisite.' Which I do not advance, with a view to *commend Mathematicks*, (which is needless,) but to demonstrate the *Certainty* of the Rules of Life and *Morality*, upon this Account, that *Natural Prudence* almost always makes Use of the *Assistance* of a *Science* that is *certain*, or of *self-evident Principles*. To this *Head* also, I think, may be *referr'd*, 'That, whereas we know not what shall hereafter happen, we may, nevertheless, know what is *possible*: And things *possible* may be *compar'd* among themselves; and it may be *certainly* known, not only, which of *two possible* Things will be of *greater* or *less Value* [*pluris aut minoris valebit*], when they do happen; but, also, which of them may be produc'd by *more*, which by *fewer*, *Causes*, that do now, or shall soon, exist. But that is *more probable*, which may happen *more ways*, and its *Chance* or *Expectation* is of *greater Value* [*plurisque valet*].' Now it is of great *Consequence*, in the Management of Affairs, 'To know certainly the *Probability*, and *Value*, of the *Hope* of the several Things, or Effects, we have occasion to consider [*certe saltem scire cujus rei, vel effectus spes major sit, plurisque aestimanda*].'" Cumberland, *A Treatise of the Laws of Nature*, 492; *De Legibus Naturae*, 183.

74. We compare the two, and from this comparison "may be *drawn* 'An universal Remedy for all irregular Affections, injurious to Others, or Destructive of our own Quiet, which generally proceed from too great a love of Ourselves.' He, who esteems nothing a *Great* Good, but what contributes *much* to the Common Happiness, will never *inordinately* desire any Thing; and, consequently, will never so offend against the Publick Good, as to be disturb'd with the Conscience of any Crime." Cumberland, *A Treatise of the Laws of Nature*, 707; *De Legibus Naturae*, 378–79.

75. Cumberland, *A Treatise of the Laws of Nature*, 686; *De Legibus Naturae*, 358.

76. This only works, however, if there is a similar measure between them. When there is a common measure, there is no difficulty in making comparisons. But when it is a matter of apples and oranges? Asking which chocolate is better makes sense; asking which of your children is better does not. Even the different types of enjoyment a single individual can have are not necessarily comparable; for example, the pleasure of a chocolate bar and the joy of seeing one's children flourish are qualitatively different, and it is impossible to express the latter joy in terms of a quantity of

chocolates. We could, of course, stick our heads in the sand and ignore the qualitative difference, claiming to reduce everything to pleasure like the utilitarian Jeremy Bentham (1748–1832), who famously wrote, "Prejudice apart, the game of push-pin is of equal value with the arts and sciences of music and poetry." Jeremy Bentham, *The Rationale of Reward* (London: Robert Heward, 1830), 206. It is not without reason that Cumberland is considered one of the founders of Utilitarianism. Frank Chapman Sharp, "The Ethical System of Richard Cumberland and Its Place in the History of British Ethics," *Mind* 21, no. 83 (July 1912): 392.

77. Cumberland, *A Treatise of the Laws of Nature*, 610; *De Legibus Naturae*, 291.

78. "For the *Common Good* is the *only End*, in the pursuit whereof *all Rational Beings can agree* among themselves; because it comprehends the *greatest possible Happiness of all*; and it is most certain, that only *that* Practical Reason is true, which discovers to *all* an *End* and *Means*, in which *all* who make a true Judgment *can agree*; and that those, therefore, act according to true Practical Reason, who have this End at heart, and make use of the Means necessary thereto." Cumberland, *A Treatise of the Laws of Nature*, 560; *De Legibus Naturae*, 247.

79. "I freely grant," writes Cumberland, "'That there are many things *indifferent*, or concerning which human Reason cannot universally pronounce, that it is necessary to the common Good, that the Matter should be transacted this way rather than that." Cumberland, *A Treatise of the Laws of Nature*, 470; *De Legibus Naturae*, 167.

80. Cumberland, *A Treatise of the Laws of Nature*, 470; *De Legibus Naturae*, 167.

81. For example, see Cumberland, *A Treatise of the Laws of Nature*, 729; *De Legibus Naturae*, 399. Cumberland takes issue with Hobbes not requiring public oaths.

82. Cf. Jon Parkin, *Science, Religion and Politics in Restoration England* (Woodbridge, Suffolk: The Boydell Press, 1999), 205. Parkin concludes his *Taming The Leviathan* by saying: "Arguably this is where one should look if one wants to establish the lasting effect of Hobbes's work; not amongst Hobbes's avowed admirers, but rather in the work of his many critics, where the critical process of taming Hobbes's ideas allowed them to be incorporated into the mainstream of seventeenth-century political thought." Jon Parkin, *Taming The Leviathan: The Reception of the Political and Religious Ideas of Thomas Hobbes in England 1640–1700* (Cambridge: Cambridge University Press, 2007), 413.

83. Newey, *The Routledge Guidebook to Hobbes' Leviathan*, 6.

84. John Locke, *An Essay Concerning Human Understanding*, ed. Peter H. Nidditch (Oxford: Clarendon Press, 1975), 356–57.

85. Locke, *An Essay Concerning Human Understanding*, 357.

86. George Orwell agrees: "[P]ublic opinion, because of the tremendous urge to conformity in gregarious animals, is less tolerant than any system of law." Orwell, *All Art Is Propaganda,* 305.

87. To the Pharisees who loved money, Christ says, "You justify yourselves in the sight of others, but God knows your hearts; for what is of human esteem is an abomination in the sight of God" Luke 16:15.

88. Locke, *An Essay Concerning Human Understanding*, 69.

89. Locke, 354–55.

90. Richard Ashcraft and M. M. Goldsmith, "Locke, Revolution Principles, and the Formation of Whig Ideology," *The Historical Journal* 26, no. 4 (2016): 773–800. The phrase has a prehistory dating back to the medieval period but without the meaning of popular sovereignty. Cf. George Boas, *Vox Populi: Essays in the History of an Idea* (Baltimore: Johns Hopkins University Press, 1969).

91. Locke, *An Essay Concerning Human Understanding*, 356.

92. Locke, 271.

93. Locke, 354.

94. Locke, 356.

95. Reinhart Koselleck, *Critique and Crisis: Enlightenment and the Pathogenesis of Modern Society* (Cambridge: The MIT Press, 1988), 55–56.

96. Hans-Georg Gadamer, "Friendship and Solidarity," trans. David Vessey and Chris Blauwkamp, *Research in Phenomenology* 39 (2009): 3.

97. Rousseau writes in his second *Discourse*: "Let us conclude that wandering in the forests, without industry, without speech, without domicile, without war and without liaisons, with no need of his fellows, likewise with no desire to harm them, perhaps never even recognizing anyone individually, Savage man, subject to few passions and self-sufficient, had only the feelings and intellect suited to that state; he felt only his true needs, saw only what he believed he had an interest to see; and his intelligence made no more progress than his vanity." Jean-Jacques Rousseau, *Discourse on the Origins of Inequality (Second Discourse), Polemics, and Political Economy*, vol. 3 of *The Collected Writings of Rousseau*, ed. Roger D. Masters and Christopher Kelly, trans. Judith R. Bush, Roger D. Masters, Christopher Kelly, and Terence Marshall (Hanover, NH: Dartmouth College Press, 1992), 3:40; 3:159–60. Citations will be given first to the volume and page number from Jean-Jacques Rousseau, *The Collected Writings of Rousseau* (Hanover, NH: Dartmouth College Press, 1990–2010), followed by Jean-Jacques Rousseau, *Oeuvres Complètes*, 5 Vols. (Paris: Bibliothèque de la Pléiade, 1959–1996).

98. "Art perished with the inventor. There was neither education nor progress; the generations multiplied uselessly." Rousseau, *Discourse on the Origins of Inequality*, 3:40; 3:60.

99. Rousseau, *Discourse on the Origins of Inequality*, 3:37–38; 3:155–57.

100. Rousseau, *Discourse on the Origins of Inequality*, 3:42; 3:161–62.

101. The critical passage of this transformation is as follows: "contacts spread and bonds are tightened. People grew accustomed to assembling in front of the Huts or around a large Tree; song and dance, true children of love and leisure, became the amusement or rather the occupation of idle and assembled men and women. Each one began to look at the others and to want to be looked at himself, and public esteem had a value. The one who sang or danced the best, the handsomest, the strongest, the most adroit, or the most eloquent became the most highly considered; and that was the first step toward inequality and, at the same time, toward vice." Rousseau, *Discourse on the Origins of Inequality*, 3:47; 3:169–70.

102. Rousseau has a keen sense of mimetic desire. It forms the major part of the powerful contrast he makes between primitive and social man, with the latter living "in the opinions of others." Rousseau, *Discourse on the Origins of Inequality*, 3:57;

3:193. Rousseau also sees the exclusionary effects of mimetic desire, writing that "if one sees a handful of powerful and rich men at the height of grandeur and fortune, while the crowd grovels in obscurity and misery, it is because the former prize the things they enjoy only insofar as the others are deprived of them; and because, without changing their status, they would cease to be happy if the People ceased to be miserable." Rousseau, *Discourse on the Origins of Inequality*, 3:63; 3:189.

103. "As soon as men had begun to appreciate one another, and the idea of consideration was formed in their minds, each one claimed a right to it, and it was no longer possible to be disrespectful toward anyone with impunity. . . . Thus, everyone punishing the contempt shown him by another in a manner proportionate to the importance he accorded himself, vengeances became terrible, and men bloodthirsty and cruel." Rousseau, *Discourse on the Origins of Inequality*, 3:47–48; 3:170.

104. Jean-Jacques Rousseau, *Social Contract, Discourses on the Virtue Most Necessary for a Hero, Political Fragments, and Geneva Manuscript*, vol. 4 of *The Collected Writings of Rousseau*, ed. Roger D. Masters and Christopher Kelly, trans. Judith R. Bush, Roger D. Masters, and Christopher Kelly (Hanover, NH: Dartmouth College Press, 1992), 4:138, 3:360.

105. Rousseau, *The Social Contract*, 4:164, 3:394.

106. The "social compact gives the body politic absolute power over all of its members." Rousseau, *The Social Contract*, 4:148, 3:372.

107. Rousseau, *The Social Contract*, 4:138, 3:360–61.

108. "The Sovereign," writes Rousseau, "by the sole fact of being, is always what it ought to be." Rousseau, *The Social Contract*, 4:140, 3:363.

109. For Rousseau, freedom is autonomy, not needing others, which is incompatible with the political relationship of suggestion-response, which involves dependence on others. Rousseau is a political theorist who imagines a world without politics, only administration. For him, politics is the utopian restoration of original innocence where I only obey myself.

110. "It up to public esteem," Rousseau writes, "to establish the difference between evil and good men. The Magistrate is judge only of rigorous right; but the People are the genuine judges of morals: an upright and even enlightened judge on this point, sometimes deceived but never corrupted." Rousseau, *Discourse on the Origins of Inequality*, 3:95; 3:222–23.

111. When multiple people consider themselves united in a single group and "they have only a single will, which relates to their common preservation and the general welfare," then "all the mechanisms of the State are vigorous and simple, its maxims are clear and luminous, it has no tangled, contradictory interests; the common good is clearly apparent everywhere, and requires only good sense to be perceived." Jean-Jacques Rousseau, *The Social Contract*, 4:198, 3:437.

112. Rousseau, *Discourse on Political Economy*, 3:144, 3:246.

113. Rousseau, 3:144, 3:246.

114. "[W]e must govern ourselves by rules, which are more general in their application, and more free from doubt and uncertainty." David Hume, *A Treatise of Human Nature*, 2nd ed., ed. L. A. Selby-Bigge and P. H. Nidditch (Oxford: Oxford at the Clarendon Press, 1978), 3.2.4.1, 514. Citations to Hume refer to the Book, Part, Section,

and Paragraph, followed by page references to the Selby-Bigge/Nidditch editions. "The imagination adheres to the *general* views of things, and distinguishes betwixt the feelings they produce, from those which arise from our particular and momentary situation." Hume, *Treatise*, 3.3.1.23, 587.

115. "[V]irtue is distinguished by the pleasure, and vice by the pain, that any action, sentiment or character gives us by the mere view and contemplation. This decision is very commodious; because it reduces us to this simple question, *Why any action or sentiment upon the general view or survey, gives a certain satisfaction or uneasiness,* in order to shew the origin of its moral rectitude or depravity, without looking for any incomprehensible relations and qualities, which never did exist in nature, nor even in our imagination, by any clear and distinct conception. I flatter myself I have executed a great part of my present design by a state of the question, which appears to me so free from ambiguity and obscurity." Hume, *Treatise*, 3.1.2.11, 475–76. "When a man denominates another his *enemy*, his *rival*, his *antagonist*, his *adversary*, he is understood to speak the language of self-love, and to express sentiments, peculiar to himself, and arising from his particular circumstances and situation. But when he bestows on any man the epithets of *vicious* or *odious* or *depraved*, he then speaks another language, and expresses sentiments, in which he expects all his audience are to concur with him. He must here, therefore, depart from his private a particular situation, and must choose a point of view, common to him with others." David Hume, *Enquiries Concerning the Human Understanding and Concerning the Principles of Morals*, ed. L. A. Selby-Bigge (London: Oxford at the Clarendon Press, 1902), 9.6, 272.

116. Hume writes that "a single act of justice, consider'd in itself, may often be contrary to the public good; and 'tis only the concurrence of mankind, in a general scheme or system of action, which is advantageous." Hume, *Treatise*, 3.3.1.12, 579.

117. It is "that particular feeling or sentiment, on which moral distinctions depend." Hume, *Treatise*, 3.3.1.30, 591.

118."Loving one's neighbor as oneself" is actually *selfishness* in Hume's view. He gives an example of fatherly love and virtue, as if it were a natural, everyday humdrum occurrence. Cf. Hume, *Treatise*, 3.2.2.5, 487. Today, perhaps we know better than to take this for granted? Especially if we reduce, as Hume does, wanting good things for ourselves and our friends to our narrow interest: "instead of fitting men for large societies," he writes, such endearing ties are "almost as contrary to them, as the most narrow selfishness." Hume, *Treatise*, 3.2.2.6, 487. Thus, friendship would not be something that builds up society, but rather something that falls in the category of private interest and, as such, is a *threat* to the social order. Cf. Hume's take on how greed for property tears society apart. "All the other passions, besides this of interest, are either easily restrain'd, or are not of such pernicious consequence, when indulg'd. . . . This avidity alone, of acquiring goods and possessions for ourselves *and our nearest friends*, is insatiable, perpetual, universal, and directly destructive of society." Hume, *Treatise*, 3.2.2.12, 491–92. Italics added. Men have a narrow circle of loyalty, and this "confined generosity" of men means that the interests they pursue—their own interest, or the interest of their family, friends and social circle—are not the same as the interests of the whole society. Pursuing only the interest of their groups, men run into "every kind of injustice and violence." Hume, *Treatise*, 3.2.2.21, 497.

119. The republican thinker James Harrington (1611–1677), who was cited frequently in the U.S. Constitutional Convention, and who coined the phrase "a government of laws and not of men," was the first thinker to use the phrase "intrinsic value," which he used to refer to virtue in his great work *The Commonwealth of Oceana* (1656), published only five years after Hobbes's *Leviathan*. James Harrington, *The Commonwealth of Oceana, and A System of Politics*, ed. J. G. A. Pocock (Cambridge: Cambridge University Press, 1992), 138, 141.

120. "Our servant, if diligent and faithful, may excite stronger sentiments of love and kindness than *Marcus Brutus*, as represented in history; but we say not upon that account, that the former character is more laudable than the latter. We know, that were we to approach equally near to that renown'd patriot, he would command a much higher degree of affection and admiration." Hume, *Treatise*, 3.3.1.16, 582. Hume does not talk about the *relationships* we have with others, but rather the *feelings* we have in their presence ("sentiments of love and kindness"). He uses the two examples of a servant and a historical figure, carefully chosen examples which render this way of speaking plausible, since English aristocrats were not involved in the lives of their servants. If instead of "servant," Hume had written "spouse," it would render his conclusion ridiculous, snapping us out of the delusion that a character out of ancient Roman history would win our "affection and admiration" to a greater degree than our spouse. Emotions should be understood instead in the context of our being towards others. Cf. Lawrence A. Blum, *Friendship, Altruism, and Morality* (London: Routledge & Kegan Paul, 1980).

121. Hume, *Treatise*, 3.2.7.8, 538.

122. "When we consider any objects at a distance, all their minute distinctions vanish, and we always give the preference to whatever is in itself preferable, without considering its situation and circumstances." Hume, *Treatise*, 3.2.7.5, 536.

123. "Such corrections are common with regard to all the senses; and indeed 'twere impossible we cou'd ever make use of language, or communicate our sentiments to one another, did we not correct the momentary appearances of things, and overlook our present situation." Hume, *Treatise*, 3.3.1.16, 582.

124. "[E]very particular person's pleasure and interest being different, 'tis impossible men cou'd ever agree in their sentiments and judgments, unless they chose some common point of view, from which they might survey their object, and which might cause it to appear the same to all of them." Hume, *Treatise*, 3.3.1.30, 591.

125. Disagreeing with the general system of valuation means you are no longer on the side of humanity: "these principles, we must remark, are social and universal: They form, in a manner, the *party* of humankind against vice or disorder, its common enemy." Hume, *Enquiries Concerning the Human Understanding and Concerning the Principles of Morals*, 9.9, 275.

126. Hume, *Treatise*, 3.2.7.6, 537.

127. Manfred Kuehn, *Kant: A Biography* (Cambridge: Cambridge University Press, 2001), 265.

128. Cf. Abraham Anderson, *Kant, Hume, and the Interruption of Dogmatic Slumber* (Oxford: Oxford University Press, 2020).

129. Kant introduces the concept of "value" into German. H. van Oyen, "Wertethik," in *Die Religion in Geschichte Und Gegenwart: Handwörterbuch Für Theologie Und Religionswissenschaft*, ed. Kurt Galling (Tübingen: J.C.B. Mohr (P. Siebeck), 1962), 1647. In the *Groundwork of the Metaphysics of Morals*, he distinguishes between two types of value: inner and outer. Outer value is the esteem that is contextualized and relative; Kant calls it "price." Inner value is the core of morality; Kant calls it "dignity" (*Würde*). Immanuel Kant, *Practical Philosophy*, ed. and trans. Mary J. Gregor, The Cambridge Edition of the Works of Immanuel Kant (Cambridge: Cambridge University Press, 1996), 84. AA 4, 434. Citations to Kant will be given in the English translation, followed by the Collected Works volume and page number. Dignity is value that is not dependent or changeable; it is unconditional, absolute, something for which everything could be sacrificed—as Kant puts it, a value that "could compensate us for the loss of everything that provides a worth to our condition." Kant, 97. AA 4, 450. It corresponds to the delight of an impartial spectator: "an impartial rational spectator can take no delight in seeing the uninterrupted prosperity of a being graced with no feature of a pure and good will, so that a good will seems to constitute the indispensable condition even of worthiness (*Würdigkeit*) to be happy." Kant, 49. AA 4, 393.

130. Kant writes that "the command, Obey authority! is also a moral one." Immanuel Kant, *Religion and Rational Theology*, ed. and trans. Allen W. Wood and George di Giovanni, The Cambridge Edition of the Works of Immanuel Kant (Cambridge: Cambridge University Press, 1996), 60. AA 6, 8. With the categorical imperative, Kant is trying to get at the core of morality independent of the vagaries of positive law, to the obedience which is not "demonstrated merely by attending to the law in a single state regulation while [remaining] blind to all others, but concomitantly, only through coherent respect for all regulations." Kant, 61. AA 6, 8.

131. Kant, *Practical Philosophy*, 101. AA 4, 454.

132. Kant, 97. AA 4, 449–50.

133. Kant, 101. AA 4, 454.

134. Cf. Jonathan Culp, "Justice, Happiness, and the Sensible Knave: Hume's Incomplete Defense of the Just Life," *The Review of Politics* 75, no. 2 (2013): 193–219.

135. The courts' decisions have less respect for the political process, and they look less to the text and intent of a political document but, instead, to "values" and moral principles. Cf. Ronald Dworkin, *Freedom's Law: The Moral Reading of the American Constitution* (New York: Oxford University Press, 1999); and Brian Bird, "The Charter of Rights and Freedoms—and Values?" *Policy Options*, November 2018, https://policyoptions.irpp.org/magazines/november-2018/the-charter-of-rights-and-freedoms-and-values/.

136. Hobbes, *Leviathan*, 30.19. CE 4, 540.

137. "Plenty dependeth (next to Gods favour) meerly on the labour and industry of men," and "a mans Labour also, is a commodity exchangeable for benefit, as well as any other thing." Hobbes, *Leviathan*, 24.3, 4. CE 4, 386.

138. William Petty, *The Economic Writings of Sir William Petty, Volume 1.* (Cambridge: Cambridge University Press, 1662), 98.

139. John Locke, *Two Treatises of Government*, ed. Peter Laslett (Cambridge: Cambridge University Press, 1988), 288.

140. Adam Smith, *An Inquiry into the Nature and Causes of the Wealth of Nations*, ed. Kathryn Sutherland (Oxford: Oxford University Press, 1993), 36.

141. David Ricardo, *On the Principles of Political Economy and Taxation* (London: John Murray, 1821).

142. Property arises from manual labor "because one cannot see what man can add, other than his own labor, in order to appropriate things he has not made." Rousseau, *Discourse on the Origins of Inequality*, 3:50, 3:173.

143. Cf. Arendt, *The Human Condition*, 79–174.

144. "But since Gold and Silver, being little useful to the Life of Man in proportion to Food, Rayment, and Carriage, has its *value* only from the consent of Men, whereof Labour yet makes, in great part, *the measure*, it is plain, that Men have agreed to disproportionate and unequal Possession of the Earth, they having by a tacit and voluntary consent found out a way, how a man may fairly possess more land than he himself can use the product of, by receiving in exchange of the overplus, Gold and Silver, which may be hoarded up without injury to any one, these metals not spoileing or decaying in the hands of the possessor." John Locke, *Two Treatises of Government*, ed. Peter Laslett (Cambridge: Cambridge University Press, 1988), 301–2.

145. "In civilized society," writes Adam Smith, a man "stands at all times in need of the co-operation and assistance of great multitudes, while his whole life is scarce sufficient to gain the friendship of a few persons." He continues, "But man has almost constant occasion for the help of his brethren, and it is in vain for him to expect it from their benevolence only. . . . It is not from the benevolence of the butcher, the brewer, or the baker, that we expect our dinner, but from their regard to their own interest." Adam Smith, *The Wealth of Nations*, 22.

146. During the period in which Marx was writing *Das Kapital*, the average working week in Germany was seventy-five hours, and prior to the 1844 Factory Act, the normal working day in Britain was twelve hours a day. Ha-Joon Chang, *Kicking Away the Ladder: Development Strategy in Historical Perspective* (London: Anthem Press, 2003), 109.

147. Jane Humphries, *Childhood and Child Labour in the British Industrial Revolution* (Cambridge: Cambridge University Press, 2010), 7–11, 252.

148. Alfred F. Havighurst, *Britain in Transition: The Twentieth Century* (Chicago: University of Chicago Press, 1985), 13.

149. Alessandro Roncaglia, *The Wealth of Ideas: A History of Economic Thought* (Cambridge: Cambridge University Press, 2005), 162.

150. Alessandro Roncaglia, *The Wealth of Ideas*, 161–62.

151. Spencer coined the term "survival of the fittest" in a conversation with Charles Darwin. Mark Francis, *Herbert Spencer and the Invention of Modern Life* (Ithaca, New York: Cornell University Press, 2007), 3. Social Darwinism "served to both justify amoral business practices and confer social status on the upwardly mobile. . . . By the 1870s, social Darwinism was the hegemonic social philosophy within the

United States." Robert E. Weir, *Workers in America: A Historical Encyclopedia*, vol. 2 (Santa Barbara, California: ABC-CLIO, 2013), 709.

152. Karl Marx. *Capital, Vol. 1*, in *Marx and Engels Collected Works,* vol. 35, trans. Samuel Moore and Edward Aveling (New York: International Publishers, 1996), 8. Marx's analysis has baffled many commentators as well. For example, see, Leszek Kolakowski, *Main Currents of Marxism: The Founders, the Golden Age, the Breakdown* (New York: W. W. Norton and Company, 2005), 271–72.

153. Locke, *Two Treatises of Government*, 284.

154. Rousseau, *Discourse on the Origins of Inequality*, 3:59, 3:184.

155. Karl Marx, *Value, Price, and Profit, in Collected Works, vol. 20, Marx and Engels: 1864–1868* (New York: International Publishers, 1985), 157–58.

156. Locke, *Two Treatises of Government*, 289.

157. Locke, 284.

158. Isaak Illich Rubin, *Essays on Marx's Theory of Value*, trans. Miloš Samardžija and Fredy Perlman (Detroit: Black & Red, 1972), 68. Italics removed. Rubin notes that irreproducible objects, like great works of art, are not covered in Marx's theory of value, since they cannot be copied by labor. Rubin, 166n15.

159. Karl Marx, *Marginal Notes on the Programme of the German Workers' Party, in Collected Works, vol. 24, Marx and Engels: 1874-1873*, (New York: International Publishers, 1989), 114.

160. Marx, *Marginal Notes on the Programme of the German Workers' Party*, 115.

Chapter 5

The Concept of "Value"

"Everybody uses the word 'values' to describe our making of the world," writes George Grant in 1969. "The word comes to us so platitudinously that we take it to belong to the way things are. It is forgotten that before Nietzsche and his immediate predecessors, men did not think about their actions in that language. They did not think they made the world valuable, but that they participated in its goodness."[1]

In this final chapter, we will look at the creation of "value" as a philosophical theme. This occurred in the nineteenth century in Germany with Nietzsche's immediate predecessors and successors, including above all Hermann Lotze (1817–1881), who invented the philosophical concept of "value"; his influential predecessor Johann Friedrich Herbart (1776–1841); and his epigones: Wilhelm Windelband (1848–1915), Windelband's student Heinrich Rickert (1863–1936), and Rickert's friend and colleague, the great Max Weber (1864–1920), who borrowed heavily from him. We shall show how the tradition of value philosophy was created and developed by these five thinkers. While the idea of value becomes philosophically thematic in the nineteenth century, it is nothing new, but rather an adumbration of the tradition of modern political thought reaching back to Martin Luther.

THE CREATORS OF "VALUE": HERBART, LOTZE, WINDELBAND, RICKERT, AND WEBER

Johann Friedrich Herbart (1776–1841) is known today for his pedagogy and is considered a founding father of the science of education. The "Herbartian" school of thought was popular at the turn of the nineteenth century and spread to many countries, while exercising particular influence in his native Germany and the United States. The generation of German professors after Herbart had to train future teachers in psychology and pedagogy, and to do this, they turned to Herbart's theories, as he had grounded both of these disciplines as sciences.[2]

Herbart's career paralleled G.F.W. Hegel's. He studied in Jena before Hegel went there as a *Privatdozent*. The Kantian Johan Gottlieb Fichte (1762–1814) was still teaching in Jena, and Herbart was his best student. But Herbart became dissatisfied with Fichte's idealism, which pitted the empirical against the transcendental and came down decisively in favor of the latter. Fichte aimed to build a system of all science, or *Wissenschaftslehre*; Herbart, by contrast, acknowledged the aspiration towards systematic unity but held that, as Frederick Beiser explains, "[T]here is one basic dualism that no system will ever surmount: that between norm and fact, between practice and theory. There is no 'principle of unification' for such distinct kinds of discourse."[3] Herbart is a key figure anticipating Neo-Kantianism, which became the preeminent force in German philosophy during the German Empire.[4] The relevant text for our purposes is his 1808 book, *Allgemeine praktische Philosophie*, where Herbart grounds ethics in aesthetics.[5] There Herbart places the standard of morality in the emotions and held that there is a plurality of moral ideas which serve as models for our desires. Herbart used value language without making it a theme, and it was left to Lotze to work out this final step.[6] Notably, Herbart also laid the groundwork for the concept of "culture."[7]

It was into a strongly Herbartian milieu that Hermann Lotze (1817–1881) entered when he matriculated at the University of Leipzig.[8] He studied Herbart intensely after graduating with a medical degree and preparing for an academic career in his home town of Zittau. Ultimately, Lotze became the successor to Herbart in 1844 at Göttingen, where he ended up teaching for over thirty-five years. Lotze denied he was influenced by Herbart. Nevertheless, he did develop his thought in Herbart's ambit and saw him as major antagonist.[9] And as we shall see, Herbart's separation of the normative and natural and his placement of ethics into aesthetics is a major component of Lotze's concept of value. Lotze was preoccupied by ethics from the very beginning of his career; his first major book was the 1841 *Metaphysik*, in which he turns to ethics as the only escape from nihilism, while in his second major book, the 1843 *Logik*, he argues that the basis of logic lies in ethics. Lotze wanted to keep morality objective, referring to something outside of our own desires.[10] He ultimately offered "values" as a way to do this without resorting to absolutism.[11]

Lotze was a hugely influential figure. First of all, like Herbart, Lotze was also an important precursor to neo-Kantianism.[12] He taught Otto Liebmann (1840–1912), whose book on Kant gave rise to the movement of Neo-Kantianism, but his most important student was Wilhelm Windelband (1848–1915), who was the father of one of the major schools of neo-Kantianism, the Southwest school (also known as the Baden school or value-theoretical school). In 1911 Windelband paid tribute to Lotze as the greatest thinker of German philosophy in the period after Hegel, whose fundamental thoughts were assimilated and transformed in the development of neo-Kantianism.[13]

Important American philosophers studied under Lotze and brought his thought back to the United States, including Josiah Royce (1855–1916) and Borden Parker Bowne (1847–1910). One of the most important thinkers America has ever produced, William James (1842–1910), studied Lotze's work intently and named him in the preface of his masterpiece, *The Principles of Psychology*, as one of the handful of thinkers who had inspired him.[14] British philosophers were also influenced by Lotze, including political theorist Bernard Bosanquet (1848–1923), and some of them had studied with Lotze, including James Ward (1843–1925) and John Cook Wilson (1849–1915). A historian of philosophy, writing in 1938, noted that Lotze's "striking success in England was due to the far greater ease with which his writings could be read and digested as compared with the impenetrability of Hegel and the sluggishness of Kant."[15]

The school of Franz Brentano (1838–1917) was greatly influenced by Lotze, as were two important figures in life philosophy: Rudolf Eucken (1846–1926), who studied with Lotze, and Wilhelm Dilthey (1833–1911), who read Lotze's book *Microcosmus* when he was twenty-five and was greatly impressed by it. [16]

But even beyond all this, Lotze was the "grandfather" of both the dominant philosophical traditions in the twentieth century to today: analytic philosophy and phenomenology.

Phenomenology was founded by Edmund Husserl (1859–1938), and Lotze had taught and mentored Husserl's teacher Carl Stumpf (1848–1937). Husserl called Lotze "one of the greatest German philosophers since Kant."[17] In the founding text of phenomenology, the *Logical Investigations*, Husserl speaks of Lotze's "decisive influence" on him, and he wrote an extensive manuscript on Lotze that he had originally intended to append to that work.[18] Lotze was also in the background for the development of analytic philosophy as well, as he "was one of the most influential of German philosophers in England in the later nineteen century."[19] Gottlob Frege (1848–1925), one of the fathers of analytic philosophy (and the thinker who introduced the term *truth-value* into logic), studied under Lotze and, by some accounts, was strongly influenced by him.[20] Two other founding figures of that tradition, G. E. Moore (1873–1958) and Bertrand Russell (1872–1970), both studied under James Ward (1843–1925), who himself was a student of Lotze and had a deep respect for him. Ward held a chair at the University of Cambridge; he was succeeded in this position first by Moore in 1925, and then by Ludwig Wittgenstein (1889–1951) in 1939, another founder of the analytic tradition.

But by the 1930s, things had drastically changed. Lotze was ignored and his historical importance underestimated.[21] Wittgenstein described Lotze to a student as "probably a man who shouldn't have been allowed to write philosophy."[22]

Lotze did not start a school of his own, with disciples carrying on and developing his legacy. Part of the reason Lotze was forgotten lies in the fact that he could not be claimed by either of the schools that dominated philosophy in the twentieth century.[23] But deeper than this is the reality that he *won*. It was Lotze's wider vision and way of posing the questions that seduced even those who rejected his answers.[24] And his singular achievement was the creation of the philosophical concept of value. "Neither Plato, nor Kant, nor Rickert invented the notion of values in the requisite sense," writes Manfred Kühn, "that honor goes to Rudolf Hermann Lotze."[25] In the decades following his death, Lotze struggled to be acknowledged for this, however. For example, the Danish philosopher Harald Høffding (1843–1931), who wrote on the concept of value and coined the phrase "the problem of values," gave no credit to him.[26] But certainly as time went on, the concept was so thoroughly assimilated and absorbed by everyone—from the neo-Kantians, to the phenomenologists, to the life philosophers and the analytic philosophers—that it became the conventional wisdom. And since no serious thinker reads philosophy to be informed of conventional wisdom—that's what journalism is for—the point of reading Lotze was lost, and he fell into the obscurity of obviousness.

Lotze's was a particular kind of achievement, the opening of a tradition rather than a dogmatic solution. It was a task, a way of speaking and of framing the problem, which Lotze introduced, most prominently in his magnum opus *Microcosmus*, a three-volume work published in 1856, 1858, and 1864. One of the most widely read books of philosophy of its day, going through edition after edition in Germany, it was immediately translated into French and Russian and then into English by 1887. There Lotze did not solve the problem of value, but rather he introduced it as a way to address a different problem: the problem of morality not being absolute, but without resorting to skepticism. As we shall see, values allow us a measured skepticism, and by speaking of them, we can have meaningful (if ultimately pointless) ivory-tower discussions about morality. But the contradictions of the concept create their own problems. As Thomas Willey writes, Lotze "wanted a value theory derived from individual moral experience but sanctioned by a universal and transcendent moral ideal."[27] This is the *problem of value*—attempting to get to something objective and universal from a particular, subjective feeling.

It was left to others to work on this problem. And the great thinkers of Southwest German Neo-Kantianism, Wilhelm Windelband (1848–1915) and Heinrich Rickert (1863–1936), took up the challenge. Together, both of these thinkers formed the core of the Baden school of Neo-Kantianism. "If any single enterprise typifies Baden philosophy," writes Thomas Willey, "it is the theory of value"[28]—and indeed, another name for the tradition was the value-theoretical school.

Windelband studied under Lotze and followed his approach in writing his doctoral dissertation, which Lotze directed.[29] He taught from 1903 until his death in 1915 at Heidelberg, which became the center of the Baden school. Windelband was an ambitious historian of philosophy and wrote handbooks that covered its entire history, with an approach that was not just "a post-factum narration," as Paul Ziche writes, but rather as something that "becomes inseparable from philosophy itself."[30] The important text, for our purposes, is his collection of essays and lectures, *Präludien* (Preludes), where Windelband lays out his basic philosophical positions.

The successor to Windelband's chair in Heidelberg was Heinrich Rickert. Windelband had had a profound impact on Rickert's intellectual development. Rickert was repelled by positivism while a student at the University of Berlin and, afterwards, by the materialist interpretation of history in Marxism that he read in Zürich, but it was only when studying under Windelband that he found an alternative to positivism. Rickert wrote his dissertation in 1888 under Windelband at Strassburg, and the rest of Rickert's career was dedicated to developing the concept of value he got from Windelband.[31] "Rickert, it could be said, built his career on the modest outline presented by Windelband in his 1894 lecture,"[32] writes Thomas Willey, referring to Windelband's best-known text, his rectorial address at Strassburg, "History and Natural Science." Rickert's magnum opus was a long, rambling tome entitled *The Limits of Concept Formation in Natural Science*, published in 1902 and revised in five editions up until 1929.

Rickert heavily influenced Max Weber (1864–1920), the greatest social scientist of the twentieth century.[33] Weber's influence was enormous, far-reaching, and profound: he is the founder of sociology and his works have been read uninterruptedly since they appeared, while retaining their vitality. "Of all the nineteenth and twentieth century theories which most persistently animate discussion and social research, none will survive so much intact as Weber's—not those of Freud, Marx, Jung, Piaget, nor anyone else."[34] Part of this staying power and contemporary appeal is the aura of a *scientific* study of society. "Max Weber is the only non-metaphysical social scientist of modern times (except Montesquieu)," writes Daniel Rossides, because Weber is "the only one to develop a genuinely scientific social science."[35] And the reason for that is the concept of value, which Weber took wholesale from Rickert, without alteration. Rickert was Weber's colleague at Heidelberg, their families became friends, and after reading *The Limits of Concept Formation in*

Natural Science, Weber told his wife he found it very good and was in fundamental agreement with it.[36]

THE NATURE OF "VALUE"

Throughout this work, we have tried to contrast the concept of value with that of a relationship. A value is a private good; a relationship is a public good. Just because two or more people share a value does not make it less of a private good. A relationship is a public good because it involves people who participate in it but do not control it; the nature of a relationship is not totally dependent upon the interpretation or desire of one individual. A relationship is a reality, not a desire, for those who participate in it and for those who encounter it. Healthy relationships are a common good—they benefit not only those directly participating in them but also those at other degrees of separation. The common good itself, we have argued, must be defined in terms of the bond of loyalty within any social group. Other fringe benefits follow upon a healthy civic friendship (in the case of the nation state, for instance), but primacy of place must always be given to the relationship shared by participants in a social whole. The effects of that relationship can be seen in good laws, social programs, and flourishing institutions, but the innermost substance of the common good is not to be found in those things but in the social loyalty and friendship that makes all of them possible. We can cooperate to fulfill our needs only when we care about each other's needs because of the relationship in which we mutually share.

By contrast, values are private goods, as the tradition of value philosophy confirms. Values in that tradition are a matter of individual human beings having unmediated access to and choosing voluntaristically between incommensurable units of non-neutral significance that stem from mimetic desire.

The concept is but a recapitulation of the modern tradition of thought going back to Martin Luther, and indeed, it follows closely Luther's revolution in thought. As we have seen, Luther's doctrine of the priesthood of all believers makes the individual the locus of access to truth. The meaning of the Bible must be clear, therefore; otherwise, a certain type of community would be necessary to understand deeper truths.[37] For Luther, the individual possesses faith and knows that he possesses it. Faith is immediacy, not trust, and therefore cannot be a participation in a personal relationship. It is certainty; the opposite of this type of "faith" is not mistrust but intellectual doubt. A "religious faith" is therefore something we know religiously, a certainty of content known immediately, not a personal relationship in which there is a lot we do not know and therefore requires trust in another person. Religious certainty is partial, as it does not tell us everything we need to know about what to do. That only means that everything else is insignificant, however. We do not need others for salvation; our fundamental relation to each other is one of indifference. For Luther, everything outside of salvation is the realm of neutral indifference; fact and value are separated, we might say. Finally, the realm of value is mimetic; the aim is not to become a just person, but rather to gain God's esteem, and there is nothing more mimetic than aiming for esteem.

The value philosophers likewise think we have an *immediate access* to value. The opening sentence of Herbart's section of aesthetics in his introduction to philosophy textbook runs, "The beautiful and the ugly, especially the praiseworthy and the disgraceful, possess a primary evidence, by virtue of which they are clear, without being learned or proven."[38] We cannot prove on theoretical grounds what must be liked or disliked.[39] For Lotze, we as individuals find things in the world that we approve of and that are good. Similar things form a similar class of goodness, and we can abstract from these individual instances to get the "invariable condition in virtue of which any content is good."[40] That is the value of the thing, which is inherent in all willing and all desire.[41] For Lotze, values are what are experienced by an individual; if we sacrifice for someone else, for example, we cannot say that that sacrifice is good unless that person experiences the value: the sacrifice must be "transformed into enjoyment."[42] For Windelband, philosophy itself is a normative science of value, and he is very clear that absolute value is not determined by the power of the majority.[43] Rather, it is our individual reflection that shows us with direct evidence the basis for general moral judgment, overcoming what we see in society—namely, a proliferation of opinions concerning morality.[44] For Rickert and Weber, individuals make valuations, while social science only registers these valuations and makes no judgment on their correctness.[45]

Secondly, for the value thinkers, value is *separate from fact*. For Herbart, the feeling of value arises when we consider the proportions between desires. These propositions can be judged according to an aesthetic standard, which stands over and above the realm of reality. He makes it clear that the aesthetic realm of proportions between desires does not refer to reality, that is, it is not an actual person with concrete desires that are the objects of our aesthetic judgment, but rather the connection of desires that anyone could have, a connection in the subjunctive mood, an abstract conception.[46] Additionally, the desires are in themselves complete and unable to be assessed; it is rather the proportions between them that form a picture that appeals to our sense of beauty. When we are presented with a picture of willingness, the form desires take when put together can be beautiful, like a piece of music that connects singular notes. The desires themselves, for Herbart, are neutral, bare facts, which do not repel or attract.[47] This is very important, and any value thinker thereafter who wants to prove the reality of value always refers to the idea of a neutral, bare fact as a necessary contrast to bring the idea of value into a kind of intuitive obviousness. We have seen in chapter 3, however, that the idea of a neutral fact is itself constructed by modern thought.

Matthias Heesch points out that this dualism in Herbart is latent and not reflected upon: on the one hand, Herbart offers a science of psychology and pedagogy that can be made into a system of equations and rules, but on the other hand, these get their orientation by being connected to values (and though Herbart does not yet call them that, Heesch is not wrong to give them this name), which themselves cannot be grounded. Herbart is insouciant concerning this separation. It has serious consequences nevertheless; Herbart is not just saying that reality appears divided because of our limited abilities to know, but rather that *reality itself is divided*.[48]

The cleaving of reality into separate spheres continues with Lotze, who ends up with three categories in *Microcosmus*: empirical facts we know from experience, truths that are eternally valid, and values that we feel.[49] The concept of empirical fact is familiar to us. Truths, Lotze now claims, are *valid*. Things have being, events happen, relations hold, but propositions have validity.[50]

Can we find valid values? It is not certain that we can, and Lotze does not definitely solve this problem, offering only a language and a puzzle.[51] Yet this is why his influence is so long lasting: instead of a dogmatic answer offering us a Hobson's choice, he gives us a task for investigation, which the different thinkers and traditions of late modernity pursue in different ways.

Windelband follows in Lotze's footsteps in contrasting value with neutral existence. Philosophy for him is the science of values, while natural science is a value-free worldview. The highest task of philosophy is to put these two realms together.[52] Rickert and Weber assume that values are of non-neutral significance and that the social task is to develop culturally valid values. For Rickert, the social scientist treats values *as factual*. That is to say, values are relevant to a certain historical and social configuration. That such and such a group of people hold such and such values is objectively true, and this is the kind of truth social science can reach. Seeing the value relevance of things in a cultural milieu is different from giving one's assent to them; there are positive valuations, negative valuations, and then there is "the purely theoretical *value relation* that is completely independent of this alternative."[53] As Beiser writes, "Rickert's foremost concern was to defend the autonomy and integrity of theoretical reason from interference from all practical values."[54] Max Weber famously agreed.[55]

Thirdly, the phenomena of values originate from *mimetic desire*. Herbart lays the groundwork here by seeing abstract value as the goal of moral action, rather than concrete acting with unique people. For him, the previous attempts of moralists to tell us what to do give us a moral philosophy that "always only reaches will, but not the *value* (*Würde*) of the will."[56] Herbart does not want to determine the will, that is, tell us what the "moral" choice would be in any given situation. Rather, for him, moral philosophy presents pictures of willingness that are apart from any actual concrete choices. The value does not determine our actions, but rather attracts us through its "moral beauty." Herbart begins *Allgemeine practische Philosophie* by referring to the classic mimetic goal, the opinions of others: practical philosophy has to do with general judgments of praise and blame.[57]

Lotze has a strong awareness of mimeticism, speaking of "our unconquerable impulse towards imitation"[58] and writing how, "even before the encounter of individuals who have conflicting claims to the same object, each one compares and measures himself with others."[59] This measuring and comparing is essential to our willing and desiring: "it is incomprehensible," Lotze writes, "[T]hat any person should aim at being the only one of his kind who has ever existed. . . . Any wholly unique superiority, however great it may be, is unintelligible; hence it is natural that self-regard should always seek association with a class to which many belong, and that which is anywhere regarded as supreme has always begun by being susceptible of comparison."[60] There is no personal uniqueness in our willing and desiring that would be beyond comparison. If there was, we could not understand it. Everything that exists is comparable. This is necessary in order that "there can be one universal truth, valid throughout the world."[61] "While our judgment tells us what is true or false for all," as one commentator summarizes Lotze's position, "so our feelings of pleasure and pain tell us what is of value for all."[62] While Lotze says a thing may have a "value of its own,"[63] we cannot assume "that anything whatever can have a content absolutely unconditioned or unique; at most it could only be the sole actual example of one content which, whether simple or compound, may be thought as a universal occurring in various examples."[64] For Lotze, knowledge as getting to know something must be made compatible with categorical knowledge.[65] When we experience something as good, we have to move past the idiosyncrasies of the context, including the people involved, in order to get at the value. Only something that could become an object of mimetic striving—something repeatable—can be a value.

For us, by contrast, it is the uniqueness of our desire that makes it non-mimetic, one that is not a matter of copying the desires of others. Also, we cannot get to know other people through general knowledge. "It is not enough to *know about* concrete beings; we have to experience them in their concreteness, if we are ever to gain a real apprehension of the propositions expressing them."[66] No matter how many general descriptors you tick off, actual knowledge of a person only comes when you hear something about them in particular, like something they did, an anecdote.[67] When we know our neighbor's story, we cannot help but be on his side to some degree.[68]

The idea of a unique, individual human personality at the root of freedom is explicitly considered—and rejected—by Windelband. He knows that such an idea is incompatible with his system, since putting personal uniqueness at the core of freedom would be to deny ultimate importance to the concept of validity. For Windelband, a unique individual essence is incompatible with the unity of the world, by which he means that it raises all sorts of questions—how choice can be made intelligible, why some people choose good and others evil, theodicy—that theory cannot answer. We can only accept the experience of freedom as a psychological fact, but we cannot think of it as a reality of persons that is deeper than desire.[69] Desire is the intelligible thing for Windelband.[70]

Rickert follows Windelband in understanding human community in terms of "general values."[71] We can place Rickert's contention, "Values as such are never real. On the contrary, they hold validly,"[72] in the light of our contention that mimetic conflict is not about a concrete object of desire, but rather about nothing. Perhaps most revealing for Rickert's understanding of value is the famous contention made by him and his colleague Max Weber—that science must be *value neutral*. If values are positive goods, and not fraught objects of mimetic desire, there would seemingly be no reason to bracket them. Nevertheless, for Rickert and Weber, to be scientific, the social sciences must abstain from value judgments. There has to be some way to distinguish academic work from partisan propaganda. There, of course, is a valuation that answers the question why we would be interested in a particular topic as a matter of study in the first place; nevertheless, it must be distinguished from the way in which the investigation is conducted, which holds judgments of value.[73] Value freedom becomes a popular dogma after Max Weber's championing of the notion. Weber's thoughts on values are presented in a handful of famous essays on social science methodology, the first of which was the 1904 essay "Objectivity in Social Science and Social Policy," as well as his "Vocation" essays—"Science as a Vocation" and "Politics as a Vocation," both published in 1919—which present a vision of a clash of irreconcilable worldviews. These texts have proved extraordinarily influential and have set the tone for most of the debate over valuations in science and knowledge.[74]

The doctrine of value neutrality is attractive precisely because values correspond to mimetic desires, and science must understandably distance itself from them in order to be scientific. Yet the unintended consequence is that values language leaves us unable to rationally discuss that which is most important to us. To discuss fundamental values is to descend into irrationality.[75]

Finally, then, the theorists of value fail to escape the Böckenförde dilemma, that values are plural and the choice between them cannot be rationally grounded. Already, for Herbart, ethics forms a part of aesthetics, as morality becomes a private matter of taste.[76] For Lotze, we experience values in the plural, and absolute value is not in the cards.[77] The world is split up into three realms of being: empirical facts we know from experience, truths that are eternally valid, and values that we feel. A viewpoint which would see the whole in its total unity, the grasping of absolute value from which everything could be explained, is out of reach.[78] Lotze does think that all the different aspects of the world could be explained by one principle, and he offers in this chapter a statement of his "philosophic faith" that the principle is divine benevolence, the living love of God; however, this principle cannot be present to our finite minds.[79] Windelband follows Lotze in making value plural. There are three separate realms of validity for him as well: logic, ethics, and aesthetics, corresponding to the values of the true, the good, and the beautiful. For Windelband, however, we *must* have absolute value. For him, Lotze's philosophic faith is a pressing question because of the specter of "relativism." As Katherina Kinzel shows, Windelband *discovered* the problem of relativism, which had not been an issue previously.[80] Relativism is only a problem when we take values too seriously; the problem of relativism arises on the heels of Lotze inventing value as a philosophical concept.

Windelband solves this new problem by claiming that we do have an absolute measure. However, the consciousness of norms (*Normalbewußtsein*) is only partially accessible to us.[81] "It is true that the interconnexions whose validity, we are certain, reaches beyond our human nature, imply the postulate of a last unifying interconnexion of all reality. But this whole is closed to our knowledge: we shall never know more than a few fragments of it, and there is no prospect of our ever being able to patch it together out of the scraps that we can gather."[82] Windelband claims that reaching the determining norm of value does not require a picture of the totality of the real.[83] The concept of value, then, is the ersatz shorthand by which we make do, given the failure of science.[84] No single system can explain all values, which must then remain pluralistic. Windelband's own corpus mirrors this inherently unsystematic nature of inquiry into values: "Windelband never came close to a system of his own," writes Beiser. "His chief philosophical legacy is fragmentary."[85]

Nevertheless, the point of philosophy for Windelband remains the search for valid values. Klaus Christian Köhnke concludes that Windelband marks a watershed in neo-Kantianism, moving it from a critical philosophy to a positive philosophy searching for absolutely valid values, a denial of which is rejected as "relativistic."[86] For Köhnke, this insistence on absolute validity "constituted a leap into *irrationality*," since, for Windelband, "in logic, ethics and aesthetics there were absolutely valid—but undemonstrable—norms whose universal validity was not a factual but an 'ideal' one: 'one which is not actual but ought to be,'" which Köhnke aptly labels Windelband's "apologia for the *status quo*."[87] The values that a critical mass of people in fact hold—the cultural or mimetic basis of a society—are valid from their perspective, and we have to remain *within that perspective* if fact and value are going to remain separated, as they ought to be. This is the "normal" perspective.

Rickert's philosophy begins where Windelband's ends. In *The Limits of Concept Formation in Natural Science*, originally published in 1902, Rickert investigates how historical knowledge is possible. Knowledge for Rickert comes when we have a *concept* to represent reality. In the whole gigantic mess of social facts—a kind of chaotic state of nature—we can isolate some aspects with a concept. When we do this, we can have knowledge. However, the question is how concepts are formed and justified. Key to Rickert's answer is the concept of *Wertbeziehung*, of value relation: various aspects of society are related to different values, and this allows us to conceptualize them. Historical actors have made commitments to certain values and by defining them in relation to those values, we have the concepts we need for knowledge.[88] Note that the historian or social scientist himself is writing an "objective" account. The values of the researcher do not come into play, only the values of the social actors being studied; the value relation (*Wertbeziehung*) is different from a value *judgment*. For Rickert, value judgments are irrational and conflicts between them cannot be solved. "Despite his Kantian pretensions, Rickert did not believe in the powers of *practical* reason. He insisted that reason has no jurisdiction over the spheres of aesthetics, morality and religion."[89] According to him, social science and history can have knowledge that is as rigorously objective as natural science by abstaining from value judgments and sticking only to the value relations at stake.[90]

If value judgments are ultimately irrational, however, it would be tempting to conclude that the only thing that matters would be the efficient production that would serve the de facto valuations of individual human beings. Positive science would show the way towards both the technological domination of nature in the natural sciences and the expansion of power in sociopolitical life in the social sciences. Any sense of meaning or purpose to this whole enterprise, to persons in their inner being, to humanity itself, would only be an obstacle to the expansion of the appetite for the domination of nature and other human beings, something to be pushed aside as a fictitious relic of an earlier era. Rickert himself wanted to avoid such a grim conclusion. As Frederick Beiser writes,

> All his life, whether as a young man or an old sage, Rickert was deeply troubled by historicism. He feared that it would lead to relativism, undermining the claims of philosophy to provide universal and necessary truth. If historicism

> were true, each philosophy would be only the self-awareness of its own age, an epitome of the beliefs and values of a specific culture. But the ultimate result of historicism, Rickert warned, is nothing less than nihilism, loss of belief in any ultimate values.[91]

It was listening to Windelband's lectures on the history of philosophy that cured him of his relativism and skepticism.

Rickert gives an answer to this dilemma in *The Limits of Concept Formation*. He senses that his value theory leads to relativism, for if every society is to be understood on its own terms according to the values that it finds important, whatever standard you apply would only be "the standard of such-and-such a society," with no objectivity possible. Rickert's solution to this problem is to say that there must be absolute values, while simultaneously refusing to tell us *which* values are absolute: "[A]s the sole metaempirical factor in empirical history," he writes, "we can also stop with the purely formal presupposition that some values or other are absolutely valid."[92] Beiser writes how "Rickert himself realized that his system could not provide much of a field guide to questions of practice." Beiser continues,

> At the close of "Vom System der Werte" he concedes that the purely formal principles of his system will not suffice to decide which values are central or most important. In the end, he admits that philosophy cannot do more than sketch the alternative worldviews, leaving it for the individual to decide for himself. And with that, Rickert threw in the towel to the voluntarist whom he so loved to hate.[93]

This is not such a bad strategy, all things considered. It is the same as Locke not telling us the content of true morality. As soon as Rickert, or anyone, starts explaining *which* values should be considered absolute and ranks all others, it instantly becomes more or less clear that we are dealing merely with the social prejudices of the age. "One era's unquestioned good is another's certain evil."[94] The unquestioned prejudices of unreflective common opinion can function as a kind of absolute value, viz. a taboo, the violation of which means expulsion from the group. Sacred cows change: progress and democracy give way to multiculturalism and tolerance, which gives way to diversity, inclusion, and equity. This problem is particularly acute for transcendental theory, which, as we have seen, is a matter of mutually exclusive systems, and change involves replacing one of them with another. Modern political thought sees itself as "the overcoming of the dark past of prejudice and unreason—a past that is itself always in motion, so that the night of unreason may well suddenly come to mean what everyone believed last year."[95]

Rickert keeps a wise silence on the content of absolute value, lest he expose and dramatically shorten the shelf life of his theory. That theory does explain very well, however, how the Whig historian and the positivist social scientist in fact operate—their pretension to objectivity is rock solid as long as everyone unquestioningly accepts their valuations. The depressing observation that the passage of time always destroys this "objectivity," relegating their texts to a dusty used-bookstore markdown shelf, is countered with nothing but the formal possibility and hope that someday the absolute values will be found. But this is no argument; it is rather a *cri de cœur*: "Relativism *can't* be correct! Therefore . . . "

Max Weber infused this depressing cul-de-sac with tragic, noble pathos in a famous and telling passage in his essay "Science as a Vocation." "'Scientific' pleading is meaningless in principle," Weber says, "because the various value spheres of the world stand in irreconcilable conflict with each other. The elder Mill, whose philosophy I will not praise otherwise, was on this point right when he said: If one proceeds from pure experience, one arrives at polytheism."[96]

We pause here to note that, since the 1960s, the phrase "sacred values" has been more prevalent in English than "virtuous citizens."[97] It is arresting to consider that the "polytheism" we face is perhaps more than a metaphor. We have seen that the defining principle of modern political thought is the *sacred* nature of sovereignty, that is, an abstract and exclusive loyalty that is proved through the sacrifice of other loyalties. Thus, we can recognize the incongruence of Weber having just finished his claim that science has disenchanted the world, yet turning around and writing: "We live as did the ancients when their world was not yet disenchanted of its gods and demons, only we live in a different sense." He continues:

> As Hellenic man at times sacrificed to Aphrodite and at other times to Apollo, and, above all, as everybody sacrificed to the gods of his city, so do we still nowadays, only the bearing of man has been disenchanted and denuded of its mystical but inwardly genuine plasticity. Fate, and certainly not 'science,' holds sway over these gods and their struggles.[98]

Concerning ultimate things, science can only be quiet; they are a matter for personal, private—and voluntaristic—decision. The "ultimately possible attitudes toward life are irreconcilable, and hence their struggle can never be brought to a final conclusion. Thus it is necessary to make a decisive choice."[99] The individual must choose his religion—an idea fundamentally incompatible with Christianity, since scripture is not philosophy, and it tells of God's search for man, not man's search for God.

The ancients believed in the gods of their society; we moderns believe in "values."[100] Both form convenient explanations for social problems and the structures of domination, convenient because they divert attention away from how we actually treat others within our web of personal relationships. By a show of fealty to the gods/values of the state, one's behavior can evade scrutiny; those who occupy the high ground of correct cultic belief are not to blame when bad consequences result from their actions and decisions. Instead of looking concretely at how our mimeticism affects our relationships, especially with those we encounter who are vulnerable and marginal, we can focus on impersonal values, which are inevitably a set of beliefs that flatters those in power, since the social climbers are the most assiduous in following a society's political correctness, its sacred values: "The more one is concerned with social respectability and prestige, the more one will adjust, consciously and unconsciously, one's talk and thinking to harmonise with that of one's dominant neighbours (in the social plural), and the less one will listen for the voice or the cry of one's neighbour (in the biblical singular)."[101]

As we have seen, the popular narrative of secularization is but our conformity to Luther's vision of Christianity's relationship to the world. For Luther, churches ought not to exist except as religious sects, and the violence of the ruling power/authority is always justified. It is only if we accept these premises that we can believe in "secularization." If we were actually secular, we would never believe that the political authority is sacred. Insofar as the political thought of the past five hundred years of western history has a different assumption, we should consider it a reversion back to myth—just-so stories of the state of nature and social contracts, of the labor theory of value and the polytheism of values—fictions that are not only unscientific but harmful insofar as they blind us to what matters for our network of human relationships, the everyday reality right in front of us. Hobbes devoted half of *Leviathan* to arguing that the sovereign is also the high priest of the state, determining the true religion. For him, the distinction between the secular and the sacred does not make sense. "Men cannot serve two masters," he writes. "For this distinction of Temporall, and Spirituall Power is but words."[102]

CONCLUSION

The concept of value is attractive to us moderns. As with faith for Luther, it provides us absolute immediacy and certainty. We do not need others to know the good and, therefore, we can have autonomy. I have all I need in my own consciousness of value. "What is good-in-itself is some felt bliss,"[103] writes Lotze. We learn "by immediate feeling the presence of worth and of unworth."[104]

The problem lies with the obverse of this immediacy: values are plural, and other people disagree. Like the proliferation of Protestant sects, one's adherence to a value inevitably meets with the disagreement and opposition of others. Values bring the intractable problem of relativism in their train, as Windelband quickly discovered. The solution of the value theorists is to adhere to absolute value in principle, while not saying what it consists in. Agreement on absolute value then becomes the goal towards which we must work—though we cannot, at this moment, point to the content of a clear value as absolute such that we gain everyone's immediate approval, that is at least the objective towards which we must work. And we can be certain that the solution will take the form of a value, and not of personal loyalty. Therefore, the less purchase loyalties have, the better. For Lotze, personal attachments are primitive, a relic of an earlier era.[105] Moral progress involves breaking down loyalties, as these are incompatible with pursuing general principles.[106] A political order based on loyalty is uncivilized and narrow.[107]

The concept of value in this way misinterprets and undermines our pursuit of the good, which is always properly personal and communal. That which we seek in our pursuits and actions, in our arts and inquiries, is not a perspicuous competitive good, not a value, but rather something that is complex and partially concealed, at least to an individual mind, because knowing it and realizing it always requires the contribution and cooperation of others. That which is the deepest and most important in life takes place between persons. This includes science, politics, and ethics. The search for truth is not a matter of following the values of science, but rather of loyalty to a scientific community and its framework of personal commitment. Politics is suggestion-response between persons, not the action of a sovereign state.[108] Ethics is the study of human character and ethos, not the crafting of an abstract morality of values. Christianity is the life-changing love of Christ, not adherence to metaphysical convictions.

Our ultimate and complete good is always sought in community, not competition. Persons are not isolated individuals, reducible to their functions, but are rather nodes of all possible relationships. Those to whom we are loyal are themselves actually and potentially loyal to others. The circle of friendship expands. As a result, there can be conflicts of loyalties that must be navigated. The measure of the quality of our loyalty to each other is the noncompetitiveness that is witnessed in this expansion, the nonviolence towards and integration of this greater context of relationships. This is our task: harmonizing our relationships, not our formulations of value. While the latter are mutually exclusive objects of thought, our relationships by contrast define the very timeliness of our being, connecting us to others and, through them, to everyone else.[109] This expansion is the task of justice, with results that cannot be known in advance. As Stephen McKenna writes, we cannot really "build" trust. "All you can do is demonstrate your own trustworthiness, hope for the best, and even be willing to have it fail—and this is essential—at expense to yourself."[110] We cannot do away with human freedom. We have to live our life, not short-circuit it by justifying our behavior with supposedly timeless values. Loyalties must be enacted, not substituted with values that would leap over our particular attachments, gaining cosmopolitanism in a single bound.

Values are the opiates of the elites. Inducing a cheap euphoria—we are better than others because of our values—they only temporarily combat the hollowness of our *mores*, the misery that flows from how we actually treat each other. As with any addiction, they undercut real attempts towards reconciliation and mutual friendship. The language of values expresses social life as a perpetual conflict: it is the symbol for that over which we will always fight. Any social unity around values is a truce between those who would otherwise be fighting as their natural condition.[111] Thinking in these terms incapacitates us from recognizing friendship as the substance of the common good.

For Aristotle, moral virtue aims at the beauty that is praiseworthy (τὸ καλόν) and finds its culmination in the great-souled man, the one who is worthy of esteem, the one who has the most value. However, for him, moral virtue is not the sum of what makes a human being good—that requires as well the non-moral, intellectual virtue of prudence—and it cannot effectively lead to happiness without friendship. If one cuts striving for good character off from intellectual virtue and friendship, it loses its purpose. If we are solely motivated by a search for value in morality, our relation to others becomes competitive and we miss the point of virtue, which is to fit us for certain types of relationships. When the moral virtues are put within the context of friendship and flourishing, as Aristotle does, they can be seen as relative to particular circumstances, rather than as ossified into abstract rules of preference, principles for the distribution of moral value as an external good. Likewise, the moral virtues can also be seen as necessary for prudence, the ability to perceive the action appropriate to circumstances, the action that does not simply follow a clear desire, but rather attends to the habits that are formed through them and the ways in which these habits enable or disable us to live in relation with each other. I am only capable of deep friendship if I am a trustworthy person. Likewise, I am only free if I can live in peace and friendship with others. Concrete freedom is not the bare possibility of choice but the actuality of participating in community and friendship.[112] The concrete social customs that enable and support friendships while drawing them into unity with each other are the substance of political prudence. Good political action and response builds up a healthy, noncompetitive, shared loyalty. Far from being a competition for value, therefore, my pursuit of what is higher has a purpose for the personal and political task of friendship.

Esteem is competitive, while true loyalty can never be. Thinking that the "common good consists of our shared values"[113] exacerbates the inherent problem of in-group solidarity leading to hostility against the out-group. Values language should be therefore either abandoned or used warily, for example, only as a rough index for a deeper reality.[114] We should take our loyalties seriously, but not our values.

NOTES

1. George Grant, *Time as History*, ed. William Christian (Toronto: University of Toronto Press, 1995), 58.

2. Horst U. K. Gundlach, "Germany," in *The Oxford Handbook of the History of Psychology: Global Perspectives*, ed. David. B Baker (Oxford: Oxford University Press, 2012), 263–64.

3. Frederick C. Beiser, *The Genesis of Neo-Kantianism, 1796–1880* (Oxford: Oxford University Press, 2014), 125.

4. Beiser, 89–141.

5. Croce called Herbart's book *Allgemeine praktische Philosophie* one of the classics of the ethical imperative, ranking it with Kant's *Critique of Pure Reason*. Benedetto Croce, *Historical Materialism and the Economics of Karl Marx*, trans. C. M. Meredith (New York: The Macmillan Company, 1914), 24.

6. Herbart critiques all previous ethical theories as wanting to regulate the will and failing to reach the "value (*Würde*) of the will." Johann Friedrich Herbart, *Allgemeine praktische Philosophie (1808)*, in *Sämtliche Werke in chronologischer Reihenfolge, Zweiter Band*, ed. Karl Kehrbach (Langensalza: Hermann Beyer & Söhne, 1887), 338. He says that "value (*Würde*) is the most adequate name for the whole excellence, into which all associations are united." Herbart, *Allgemeine praktische Philosophie*, 408. Herbart used "value" to defend the importance of the particular in the face of generalization. Herbart, 350. This was also important to Hermann Lotze, who absorbed this lesson at the feet of Christian Hermann Weiße (1801–1866), his teacher at the University of Leipzig. Cf. Frederick C. Beiser, *Late German Idealism: Trendelenburg and Lotze* (Oxford: Oxford University Press, 2013), 141–42.

7. Ernst Wolfgang Orth, "Kultur und Vorstellungsmassen. Ansätze zur Entwicklung eines Neuen Kulturbegriffs im 19. Jahrhundert Bei Johann Friedrich Herbart," in *Herbarts Kultursystem: Perspektiven der Transdisziplinarität im 19. Jahrhundert*, ed. Andreas Hoeschen and Lothar Schneider (Würzburg: Königshausen & Neumann, 2001), 27.

8. The University of Leipzig, where Lotze studied philosophy as an undergraduate in the 1830s, was dominated by Herbartian professors. William R. Woodward, *Hermann Lotze: An Intellectual Biography* (Cambridge: Cambridge University Press, 2015), 68–71.

9. As Beiser notes, while Lotze does not usually cite his sources, he often has Herbart in mind. Beiser, *Late German Idealism*, 196n12, 272n74. "It was Herbart whom

Lotze saw as the chief antagonist of the idealist tradition, and indeed as the main obstacle to reinstating his romantic worldview." Beiser, 159–60. Lotze "defends the idealist tradition against its most compelling contemporary foe, Herbart." Beiser, 154.

10. Lotze "feared that the critical limits of transcendental idealism would result in a kind of solipsism or skepticism, according to which the individual subject could know nothing beyond its own representations. . . . [O]ne purpose behind his own distinction between the realms of existence and validity was to escape the solipsistic snares of skepticism or subjective idealism. The truths of the Lotzean realm of validity are objective not in the sense that they exist independent of the mind, but in the sense they are true even if no one ever thinks of them. Though Lotze's doctrine of validity will later become the source of the theory of value of the Southwestern school, it is worthwhile to note that its original intention was to avoid the unpalatable consequences of skepticism and Kant's subjective idealism." Beiser, *The Genesis of Neo-Kantianism, 1796–1880*, 194–95.

11. Herbert Schnädelbach claims Lotze took the concept over from the political economy of the 1840s. Herbert Schnädelbach, *Philosophy in Germany, 1831–1933*, trans. Eric Matthews (Cambridge: Cambridge University Press, 1984), 161.

12. Thomas E. Willey, *Back to Kant: The Revival of Kantianism in German Social and Historical Thought, 1860–1914* (Detroit: Wayne State University Press, 1978), 40–57.

13. Wilhelm Windelband, *Die Philosophischen Richtungen der Gegenwart*, ed. Ernst von Aster (Leipzig: Quelle & Meyer, 1911), 376.

14. William James, *The Principles of Psychology* (Cambridge: Harvard University Press, 1981), 7.

15. Rudolf Metz, *A Hundred Years of British Philosophy* (London: Routledge, 2013), 256.

16. Reinhardt Pester, *Hermann Lotze: Wege seines Denkens und Forschens: ein Kapitel deutscher Philosophie- und Wissenschaftsgeschichte im 19. Jahrhundert* (Würzburg: Königshausen & Neumann, 1997), 255.

17. Peter Andras Varga, "The Missing Chapter from the Logical Investigations: Husserl on Lotze's Formal and Real Significance of Logical Laws," *Husserl Studies* 29, no. 3 (2013), 182n8.

18. Edmund Husserl, *Logical Investigations, Volume I*, trans. J. N. Findlay (London: Routledge & Kegan Paul, 1970), 218n1.

19. Peter M. Simons, *Philosophy and Logic in Central Europe from Bolzano to Tarski: Selected Essays* (Dordrecht: Springer, 1992), 153.

20. Frege's ideas "are deeply indebted to the thought of Hermann Lotze." Hans D. Sluga, *Gottlob Frege* (London: Routledge & Kegan Paul, 1980), 5.

21. Cf. Philippe Devaux, *Lotze et son influence sur la philosophie anglo-saxonne* (Bruxelles: Maurice Lamertin, 1932), 47.

22. Rush Rhees, ed., *Ludwig Wittgenstein: Personal Recollections* (Totowa, NJ: Rowman & Littlefield, 1981), 121.

23. "My guess is that the reason [Lotze was forgotten] was the analytic-continental divide in philosophy, which reigned for the last eighty years with almost uncompromising insensitivity. Forgetting all other styles of doing their discipline, philosophers

enthusiastically sided with one of the two camps." Nikolay Milkov, "Hermann Lotze's Microcosm," in *Islamic Philosophy and Occidental Phenomenology on the Perennial Issue of Microcosm and Macrocosm*, ed. Anna-Teresa Tymieniecka (Dordrecht: Springer, 2006), 41.

24. Cf. Devaux, *Lotze et son influence sur la philosophie anglo-saxonne*, 47–48. As George Santayana puts it, it is "hard to classify and label [Lotze's] conclusions," but even when they are not satisfactory, "his treatment of the question is full of suggestions and opens up a great variety of problems." George Santayana and Paul Grimley Kuntz, *Lotze's System of Philosophy*, ed. Paul Grimley Kuntz (Oxford: Indiana University Press, 1971), 109, 173.

25. Manfred Kühn, "Interpreting Kant Correctly: On the Kant of the Neo-Kantians," in Neo-Kantianism in Contemporary Philosophy, ed. Sebastian Luft and Rudolf A. Makkreel (Bloomington: Indiana University Press, 2010), 124.

26. Lotze's student, John Merz, found it remarkable "that in this, his original development of a distinctly Lotzian idea, he expresses no allegiance to Lotze." John Merz, *A History of European Thought in the Nineteenth Century, Volume Three* (Edinburgh: William Blackwood and Sons, 1912), 409n1.

27. Willey, *Back to Kant,* 52.

28. Willey, 134.

29. A central thesis of Lotze's philosophy was that we can have a scientific worldview and still have faith in unconditioned causes. Windelband's dissertation—written under Lotze—defended this point. That is to say, there is a role for contingency, for facts we just have to accept; everything is not determined by reasons we can discern. Cf. Frederick C. Beiser, *The German Historicist Tradition* (Oxford: Oxford University Press, 2011), 371–72.

30. Paul Ziche, "Indecisionism and Anti-Relativism: Wilhelm Windelband as a Philosophical Historiographer of Philosophy," in *From Hegel to Windelband: Historiography of Philosophy in the 19th Century*, ed. Valentin Pluder and Gerald Hartung (Berlin: Walter de Gruyter, 2015), 208.

31. Willey, *Back to Kant*, 140–41.

32. Willey, 139.

33. Guy Oakes, "Value Theory and the Foundations of the Cultural Sciences. Remarks on Rickert," in *Methodology of the Social Sciences, Ethics, and Economics in the Newer Historical School*, ed. Peter Koslowski (Berlin: Springer, 1997), 59–60.

34. Alan Sica, *Max Weber and the New Century* (New Brunswick: Transaction, 2004), 2.

35. Daniel W. Rossides, "The Legacy of Max Weber: A Non-Metaphysical Politics," *Sociological Inquiry* 42, no. 3–4 (1972): 183.

36. Willey, *Back to Kant*, 161–62.

37. For Luther, the articulation of a community is unnecessary for truth; the book of scripture is sufficient, and even just nature suffices, given what Luther says about Romans 1:20. WA 26, 174–177. LW 25, 154–58.

38. "Das Schöne und Hässliche, insbesondere das Löbliche und Schöndliche, besitzt eine ursprüngliche Evidenz, vermöge deren es klar ist, ohne gelernt und bewisen zu seyn." Johann Friedrich Herbart, *Lehrbuch zur Einleitung in die Philosophie,*

in Sämtliche Werke in chronologischer Reihenfolge, Vierter Band, ed. Karl Kehrbach (Langensalza: Hermann Beyer & Söhne, 1891), 105.

39. Herbart, *Lehrbuch zur Einleitung in die Philosophie*, 109.

40. Mic 2:719. Mik 3:606. Citations to Lotze's *Microcosmus* will be given with the volume and page number for the English and German versions.

41. "Will and desire themselves are what they are only by their consciousness of relation to something worthy in their objects. If the efforts of an intelligent being could be divorced from every shadow of pleasurable and painful interest in their object, they would be transformed into that lifeless impulse towards activity which produces indeed physical events, but certainly not actions." Mic 1:688. Mik 2:302.

42. Mic 2:721. Mik 3:608.

43. Wilhelm Windelband, *Präludien*, 3rd ed. (Tübingen: J.C.B. Mohr, 1907), 66.

44. Windelband, *Präludien*, 381.

45. Heinrich Rickert, *The Limits of Concept Formation in Natural Science: A Logical Introduction to the Historical Sciences*, ed. and trans. Guy Oakes, abridged (Cambridge: Cambridge University Press, 1986), 91. Max Weber, *The Methodology of the Social Sciences*, ed. Edward A. Shils and Henry A. Finch (Glencoe, Illinois: The Free Press, 1949), 1–2.

46. Herbart, *Lehrbuch zur Einleitung in die Philosophie*, 116–18.

47. Herbart, 113–14.

48. Mathias Heesch, *Johann Friedrich Herbart zur Einführung* (Hamburg: Junius, 1999), 9–13.

49. Mic 2:575. Mik 3:457.

50. Hermann Lotze, *Logik: Drei Bücher Vom Denken, Vom Untersuchen und Vom Erkennen* (Leipzig: S. Hirzel, 1874), 499. Hermann Lotze, *Logic, Volume II*, trans. Bernard Bosanquet (Oxford: Oxford at the Clarendon Press, 1888), 208.

51. Schnädelbach is wrong to say that for Lotze, "Values are objectively ideal, but they do not exist in the way that the real does: rather they have validity." Schnädelbach, *Philosophy in Germany*, 178. Lotze does not simply associate values with validity, as he does with propositions; this is precisely the problem of value.

52. Windelband, *Präludien*, 23.

53. Rickert, *The Limits of Concept Formation in Natural Science*, 200.

54. Beiser, *The German Historicist Tradition*, 398.

55. "When the normatively valid is the object of empirical investigation, its normative validity is disregarded. Its 'existence' and not its 'validity' is what concerns the investigator." Weber, *The Methodology of the Social Sciences*, 39.

56. Herbart, *Allgemeine praktische Philosophie*, 338.

57. Herbart, 333–34.

58. Mic 1:705. Mik 2:319.

59. Mic 1:701. Mik 2:315.

60. Mic 1: 703. Mik 2:317.

61. Mic 2:600. Mik 3:482.

62. Evan Edward Thomas, *Lotze's Theory of Reality* (London: Longmans, Green, and Co., 1921), 178.

63. Mic 2:590. Mik 3:473.

64. Mic 2:600. Mik 3:482.

65. According to him, although we first come to know the world as a coherent whole of unique individuals, the idea of universally valid truth destroys this naïve perception and shows everything to be comparable. Mic 2:591–94. Mik 3:474–77.

66. John F. Crosby, *The Personalism of John Henry Newman* (Washington, DC: The Catholic University of America Press, 2016), 39.

67. This difference is highlighted by two German verbs: *kennen* for acquaintance knowledge and *wissen* for information knowledge, which English does not distinguish between. Cf. Dietrich von Hildebrand, *What Is Philosophy?* (Steubenville, Ohio: Dietrich von Hildebrand Legacy Project, 2021), 30–34.

68. In his imprisonment in the state penitentiary for using state resources for political campaigns, former Speaker of the Pennsylvania House of Representatives Bill DeWeese shared a cell with a child molester. In getting to know him, DeWeese learned that his father had molested him as a boy. This naturally changed his empathy level for his cellmate.

69. Wilhelm Windelband, *Über Willensfreiheit* (Tübingen: J.C.B. Mohr [P. Siebeck], 1904), 161–73. Windelband even goes so far as to use Plato's myth at the end of the *Republic* as an example of how we cannot understand freedom metaphysically, but he makes an embarrassing error, reversing two elements of the story. In Plato, the souls are making a choice about their future lives before they drink of the waters of Lethe and forget all the empirical details of their past lives, but Windelband says they drink first, then make their choice. Windelband, 163–64.

70. Choosing and acting follow upon desire necessarily. Responsibility comes into play with our desire, not with our actual choosing and acting. Windelband, 75–76. For Martin Lampe, this shows the "derailment" of Windelband's views. Martin Lampe, *Das Problem der Willensfreiheit Bei Lipps, Eucken, Rindelband, v. Hartmann und Wundt* (Berlin: R. Trenkel, 1907), 38.

71. Rickert, *The Limits of Concept Formation in Natural Science*, 131.

72. Rickert, 141.

73. Cf., for example, Rickert, 97.

74. Hans Albert and Ernst Topitsch, "Einleitung," in *Werturteilsstreit* (Darmstadt: Wissenschaftliche Buchgesellschaft, 1979), ix–x.

75. For example, as Beiser writes, while Rickert held that "reason is sovereign in the domain of science" and that "truth is the dominating *sui generis* value in the realm of theory," he "also insisted on recognizing the irrational powers of the will and feeling in the spheres of politics, art and religion." Beiser, *The German Historicist Tradition*, 399.

76. Cf. Heesch, *Johann Friedrich Herbart zur Einführung*, 108–9.

77. This is the case for Lotze from the middle of the 1940s. Cf. Fritz Bamberger, *Untersuchungen zur Entstehung des Wertproblems in der Philosophie des 19. Jahrhunderts* (Halle a. S.: Max Niemeyer, 1924), 85–86.

78. "For we do not possess either of Nature or of History such complete knowledge as would enable us to guess the whole of the divine plan of the universe; the attempts that have been made to determine this from meagre earthly experience betray only too plainly the unfavourable nature of our standpoint, which, with all the one-sidedness

of its limited outlook, wishes to be taken for that topmost summit, from which the whole world may plainly be seen spread out below." Mic 2:723–24. Mik 3:610–11.

79. Mic 2:716ff. Mik 3:604ff.

80. Katherina Kinzel, "Wilhelm Windelband and the Problem of Relativism," *British Journal for the History of Philosophy* 25, no. 1 (2017): 84–107.

81. Windelband, *Präludien*, 77, 429. Religion (our connection with the transcendental) must be mysterious and cannot be completely known. Windelband, 428.

82. Wilhelm Windelband, "The Principles of Logic," in *Encyclopaedia of the Philosophical Sciences*, ed. Henry Jones, trans. B. Ethel Meyer (London: Macmillian and Co., 1913), 65.

83. Windelband, *Über Willensfreiheit*, 195–96.

84. All scientific knowledge "presents a *piece cut out of Reality*, which, as synthetically complete, never really exists. We must, in this sense, attribute not existence but value to the object; still it contains pure moments of being and it includes them in an interconnexion which is valid for that object. No description of facts can ever completely comprise or imitate the reality with which it is concerned: but it can weave the selected constituents into a form which agrees with their real interconnexion." Windelband, "The Principles of Logic," 64.

85. Beiser, *The Genesis of Neo-Kantianism, 1796–1880*, 493.

86. Klaus Christian Köhnke, *The Rise of Neo-Kantianism: German Academic Philosophy between Idealism and Positivism*, trans. R. J. Hollingdale (Cambridge: Cambridge University Press, 1991), 272, 280.

87. Köhnke, 271.

88. Guy Oakes, "Value Theory and the Foundations of the Cultural Sciences," 66–67.

89. Beiser, *The German Historicist Tradition*, 439.

90. Oakes, "Value Theory and the Foundations of the Cultural Sciences," 68.

91. Beiser, *The German Historicist Tradition*, 395.

92. Heinrich Rickert, *The Limits of Concept Formation in Natural Science*, trans. and ed. Guy Oakes (Cambridge: Cambridge University Press, 1986), 235. Anton Zijderveld calls Rickert a "relative relativist." "[A]s far as the non-theoretical (religious, ethical, aesthetic, hedonistic) values are concerned, Rickert seems to be a relative relativist himself—a position, incidentally, which he compares with agnosticism. The absolute, radical relativist is an atheist who radically rejects the notion of the absolute. But the relative relativist is an agnostic who will not categorically deny that there is an absolute, but who is unable to acquire a firm knowledge of it and therefore settles for the relative." Anton C. Zijderveld, *Rickert's Relevance: The Ontological Nature and Epistemological Functions of Values* (Leiden: Brill, 2006), 161.

93. Beiser, *The German Historicist Tradition*, 412.

94. Jon Meacham, *American Lion: Andrew Jackson in the White House* (New York: Random House, 2008), 211–12.

95. Adrian Vermeule, "Integration from Within," *American Affairs* II, no. 1 (2018): 208.

96. Max Weber, *From Max Weber: Essays in Sociology*, ed. C. Wright Mills and H.H. Gerth (Oxford: Oxford University Press, 1958), 147.

97. Google Ngram Viewer search performed March 5, 2021, https://books.google.com/ngrams.

98. Weber, *From Max Weber*, 148.

99. Weber, 152.

100. The ancient gods were powers effective in the world, like the "market" in modern times. Cf. Andrew Willard Jones, *The Two Cities: A History of Christian Politics* (Steubenville, Ohio: Emmaus Road Publishing, 2021), 54, 270. Our belief in "values" enables there to be "religion without God," as Ronald Dworkin put it at the end of his life. Ronald Dworkin, *Religion Without God* (Cambridge, Massachusetts: Harvard University Press, 2013), 10.

101. Joel Backström, "Of Dictators and Greengrocers: On the Repressive Grammar of Values-Discourse," *Ethical Perspectives* 22, no. 1 (2015): 54.

102. Thomas Hobbes, *Leviathan*, 42.122. CE 5, 912.

103. Mic 2:721. Mik 3:608.

104. Mic 2:385. Mik 3:242.

105. Primitive morality is "not regulated by general laws of feeling," Lotze writes, "but is grounded on the personal worth of those whom the actions in question affect. Here evil means wounding the soul of him whom we love, and whilst towards such a one all the virtues of benevolence may be developed, even to the point of refined tenderness, fierce hatred and revenge towards all enemies may go on undisturbed." Mic 1:705. Mik 2:319. The foundational relationship is one of minimum loyalty: "A man only comprehends what he owes to his fellows when he comes into contact with those who are nothing to him; it is only when all the claims to consideration, friendship, love, and reverence founded upon those special natural conditions have fallen away, that general duties and their necessary general motives become clear." Mic 2:498. Mik 3:383.

106. Families, for instance, are united by feelings "which do not flow from general duties of men towards their fellows"; while they "incidentally" enrich our life, "far from illuminating men's consciousness of general moral duties," these personal bonds "only obscure it." Mic 2:497. Mik 3:382.

107. The loyal person in an undeveloped society strives for ends which are "less distant and many-sided." He is "inclined to admire the strength and grandeur of others and to submit his own power to theirs," which Lotze describes as a "faith and devotion towards chiefs and leaders." Mic 1:705. Mik 2:319. Notice that it is not a matter of showing loyalty to other people who have shown loyalty to us, but rather of admiring the winners in a mimetic contest.

108. It is not surprising that it was ignored by the value theorists. The Baden School discussed values, but not political life. "Moral questions were important to the Baden philosophers only in the theoretical sense," as they gave primacy to theoretical over practical problems. Willey, *Back to Kant*, 132. "The analysis of political realities was neglected, and relatively little attention was paid to questions of political technique. These matters were generally felt to be trivial." Fritz K. Ringer, *The Decline of the German Mandarins: The German Academic Community, 1890–1933* (Cambridge: Harvard University Press, 1969), 121.

109. Through a kind of time travel, the future reaches back to the past and changes it. Take a marriage that ends in divorce—looking back on the honeymoon photos will be painful, because the meaning of the past has changed. Forgiveness has the opposite effect, making possible a future relationship that was previously closed off. The mutuality of persons "underpins the mutuality of past and present," writes David Walsh. "We can hold in mind and in love persons long dead and they, in turn, can hold us in mind before we are even born." David Walsh, *Politics of the Person as the Politics of Being* (Notre Dame: University of Notre Dame Press, 2016), 189, 199.

110. Stephen McKenna, "A Mimetic Perspective on Trust," in *Living in an Age of Mistrust: An Interdisciplinary Study of Declining Trust and How to Get It Back*, ed. Andrew I. Yeo and Matthew N. Green (New York: Routledge, 2017), 52. McKenna rather generously gives credit for this idea to Onora O'Neill. Onora O'Neill, *A Question of Trust* (Cambridge: Cambridge University Press, 2002), 38–39.

111. Cf., for example, Carl Schmitt, Eberhard Jungel, and Sepp Schelz, *Die Tyrannei Der Werte* (Hamburg: Lutherisches Verlagshaus, 1979); and Blake Smith, "Liberalism for Losers: Carl Schmitt's 'The Tyranny of Values,'" *American Affairs* V, no. 1 (2021): 222–40.

112. As much as this might resemble Hegel's *Sittlichkeit*, the problem is that Hegel makes ultimately the same mistake as the moralists do, of attempting only to ascend to what is higher, without an interruption by the downward movement of integration into and service to lower-level communities, tying the two together chiasmatically as macrocosm and microcosm. Cf. D.C. Schindler, *The Perfection of Freedom: Schiller, Schelling, and Hegel between the Ancients and the Moderns* (Eugene, Oregon: Cascade, 2012), 320–72. Dean Moyar argues that the concept of value is the key to understanding Hegel's philosophy of justice and freedom. Dean Moyar, *Hegel's Value: Justice as the Living Good* (Oxford, Oxford University Press, 2021).

113. Robert B. Reich, *The Common Good* (New York: Alfred A. Knopf, 2018), 18.

114. Fritz Bamberger, for instance, thinks the term "value" is good only as an index for the incommunicable individuality of what we experience. Bamberger, *Untersuchungen zur Entstehung des Wertproblems in der Philosophie des 19. Jahrhunderts*, 86–87. The greatest philosopher to reflect on values, Max Scheler responded to the quest for universal validity without reference to values, but rather by bringing out the essential interconnection of person and world. Likewise, for him, the original bearer of good and evil is the relationship between persons, which he calls the "basic moral tenor." Max Scheler, *Formalism in Ethics and Non-Formal Ethics of Values*, trans. Manfred S. Frings and Roger L. Funk (Evanston: Northwestern University Press, 1973), 393–95, 112–13.

Bibliography

Abizadeh, Arash. *Hobbes and the Two Faces of Ethics*. Cambridge: Cambridge University Press, 2018.

Albee, Ernest. "The Ethical System of Richard Cumberland. I." *The Philosophical Review* 4, no. 3 (1895): 264–90.

Albert, Hans, and Ernst Topitsch. "Einleitung." In *Werturteilsstreit*. Darmstadt: Wissenschaftliche Buchgesellschaft, 1979.

Althoff, Gerd. "Friendship and Political Order." In *Friendship and Medieval Europe*, edited by Julian Haseldine, 91–105. Thrupp: Sutton, 1999.

Anderson, Abraham. *Kant, Hume, and the Interruption of Dogmatic Slumber*. Oxford: Oxford University Press, 2020.

Andrew, Edward G. *The Genealogy of Values*. Lanham: Rowman and Littlefield, 1995.

Annas, Julia. "Ethics in Stoic Philosophy." *Phronesis* 52, no. 1 (2007): 58–87.

Anscombe, G. E. M. *Human Life, Action and Ethics*. Charlottesville: Imprint Academic, 2005.

———. "On Brute Facts." *Analysis* 18, no. 3 (1958): 69–72.

Appiah, Kwame Anthony. *The Ethics of Identity*. Princeton: Princeton University Press, 2005.

Aquinas, Saint Thomas. *On Kingship, to the King of Cyprus*. Translated by Gerald B. Phelan. Toronto: Pontifical Institute of Mediaeval Studies, 1982.

Ardito, Alissa M. *Machiavelli and the Modern State*. Cambridge: Cambridge University Press, 2015.

Arendt, Hannah. "Some Questions of Moral Philosophy." In *Responsibility and Judgment*, edited by Jerome Kohn, 49–146. New York: Schocken Books, 2003.

———. *The Human Condition*. 2nd ed. Chicago: University of Chicago Press, 1958.

———. "Thinking and Moral Considerations." In *Responsibility and Judgment*, edited by Jerome Kohn, 159–89. New York: Schocken Books, 2003.

Aristotle. *Nicomachean Ethics*. In *The Basic Works of Aristotle*, edited by Richard McKeon, translated by W. D. Ross, 927–1112. New York: Random House, 1941.

Ashcraft, Richard, and M. M. Goldsmith. "Locke, Revolution Principles, and the Formation of Whig Ideology." *The Historical Journal* 26, no. 4 (2016): 773–800.

Augustine, Saint. *Concerning the City of God against the Pagans*. Translated by Henry Bettenson. New York: Penguin, 2003.

Backström, Joel. "Of Dictators and Greengrocers: On the Repressive Grammar of Values-Discourse." *Ethical Perspectives* 22, no. 1 (2015): 39–67.

Bamberger, Fritz. *Untersuchungen zur Entstehung des Wertproblems in der Philosophie des 19. Jahrhunderts*. Halle a. S.: Max Niemeyer, 1924.

Banfield, Edward C. *The Moral Basis of a Backward Society*. Glencoe, Illinois: The Free Press, 1958.

Beiser, Frederick C. *Late German Idealism: Trendelenburg and Lotze*. Oxford: Oxford University Press, 2013.

———. *The Genesis of Neo-Kantianism, 1796–1880*. Oxford: Oxford University Press, 2014.

———. *The German Historicist Tradition*. Oxford: Oxford University Press, 2011.

Bell, Jason Matthew. "The Relevance of Royce's Applied Ethics: Studies in War, Business, and Environmental Ethics." Vanderbilt University, 2009.

Bellamy, Alex J. *World Peace (And How We Can Achieve It)*. Oxford: Oxford University Press, 2019.

Benson, Iain T. "Acton Lecture 2017: Civic Virtues and the Politics of 'Full Drift Ahead.'" Sydney: The Centre for Independent Studies, 2017. https://www.cis.org .au/app /uploads/2017/06/op155.pdf?

Bentham, Jeremy. *The Rationale of Reward*. London: Robert Heward, 1830.

Bird, Brian. "The Charter of Rights and Freedoms—and Values?" Policy Options, 2018. https://policyoptions.irpp.org/magazines/november-2018/the-charter-of -rights-and-freedoms-and-values/.

Bissinger, Buzz. *A Prayer for the City*. New York: Random House, 1997.

Blanchot, Maurice. *Friendship*. Translated by Elizabeth Rottenberg. Stanford: Stanford University Press, 1971.

Blickle, Peter. *The Revolution of 1525: The German Peasants' War from a New Perspective*. Translated by Thomas A. Brady Jr. and H. C. Erik Midelfort. Baltimore: The Johns Hopkins University Press, 1977.

Bloom, Allan. "How Nietzsche Conquered America." *Wilson's Quarterly*, Vol. 11, No. 3 (Summer 1987), 80–93.

———. *The Closing of the American Mind: How Higher Education Has Failed Democracy and Impoverished the Souls of Today's Students*. New York: Simon and Schuster, 1987.

Blum, Lawrence A. *Friendship, Altruism, and Morality*. London: Routledge & Kegan Paul, 1980.

Boas, George. *Vox Populi: Essays in the History of an Idea*. Baltimore: Johns Hopkins University Press, 1969.

Böckenförde, Ernst Wolfgang. *State, Society, and Liberty: Studies in Political Theory and Constitutional Law*. Translated by J. A. Underwood. New York: Berg, 1991.

Bossy, John. *Christianity in the West 1400–1700*. Oxford: Oxford University Press, 1985.

Brague, Rémi. *The Kingdom of Man: Genesis and Failure of the Modern Project*. Translated by Paul Seaton. Notre Dame: University of Notre Dame Press, 2018.

Brandon, Eric. *The Coherence of Hobbes's Leviathan: Civil and Religious Authority Combined*. New York: Continuum, 2007.

Breitsameter, Christof. *Individualisierte Perfektion: Vom Wert der Werte*. Paderborn: Ferdinand Schöningh, 2009.

Brooke, Christopher. *Philosophic Pride: Stoicism and Political Thought from Lipsius to Rousseau*. Princeton: Princeton University Press, 2012.

Brooks, Arthur C. *Gross National Happiness: Why Happiness Matters for American—and How We Can Get More of It*. New York: Basic Books, 2008.

Bruhn, John G., and Stewart Wolf. *The Roseto Story: An Anatomy of Health*. Norman: University of Oklahoma Press, 1979.

Bruni, Luigino. *The Genesis and Ethos of the Market*. New York: Palgrave Macmillan, 2012.

Buber, Martin. *Two Types of Faith*. Translated by Norman P. Goldhawk. New York: Macmillan, 1951.

Bumsted, Brad, and Paula Knudsen. "Powering Down: Former State Sen. Vincent J. Fumo Talks about Changes in the Political Climate since His Time Spent in Prison." *The Caucus*, July 17, 2018.

Burke, Edmund. *Reflections on the Revolution in France*. Edited by L. G. Mitchell. Oxford: Oxford University Press, 1993.

Burrell, David B. *Friendship and Ways to Truth*. Notre Dame: University of Notre Dame Press, 2000.

Carty, Jarrett A. *God and Government: Martin Luther's Political Thought*. Montreal: McGill-Queen's University Press, 2017.

Cassin, Barbara, Marc Crépon, and François Prost. "Morals/Ethics." In *Dictionary of Untranslatables: A Philosophical Lexicon*, edited by Barbara Cassin, translated by Steven Rendall, Christian Hubert, Jeffrey Mehlman, Nathanael Stein, and Michael Syrotinski, 691–99. Princeton: Princeton University Press, 2014.

Cavanaugh, William T. *The Myth of Religious Violence: Secular Ideology and the Roots of Modern Conflict*. Oxford: Oxford University Press, 2009.

Chang, Ha-Joon. *Kicking Away the Ladder: Development Strategy in Historical Perspective*. London: Anthem Press, 2003.

Christakis, Nicholas A., and James H. Fowler. *Connected: The Surprising Power of Our Social Networks and How They Shape Our Lives*. New York: Little, Brown and Company, 2009.

Chua, Amy. *Political Tribes: Group Instinct and the Fate of Nations*. New York: Penguin, 2018.

Collins, Harry, and Robert Evans. *Rethinking Expertise*. Chicago: University of Chicago Press, 2007.

Conan Doyle, Arthur. *The Adventures of Sherlock Holmes*. Minneapolis: Lerner Publishing Group, 2007.

Cowan, Donald. *Unbinding Prometheus: Education for the Coming Age*. Dallas: Dallas Institute Publications, 1988.

Crick, Bernard. *In Defence of Politics*. London: Bloomsbury, 2013.

Croce, Benedetto. *Historical Materialism and the Economics of Karl Marx*. Translated by C. M. Meredith. New York: The Macmillan Company, 1914.

Crosby, John F. *The Personalism of John Henry Newman*. Washington, DC: The Catholic University of America Press, 2016.

———. *The Selfhood of the Human Person*. Washington, DC: The Catholic University of America Press, 1996.

Culp, Jonathan. "Justice, Happiness, and the Sensible Knave: Hume's Incomplete Defense of the Just Life." *The Review of Politics* 75, no. 2 (2013): 193–219.

Cumberland, Richard. *A Treatise of the Laws of Nature*. Translated by John Maxwell. Indianapolis: Liberty Fund, 2005.

———. *De Legibus Naturae*. London: E. Flesher for Nathanael Hooke, 1672.

Curran, Eleanor. *Reclaiming the Rights of the Hobbesian Subject*. Houndmills: Palgrave Macmillan, 2007.

Dallmayr, Fred. *Horizons of Difference: Engaging With Others*. Notre Dame: University of Notre Dame Press, 2020.

———. *Post-Liberalism: Recovering a Shared World*. Oxford: Oxford University Press, 2019.

Darwall, Stephen. "Trust as a Second-Personal Attitude (of the Heart)." In *The Philosophy of Trust*, edited by Paul Faulkner and Thomas Simpson, 35–50. Oxford: Oxford University Press, 2017.

———. *The Pure Theory of Politics*. Indianapolis: Liberty Fund, 2000.

de Jouvenel, Bertrand. *Sovereignty: An Inquiry into the Political Good*. Translated by J. F. Huntington. Indianapolis: Liberty Fund, 1997.

de Lolme, Jean Louis. *The Constitution of England, or an Account of the English Government*. Indianapolis: Liberty Fund, 2007.

Deneen, Patrick J. "Friendship and Politics: Ancient and American." In *Friends and Citizens: Essays in Honor of Wilson Carey McWilliams*, edited by Peter Dennis Bathory and Nancy L. Schwartz, 47–66. Lanham: Rowman & Littlefield Publishers, 2001.

———. *Why Liberalism Failed*. New Haven: Yale University Press, 2018.

Derrida, Jacques. *Politics of Friendship*. Translated by George Collins. London: Verso, 1997.

———. *Speech and Phenomena*. Translated by David B. Allison. Evanston: Northwestern University Press, 1973.

Descartes, René. *A Discourse on the Method*. Edited by Ian Maclean. Oxford: Oxford University Press, 2006.

Devaux, Philippe. *Lotze et son influence sur la philosophie anglo-saxonne*. Bruxelles: Maurice Lamertin, 1932.

Devere, Heather. "Amity Update: The Academic Debate on Friendship and Politics" 1 (2013): 5–33.

Digeser, P. E. *Friendship Reconsidered: What It Means, and How It Matters to Politics*. New York: Columbia University Press, 2016.

Domenicucci, Jacopo, and Richard Holton. "Trust as a Two-Place Relation." In *The Philosophy of Trust*, edited by Paul Faulkner and Thomas Simpson, 149–60. Oxford: Oxford University Press, 2017.

Dworkin, Ronald. *Freedom's Law: The Moral Reading of the American Constitution*. New York: Oxford University Press, 1999.

———. *Religion Without God*. Cambridge, Massachusetts: Harvard University Press, 2013.

Easton, David. *The Political System: An Inquiry into the State of Political Science*. New York: Alfred A. Knopf, 1953.

Edel, Abraham. "Right and Good." In *Dictionary of the History of Ideas*, edited by Philip Wiener, 4:173–87. New York: Charles Scribner's Sons, 1973.

———. "The Concept of Value and Its Travels in Twentieth-Century America." In *Values and Value Theory in Twentieth-Century America: Essays in Honor of Elizabeth Flower*, edited by Murray G. Murphey and Ivar Berg, 12–36. Philadelphia: Temple University Press, 1988.

Egolf, Brenda, Judith Lasker, Stewart Wolf, and Louise Potvin. "The Roseto Effect: A 50-Year Comparison of Mortality Rates." *American Journal of Public Health* 82, no. 8 (1992): 1089–92.

Engelland, Chad. *Ostension: Word Learning and the Embodied Mind*. Cambridge: MIT Press, 2014.

———. *Phenomenology*. Cambridge: The MIT Press, 2020.

———. *The Way of Philosophy: An Introduction*. Eugene, Oregon: Cascade Books, 2016.

Erickson, Millard J. *Introducing Christian Doctrine*. Edited by L. Arnold Hustad. 2nd ed. Grand Rapids, Michigan: Baker Academic, 2001.

Estes, James M. *Peace, Order and the Glory of God: Secular Authority and the Church in the Thought of Luther and Melanchthon 1518–1559*. Leiden: Brill, 2005.

Everett, Daniel L. *Don't Sleep, There Are Snakes: Life and Language in the Amazonian Jungle*. New York: Vintage, 2008.

Faulkner, Paul, and Thomas Simpson, eds. *The Philosophy of Trust*. Oxford: Oxford University Press, 2017.

Felten, Eric. *Loyalty: The Vexing Virtue*. New York: Simon & Schuster, 2011.

Fink, Hans. "Against Ethical Exceptionalism—Through Critical Reflection on the History of Use of the Terms 'Ethics' and 'Morals' in Philosophy." *SATS* 21, no. 2 (2020): 85–100.

Fiorina, Morris P. *Culture War?: The Myth of a Polarized America*. New York: Longman, 2004.

Fish, Stanley. *Is There a Text in This Class?: The Authority of Interpretive Communities*. Cambridge: Harvard University Press, 1980.

Fletcher, George P. *Loyalty: An Essay on the Morality of Relationships*. New York: Oxford University Press, 1993.

Francis, Mark. *Herbert Spencer and the Invention of Modern Life*. Ithaca, New York: Cornell University Press, 2007.

Friedan, Betty. *The Second Stage*. Cambridge: Harvard University Press, 1998.

Fromkin, David. *A Peace to End All Peace: The Fall of the Ottoman Empire and the Creation of the Modern Middle East*. New York: Henry Holt & Co., 1989.

Funkenstein, Amos. *Theology and the Scientific Imagination*. Princeton: Princeton University Press, 1986.

Gadamer, Hans-Georg. "Friendship and Solidarity." Translated by David Vessey and Chris Blauwkamp. *Research in Phenomenology* 39 (2009): 3–12.

———. *Hermeneutics, Religion, and Ethics*. New Haven: Yale University Press, 1999.

Gambetta, Diego, ed. *Trust: Making and Breaking Cooperative Relations*. New York: Basil Blackwell, 1988.

Gbowee, Leymah, with Carol Mithers. *Mighty Be Our Powers: How Sisterhood, Prayer, and Sex Changed a Nation at War*. New York: Beast Books, 2011.

Gebhardt, Jürgen. "Die Werte." In *Anodos: Festschrift für Helmut Kuhn*, 35–54. Weinheim: VCH, Acta humaniora, 1989.

Gedder, Jeremy Seth. *Hugo Grotius and the Modern Theology of Freedom*. New York: Routledge, 2017.

Gennaro, Ivo De. "Preface." In *Value: Sources and Readings on a Key Concept of the Globalized World*, xi–xiii. Edited by Ivo De Gennaro. Leiden: Brill, 2012.

Gennaro, Ivo De, and Gino Zaccaria. *The Dictatorship of Value: Teaching and Research in the Planetary University*. Milan: McGraw-Hill, 2011.

Ghubril, Saleem. "Commencement Address," The 87th Annual Commencement of Robert Morris University. Moon Township, Pennsylvania, May 5, 2012.

Giambrone, Anthony. "Is That in the Bible?," in *Magnificat*. New York: Yonkers, 2019-22.

Girard, René. *The Scapegoat*. Baltimore: Johns Hopkins University Press, 1986.

Goodhart, David. *The Road to Somewhere: The Populist Revolt and the Future of Politics*. London: Hurst, 2017.

Grant, George. *Time as History*. Edited by William Christian. Toronto: University of Toronto Press, 1995.

Gregory, Brad S. *Rebel in the Ranks: Martin Luther, the Reformation, and the Conflicts That Continue to Shape Our World*. New York: HarperOne, 2017.

———. *The Unintended Reformation: How a Religious Revolution Secularized Society*. Cambridge: Belknap Press, 2012.

Grotius, Hugo. *The Rights of War and Peace, Book II*. Edited by Richard Tuck. Indianapolis: Liberty Fund, 2005.

Gundlach, Horst U. K. "Germany." In *The Oxford Handbook of the History of Psychology: Global Perspectives*, edited by David. B Baker. Oxford: Oxford University Press, 2012.

Haara, Heikki. *Pufendorf's Theory of Sociability: Passions, Habits and Social Order*. Cham, Switzerland: Springer Nature, 2018.

Haara, Heikki, and Aino Lahdenranta. "Smithian Sentimentalism Anticipated: Pufendorf on the Desire of Esteem and Moral Conduct." In *The Journal of Scottish Philosophy* 16.1 (2018).

Hamilton, Alexander, John Jay, and James Madison. *The Federalist Papers*. Edited by Clinton Rossiter. New York: Penguin, 1961.

Hardin, Russell. *Trust and Trustworthiness*. New York: Russell Sage Foundation, 2002.

Harold, Philip J. "Economics, Politics, and Natural Law." In *Human Rights and Natural Law: An Intercultural Philosophical Perspective*, edited by Walter Schweidler, 147–56. Sankt Augustin: Academia, 2012.

Harrington, James. *The Commonwealth of Oceana, and A System of Politics*. Edited by J. G. A. Pocock. Cambridge: Cambridge University Press, 1992.

Harris, Jared D., Adrian A. C. Keevil, and Andrew C. Wicks. "Public Trust in the Institution of Business." In *Handbook of Advances in Trust Research*, edited by Reinhard Bachmann and Akbar Zaheer, 204–23. Cheltenham, UK: Edward Elgar, 2013.

Hart, Roderick P. *Campaign Talk: Why Elections Are Good For Us*. Princeton: Princeton University Press, 2000.

Havighurst, Alfred F. *Britain in Transition: The Twentieth Century*. Chicago: University of Chicago Press, 1985.

Hayes, Carlton J.H. *Essays on Nationalism*. New York: Russell & Russell, 1954.

———. *Nationalism: A Religion*. New York: The Macmillan Company, 1960.

Heenan, John. "Putting the Plural Noun Values in Context." *Keynote Address to the Eighth National Character Education Symposium*. Wellington, 2010. http://www.pnbhs.school.nz/wp-content/uploads/2015/11/John-Heenan-Putting-Values-in-Context.pdf.

Heesch, Mathias. *Johann Friedrich Herbart zur Einführung*. Hamburg: Junius, 1999.

Heidegger, Martin. *Being and Time*. Translated by John Macquarrie and Edward Robinson. New York: Harper & Row, 1962.

———. *Gesamtausgabe*. Frankfurt am Main: Vittorio Klostermann, n.d.

———. "Letter—Forward." In *Heidegger et la critique de la notion de valeur: la destruction de la fondation métaphysique*, vi–xi. The Hague: Martinus Nijhoff, 1976.

———. *Pathmarks*. Cambridge: Cambridge University Press, 1998.

———. *Sein und Zeit*. 4th ed. Tübingen: Max Niemeyer, 1977.

———. *The Question Concerning Technology and Other Essays*. Translated by William Lovitt. New York: Harper & Row, 1977.

———. *Towards the Definition of Philosophy*. Translated by Ted Sadler. New York: Continuum, 2008.

Heilke, Thomas. "From Civic Friendship to Communities of Believers: Anabaptist Challenges to Lutheran and Calvinist Discourses." In *Discourses and Representations of Friendship in Early Modern Europe, 1500–1700*, edited by Daniel T. Lochman, Maritere López, and Lorna Huson, 225–37. Burlington: Ashgate, 2011.

Herbart, Johann Friedrich. *Allgemeine praktische Philosophie (1808)*. In *Sämtliche Werke in chronologischer Reihenfolge, Zweiter Band*. Edited by Karl Kehrbach. Langensalza: Hermann Beyer & Söhne, 1887.

———. *Lehrbuch zur Einleitung in die Philosophie*. In *Sämtliche Werke in chronologischer Reihenfolge, Vierter Band*. Edited by Karl Kehrbach. Langensalza: Hermann Beyer & Söhne, 1891.

Himmelfarb, Gertrude. *The De-Moralization of Society: From Victorian Virtues to Modern Values*. New York: Alfred A. Knopf, 1995.

Hobbes, Thomas. *Behemoth, or The Long Parliament*. In Clarendon Edition of the Works of Thomas Hobbes, vol. 10, edited by Paul Seaward. Oxford: Oxford University Press, 2009.

———. *De Cive: The English Version*. In Clarendon Edition of the Works of Thomas Hobbes, vol. 2, edited by Howard Warrender.. Oxford: Oxford University Press, 1983.

———. *Leviathan: The English and Latin Texts (i)*. In Clarendon Edition of the Works of Thomas Hobbes, vol. 4, edited by Noel Malcolm. Oxford: Oxford University Press, 2013.

———. *Leviathan: The English and Latin Texts (ii)*. In Clarendon Edition of the Works of Thomas Hobbes, vol. 5, edited by Noel Malcolm. Oxford: Oxford University Press, 2012.

Holmes, Jeremy. *Cur Deus Verba: Why the Word Became Words*. San Francisco: Ignatius Press, 2021.

Höpfl, Harro, ed. *Luther and Calvin on Secular Authority*. Translated by Harro Höpfl. Cambridge: Cambridge University Press, 1991.

Hughes, Bettany. *The Hemlock Cup: Socrates, Athens and the Search for the Good Life*. New York: Alfred A. Knopf, 2001.

Hume, David. *A Treatise of Human Nature*. 2nd ed. Edited by L. A. Selby-Bigge and P. H. Nidditch. Oxford: Oxford at the Clarendon Press, 1978.

———. *Enquiries Concerning the Human Understanding and Concerning the Principles of Morals*. Edited by L. A. Selby-Bigge. London: Oxford at the Clarendon Press, 1902.

Humphries, Jane. *Childhood and Child Labour in the British Industrial Revolution*. Cambridge: Cambridge University Press, 2010.

Husserl, Edmund. *Logical Investigations, Volume I*. Translated by J. N. Findlay. London: Routledge & Kegan Paul, 1970.

Hutter, Horst. *Politics as Friendship: The Origins of Classical Notions of Politics in the Theory and Practice of Friendship*. Waterloo, Ontario: Wilfrid Laurier University Press, 1978.

James, William. *The Principles of Psychology*. Cambridge: Harvard University Press, 1981.

Joas, Hans. *The Sacredness of the Person: A New Genealogy of Human Rights*. Translated by Alex Skinner. Washington, D.C.: Georgetown University Press, 2013.

Johnson, James Turner. *Sovereignty: Moral and Historical Perspectives*. Washington, DC: Georgetown University Press, 2014.

Jones, Andrew Willard. *Before Church and State: A Study of Social Order in the Sacramental Kingdom of St. Louis IX*. Steubenville, Ohio: Emmaus Academic, 2017.

———. *The Two Cities: A History of Christian Politics*. Steubenville, Ohio: Emmaus Road Publishing, 2021.

Jones, Karen. "'But I Was Counting On You!'" In *The Philosophy of Trust*, edited by Paul Faulkner and Thomas Simpson, 90–108. Oxford: Oxford University Press, 2017.

Jüssen, G. "Moral, Moralisch, Moralphilosophie: Lateinische Antike." In *Historisches Wörterbuch der Philosophie*, edited by Joachim Ritter, 3:149–50. Basel/Stuttgart: Schwabe & Co., 1974.

———. "Moral, Moralisch, Moralphilosophie: Lateinische Patristik und Lateinisches Mittelalter." In *Historisches Wörterbuch der Philosophie*, edited by Joachim Ritter, 3:151–53. Basel/Stuttgart: Schwabe & Co., 1974.

Kahn, Paul W. *Putting Liberalism in Its Place*. Princeton: Princeton University Press, 2005.

Kant, Immanuel. *Gesammelte Schriften*. Edited by Königlich Preußische Akademie der Wissenschaften/Berlin-Brandenburgische Akademie der Wissenschaften. Berlin, Göttingen: de Gruyter, n.d.

———. *Practical Philosophy*. Edited and translated by Mary J. Gregor. The Cambridge Edition of the Works of Immanuel Kant. Cambridge: Cambridge University Press, 1996.

———. *Religion and Rational Theology*. Edited and translated by Allen W. Wood and George di Giovanni. The Cambridge Edition of the Works of Immanuel Kant. Cambridge: Cambridge University Press, 1996.

Keller, Simon. *Partiality*. Princeton: Princeton University Press, 2013.

Kenny, Anthony. *The Rise of Modern Philosophy*. Oxford: Clarendon Press, 2006.

Kinzel, Katherina. "Wilhelm Windelband and the Problem of Relativism." *British Journal for the History of Philosophy* 25, no. 1 (2017): 84–107.

Kisiel, Theodore. *The Genesis of Heidegger's Being and Time*. Berkeley: University of California Press, 1993.

Kittelson, James M., and Hans H. Wiersma. *Luther The Reformer: The Story of the Man and His Career*. 2nd ed. Minneapolis: Fortress Press, 2016.

Kochin, Michael S. *Five Chapters on Rhetoric: Character, Action, Things, Nothing, and Art*. University Park, Pennsylvania: The Pennsylvania State University Press, 2009.

Köhnke, Klaus Christian. *The Rise of Neo-Kantianism: German Academic Philosophy between Idealism and Positivism*. Translated by R. J. Hollingdale. Cambridge: Cambridge University Press, 1991.

Kolakowski, Leszek. *Main Currents of Marxism: The Founders, the Golden Age, the Breakdown*. New York: W. W. Norton and Company, 2005.

Kolers, Avery. *A Moral Theory of Solidarity*. Oxford: Oxford University Press, 2016.

Koselleck, Reinhart. *Critique and Crisis: Enlightenment and the Pathogenesis of Modern Society*. Cambridge: The MIT Press, 1988.

Kraus, Oskar. *Die Werttheorien: Geschichte und Kritik*. Brünn: Rudolf M. Rohrer, 1937.

Krobath, Hermann T. *Werte: Ein Streifzug Durch Philosophie und Wissenschaft*. Würzburg: Königshausen & Neumann, 2009.

Kuehn, Manfred. *Kant: A Biography*. Cambridge: Cambridge University Press, 2001.

Kuhn, Helmut. "Fact and Value in Ethics." *Philosophy and Phenomenological Research* 2, no. 4 (1942): 501–10.

———. "Werte—Eine Urgegebenheit." In *Philosophische Anthropologie, Zweiter Teil*, edited by Hans-Georg Gadamer and Paul Vogler, 343–73. Stuttgart: Georg Thieme, 1975.

Kühn, Manfred. "Interpreting Kant Correctly: On the Kant of the Neo-Kantians." In *Neo-Kantianism in Contemporary Philosophy*, edited by Sebastian Luft and Rudolf A. Makkreel, 113–31. Bloomington: Indiana University Press, 2010.

Kundera, Milan. *The Art of the Novel*. Translated by Linda Asher. New York: Grove Press, 1988.

Laird, John. *The Idea of Value*. Cambridge: Cambridge University Press, 1929.

Lampe, Martin. *Das Problem der Willensfreiheit Bei Lipps, Eucken, Rindelband, v. Hartmann und Wundt*. Berlin: R. Trenkel, 1907.

Lencioni, Patrick. *The Five Dysfunctions of a Team*. San Francisco: Jossey-Bass, 2002.

Levack, Brian P. *The Witch-Hunt in Early Modern Europe*. 3rd ed. Harlow, UK: Pearson Longman, 2006.

Levinas, Emmanuel. *Ethics and Infinity: Conversations with Philippe Nemo*. Translated by Richard Cohen. Pittsburgh: Duquesne University Press, 1985.

———. "Meaning and Sense." In *Basic Philosophical Writings*, translated by Adriaan T. Peperzak, Simon Critchley, and Robert Bernasconi, 33–64. Bloomington: Indiana University Press, 1996.

———. *The Theory of Intuition in Husserl's Phenomenology*. Translated by André Orianne. Evanston: Northwestern University Press, 1973.

Lippmann, Walter. *Public Opinion*. Mineola: Dover, 2004.

Lloyd, S. A., ed. *The Bloomsbury Companion to Hobbes*. London: Bloomsbury, 2013.

Locke, John. *An Essay Concerning Human Understanding*. Edited by Peter H. Nidditch. Oxford: Clarendon Press, 1975.

———. *Two Treatises of Government*. Edited by Peter Laslett. Cambridge: Cambridge University Press, 1988.

Lotze, Hermann. *Logic, Volume II*. Translated by Bernard Bosanquet. Oxford: Oxford at the Clarendon Press, 1888.

———. *Logik: Drei Bücher Vom Denken, Vom Untersuchen und Vom Erkennen*. Leipzig: S. Hirzel, 1874.

———. *Microcosmus: An Essay Concerning Man and His Relation to the World, Two Volumes*. Translated by Elizabeth Hamilton and E. E., Constance Jones. Edinburgh: T. & T. Clark, 1885.

———. *Mikrokosmus: Ideen zur Naturgeschichte und Geschichte der Menschheit, 3 Volumes*. Leipzig: Hirzel: 1856, 1858, 1864, n.d.

Lucka, Emil. *Eros: The Development of the Sex Relation Through the Ages*. Translated by Ellie Schleussner. New York: G. P. Putnam's Sons, 1915.

Luther, Martin. "A Sermon on Keeping Children in School." In *Luther's Works, Volume 46*, edited by Robert C. Schultz, translated by Charles M. Jacobs and Robert C. Schultz, 207–58. Philadelphia: Fortress Press, 1967.

———. "Against the Heavenly Prophets in the Matter of Images and Sacraments." In *Luther's Works, Volume 40*, edited by Conrad Bergendoff, translated by Bernhard Erling and Conrad Bergendoff, 73–223. Philadelphia: Muhlenberg Press, 1958.

———. "Against the Robbing and Murdering Hordes of Peasants." In *Luther's Works, Volume 46*, edited by Robert C. Schultz, translated by Charles M. Jacobs and Robert C. Schultz, 45–55. Philadelphia: Fortress Press, 1967.

———. "An den Christlichen Adel Deutscher Nation von des Christlichen Standes Besserung." In *D. Martin Luthers Werke, 6. Band*, 404–69. Weimar: Hermann Böhlau, 1888.

———. "An Open Letter on the Harsh Book Against the Peasants." In *Luther's Works, Volume 46*, edited by Robert C. Schultz, translated by Charles M. Jacobs and Robert C. Schultz, 57–85. Philadelphia: Fortress Press, 1967.

———. "Auslegung des 101. Psalms." In *D. Martin Luthers Werke, 51. Band*, 197–264. Weimar: Hermann Böhlaus Nachfolger, 1914.

———. "Commentary on Psalm 82." In *Luther's Works, Vol. 13*, edited by Jaroslav Pelikan, translated by C. M. Jacobs, 39–72. Saint Louis: Concordia Publishing House, 1956.

———. "Commentary on Psalm 101." In *Luther's Works, Volume 13*, edited by Jaroslav Pelikan, translated by Alfred von Rohr Sauer, 143–224. Saint Louis: Concordia Publishing House, 1956.

———. "Commentary on Psalm 110." In *Luther's Works, Volume 13*, edited by Jaroslav Pelikan, translated by H. Richard Klann, 225–348. Saint Louis: Concordia Publishing House, 1956.

———. "Der Brief an die Römer." In *D. Martin Luthers Werke, 56. Band.* Weimar: Hermann Böhlaus Nachfolger, 1938.

———. "De Servo Arbitrio." In *D. Martin Luthers Werke, 18. Band*, 551–787. Weimar: Hermann Böhlaus Nachfolger, n.d.

———. "Der 117. Psalm Ausgelegt." In *D. Martin Luthers Werke, 12. Band, Erste Abteilung*, 189–218. Weimar: Hermann Böhlaus Nachfolger, 1913.

———. "Der CX. Psalm, Gepredigt und Ausgelegt." In *D. Martin Luthers Werke, 41. Band*, 79–239. Weimar: Hermann Böhlaus Nachfolger, 1964.

———. "Ein Sendbrief von dem Harten Büchlein Wider die Bauern." In *D. Martin Luthers Werke, 18. Band*, 375–401. Weimar: Hermann Böhlaus Nachfolger, 1908.

———. "Eine Predigt, Daß Man Kinder zur Schulen Halten Solle." In *D. Martin Luthers Werke, 30. Band, Zweite Abteilung*, 517–88. Weimar: Hermann Böhlaus Nachfolger, 1909.

———. "Explanations of the Ninety-Five Theses." In *Luther's Works, Volume 31*, edited by Harold J. Grimm, translated by Carl W. Folkemer, 77–252. Philadelphia: Muhlenberg Press, 1957.

———. "First Lectures on the Psalms I." In *Luther's Works, Volume 10*, edited by Hilton C. Oswald. Saint Louis: Concordia Publishing House, 1974.

———. "Lectures on Romans." In *Luther's Works, Volume 25*, edited by Hilton C. Oswald, translated by Walter G. Tillmanns and Jacob A. O. Preus. Saint Louis: Concordia Publishing House, 1972.

———. "Ob Kriegsleute Auch in Seligem Stande Sein Können." In *D. Martin Luthers Werke, 19. Band*, 623–62. Weimar: Hermann Böhlaus Nachfolger, 1897.

———. "Preface to the Complete Edition of Luther's Latin Writings, 1545." In *Luther's Works, Volume 34*, edited and translated by Lewis W. Spitz, 323–38. Philadelphia: Muhlenberg Press, 1960.

———. "Resolutiones Disputationum de Indulgentiarum Virtute." In *D. Martin Luthers Werke, 1. Band*, 525–628. Weimar: Hermann Böhlau, 1883.

———. "Sermo de Duplici Iustitia." In *D. Martin Luthers Werke, 2. Band*, 145–52. Weimar: Hermann Böhlau, 1884.

———. "Temporal Authority: To What Extent It Should Be Obeyed." In *Luther's Works, Volume 45*, edited by Walther I. Brandt, translated by J. J. Schindel, 75–128. Philadelphia: Muhlenberg Press, 1962.

———. "The Bondage of the Will." In *Luther's Works, Volume 33*, edited by Philip S. Watson. Philadelphia: Fortress Press, 1972.

———. "The Freedom of a Christian." In *Luther's Works, Volume 31*, edited by Harold J. Grimm, translated by W. A. Lambert, 327–77. Philadelphia: Muhlenberg Press, 1957.

———. *The Life of Luther Written by Himself.* Edited by M. Michelet, translated by William Hazlitt. London: George Bell and Sons, 1904.

———. "The Second Sermon, March 10, 1522, Monday after Invocavit," https://www.theologie.uzh.ch/predigten/archiv-6/eight-sermons-wittenberg.pdf.

———. "To the Christian Nobility of the German Nation Concerning the Reform of the Christian Estate." In *Luther's Works, Volume 44*, edited by James Atkinson, translated by Charles M. Jacobs, 115–217. Philadelphia: Fortress Press, 1966.

———. "Treatise on Good Works." In *Luther's Works, Volume 44*, edited by James Atkinson, translated by W.A. Lambert, 15–121. Philadelphia: Fortress Press, 1966.

———. "Two Kinds of Righteousness." In *Luther's Works, Volume 31*, edited by Harold J. Grimm, translated by Lowell J. Satre, 293–306. Muhlenberg Press, 1957.

———. "Von den Guten Werken." In *D. Martin Luthers Werke, 6. Band*, 202–76. Weimar: Hermann Böhlau, 1888.

———. "Von der Freiheit eines Christenmenschen." In *D. Martin Luthers Werke, 7. Band*, 20–49. Weimar: Hermann Böhlaus Nachfolger, 1897.

———. "Von Weltlicher Oberkeit, Wei Weit Man Ihr Gehorsam Schuldig Sei." In *D. Martin Luthers Werke, 11. Band*, 229–81. Weimar: Hermann Böhlaus Nachfolger, 1900.

———. "Vorrede Luthers Zum Ersten Bande Der Gesamtausgabe Seiner Lateinischen Schriften." In *D. Martin Luthers Werke, 54. Band*, 176–87. Weimar: Hermann Böhlaus Nachfolger, 1928.

———. "Whether Soldiers, Too, Can Be Saved." In *Luther's Works, Volume 46*, edited by Robert C. Schultz, translated by Charles M. Jacobs, 87–143. Philadelphia: Fortress Press, 1967.

———. "Wider die Himmlischen Propheten." In *D. Martin Luthers Werke, 18. Band*, 62–214. Weimar: Hermann Böhlaus Nachfolger, 1908.

———. "Wider die Räuberischen Und Mörderischen Rotten Der Bauern." In *D. Martin Luthers Werke, 18. Band*, 357–61. Weimar: Hermann Böhlaus Nachfolger, 1908.

Lynch, Sandra. *Philosophy and Friendship*. Edinburgh: Edinburgh University Press, 2005.

MacCulloch, Diarmaid. *Reformation: Europe's House Divided*. London: Allen Lane, 2003.

MacIntyre, Alasdair. *Ethics in the Conflicts of Modernity: An Essay on Desire, Practical Reasoning, and Narrative*. Cambridge: Cambridge University Press, 2016.

———. *After Virtue: A Study in Moral Theory*. Notre Dame: University of Notre Dame Press, 1984.

Manchester, William. *A World Lit Only by Fire: The Medieval Mind and the Renaissance*. New York: Back Bay Books, 1993.

Mander, W.J. *Idealist Ethics*. Oxford: Oxford University Press, 2016.

Manent, Pierre. *Beyond Radical Secularism: How France and the Christian West Should Respond to the Islamic Challenge*. Translated by Ralph C. Hancock. South Bend: St. Augustine's Press, 2016.

———. *Natural Law and Human Rights*. Translated by Ralph C. Hancock. Notre Dame: University of Notre Dame Press, 2020.

Mansfield, Harvey C., Jr. *America's Constitutional Soul*. Baltimore: John Hopkins University Press, 1991.

Manzi, Jim. *Uncontrolled: The Surprising Payoff of Trial-and-Error for Business, Politics, and Society*. New York: Basic Books, 2012.

Marietta, Morgan. *The Politics of Sacred Rhetoric: Absolutist Appeals and Political Persuasion*. Waco, TX: Baylor University Press, 2012.

Maritain, Jacques. "The Concept of Sovereignty." *The American Political Science Review* 44, no. 2 (1950): 343–57.

Markus, R. A. *Saeculum: History and Society in the Theology of St Augustine*. Cambridge: Cambridge University Press, 1988.

Martin, Aaron. *Young People and Politics: Political Engagement in the Anglo-American Democracies*. New York: Routledge, 2012.

Marx, Karl. *Capital, Vol. 1., in Marx and Engels Collected Works*, vol. 35. Translated by Samuel Moore and Edward Aveling. New York: International Publishers, 1996.

———. *Marginal Notes on the Programme of the German Workers' Party*. In *Collected Works*, vol. 24, *Marx and Engels: 1874–1873*. New York: International Publishers, 1989.

———. *Value, Price, and Profit*. In *Collected Works*, vol. 20, *Marx and Engels: 1864–1868*. New York: International Publishers, 1985.

McCormick, John P. "Fear, Technology, and the State: Carl Schmitt, Leo Strauss, and the Revival of Hobbes in Weimar and National Socialist Germany." *Political Theory* 22, no. 4 (1994): 619–52.

McDougall, Walter A. *The Tragedy of U.S. Foreign Policy: How America's Civil Religion Betrayed the National Interest*. New Haven: Yale University Press, 2016.

McGrath, Alister E. *Iustitia Dei: A History of the Christian Doctrine of Justification*. 3rd ed. Cambridge: Cambridge University Press, 2005.

McKenna, Stephen. "A Mimetic Perspective on Trust." In *Living in an Age of Mistrust: An Interdisciplinary Study of Declining Trust and How to Get It Back*, edited by Andrew I. Yeo and Matthew N. Green, 45–56. New York: Routledge, 2017.

Meacham, Jon. *American Lion: Andrew Jackson in the White House*. New York: Random House, 2008.

Merz, John. *A History of European Thought in the Nineteenth Century, Volume Three*. Edinburgh: William Blackwood and Sons, 1912.

Metaxas, Eric. *Martin Luther: The Man Who Rediscovered God and Changed the World*. New York: Penguin, 2017.

Metz, Rudolf. *A Hundred Years of British Philosophy*. London: Routledge, 2013.

Meyer, Dick. *Why We Hate Us: American Discontent in the New Millennium*. New York: Crown, 2008.

Milbank, John. *Theology and Social Theory: Beyond Secular Reason*. 2nd ed. Malden, MA: Blackwell, 2006.

Milbank, John, and Adrian Pabst. *The Politics of Virtue: Post-Liberalism and the Human Future*. London: Rowman & Littlefield, 2016.

Milkov, Nikolay. "Hermann Lotze's Microcosm." In *Islamic Philosophy and Occidental Phenomenology on the Perennial Issue of Microcosm and Macrocosm*, edited by Anna-Teresa Tymieniecka, 41–65. Dordrecht: Springer, 2006.

Mill, John Stuart. *Autobiography*. Edited by John M. Robson. New York: Penguin, 1989.

Mormann, Thomas. "Carnap's Logical Empiricism, Values, and American Pragmatism." *Journal for General Philosophy of Science* 38, no. 1 (April 21, 2007): 127–46.

Moyar, Dean. *Hegel's Value: Justice as the Living Good*. Oxford, Oxford University Press, 2021.

Muirhead, Russell. "The Case For Party Loyalty." In *Loyalty*, edited by Sanford Levinson, Joel Parker, and Paul Woodruff, 229–56. New York: New York University Press, 2013.

Nagachevskaya, Svetlana. *Pictures at an Exhibition: A Reconciliation of Divergent Perceptions About Mussorgsky's Renowned Cycle*. The University of Arizona, 2009.

Newey, Glen. *After Politics: The Rejection of Politics in Contemporary Liberal Philosophy*. New York: Palgrave, 2001.

———. *The Routledge Guidebook to Hobbes' Leviathan*. London: Routledge, 2014.

Nietzsche, Friedrich. *Beyond Good and Evil: Prelude to a Philosophy of the Future*. Translated by Walter Kaufmann. New York: Vintage, 1966.

———. *Daybreak*. Cambridge: Cambridge University Press, 1997.

———. *The Birth of Tragedy and The Genealogy of Morals*. Translated by Francis Golffing. New York: Doubleday, 1956.

———. *The Will to Power*. Edited by Kaufman. Translated by Walter Kaufmann and R. J. Hollingdale. New York: Vintage, 1967.

———. *Werke: Kritische Gesamtausgabe*. Edited by Giorgio Colli and Mazzino Montinari. Berlin: de Gruyter, n.d.

Nilbock, Jan. *Was Sind Werte? Philosophische Grundlagen zur Wertedebatte*. Norderstedt: GRIN, 2007.

Nixon, Jon. *Hannah Arendt and the Politics of Friendship*. London: Bloomsbury, 2015.

Nussbaum, Martha C. *Not For Profit*. Princeton: Princeton University Press, 2010.

Oakes, Guy. "Value Theory and the Foundations of the Cultural Sciences. Remarks on Rickert." In *Methodology of the Social Sciences, Ethics, and Economics in the Newer Historical School,* edited by Peter Koslowski, 59–78. Berlin: Springer, 1997.

O'Neil, Collin. "Betraying Trust." In *The Philosophy of Trust*, edited by Paul Faulkner and Thomas Simpson, 70–89. Oxford: Oxford University Press, 2017.

O'Neill, Onora. *A Question of Trust*. Cambridge: Cambridge University Press, 2002.

Oakeshott, Michael. *The Voice of Liberal Learning*. Indianapolis: Liberty Fund, 1989.

Oakley, Francis. *Empty Bottles of Gentilism: Kingship and the Divine in Late Antiquity and the Early Middle Ages (to 1050)*. New Haven: Yale University Press, 2010.

Oberman, Heiko A. *Luther: Man Between God and the Devil*. Translated by Eileen Walliser-Schwarzbart. New Haven: Yale University Press, 1989.

Orlinsky, Harry M. *Ancient Israel*. 2nd ed. Ithaca: Cornell University Press, 1960.

Orth, Ernst Wolfgang. "Kultur und Vorstellungsmassen. Ansätze zur Entwicklung eines Neuen Kulturbegriffs im 19. Jahrhundert Bei Johann Friedrich Herbart." In

Herbarts Kultursystem: Perspektiven der Transdisziplinarität im 19. Jahrhundert, edited by Andreas Hoeschen and Lothar Schneider, 25–37. Würzburg: Königshausen & Neumann, 2001.

Orwell, George. *1984*. New York: Signet Classics, 1977.

———. *All Art Is Propaganda*. Edited by George Packer. Boston: Mariner Books, 2008.

Osiander, Andreas. "Sovereignty, International Relations, and the Westphalian Myth." *International Organization* 55, no. 2 (2001): 251–87.

Pabst, Adrian. *Postliberal Politics: The Coming Era of Renewal*. Cambridge: Polity, 2021.

Pakaluk, Michael. "Introduction." In *Other Selves: Philosophers on Friendship*, edited by Michael Pakaluk, vii–xiv. Indianapolis: Hackett, 1991.

Parkin, Jon. *Science, Religion and Politics in Restoration England*. Woodbridge, Suffolk: The Boydell Press, 1999.

———. *Taming The Leviathan: The Reception of the Political and Religious Ideas of Thomas Hobbes in England 1640–1700*. Cambridge: Cambridge University Press, 2007.

Peirce, Charles S. *Selected Writings: Values in a Universe of Change*. New York: Dover, 1958.

Peirce, Charles Sanders. *Collected Papers of Charles Sanders Peirce, Volume V: Pragmatism and Pragmaticism*. Edited by Charles Hartshorne and Paul Weiss. Cambridge, Massachusetts: Belknap Press, 1960.

Perry, John. *The Pretenses of Loyalty: Locke, Liberal Theology, and American Political Theology*. Oxford: Oxford University Press, 2011.

Pester, Reinhardt. *Hermann Lotze: Wege Seines Denkens und Forschens: Ein Kapitel deutscher Philosophie- und Wissenschaftsgeschichte im 19. Jahrhundert*. Würzburg: Königshausen & Neumann, 1997.

Peterson, Andrew and David Civil. "Virtues, values and the fracturing of civic and moral virtue in citizenship education policy in England," *Educational Review*. DOI: 10.1080/00131911.2021.2023105.

Peterson, Jordan B. *Maps of Meaning: The Architecture of Belief*. New York: Routledge, 1999.

Petty, William. *The Economic Writings of Sir William Petty, Volume 1*. Cambridge: Cambridge University Press, 1662.

Plato. *Republic*. In *The Collected Dialogues of Plato*, edited by Edith Hamilton and Huntington, translated by Paul Shorey. Princeton: Princeton University Press, 1989.

Pocock, J. G. A. *Politics, Language, and Time: Essays on Political Thought and History*. Chicago: Chicago University Press, 1971.

———. *The Machiavellian Moment*. Princeton: Princeton University Press, 1975.

Polanyi, Michael. *Personal Knowledge: Towards a Post-Critical Philosophy*. Chicago: University of Chicago Press, 1958.

Porter, Theodore M. *Trust in Numbers: The Pursuit of Objectivity in Science and Public Life*. Princeton: Princeton University Press, 1995.

Postman, Neil. *Technopoly: The Surrender of Culture to Technology*. New York: Vintage, 1992.

Pufendorf, Samuel. *On the Duty of Man and Citizen According to Natural Law*. Edited by James Tully. Translated by Michael Silverthorne. Cambridge: Cambridge University Press, 1991.

———. *Two Books of the Elements of Universal Jurisprudence*. Edited by Thomas Behme. Translated by William Abbott Oldfather. Indianapolis: Liberty Fund, 2009.

———. *Elementa jurisprudentiae universalis*. Edited by Frank Böhling. In *Samuel Pufendorf: Gesammelte Werke*, vol. 3. Edited by Wilhelm Schmidt-Biggemann. Berlin: Akademie Verlag, 1999.

———. *De officio*. Edited by Gerald Hartung. In *Samuel Pufendorf: Gesammelte Werke*, vol. 2. Edited by Wilhelm Schmidt-Biggemann. Berlin: Akademie Verlag, 1997.

Putnam, Robert D. *Bowling Alone: The Collapse and Revival of American Community*. New York: Simon & Schuster, 2000.

Raphael, D.D. *Concepts of Justice*. Oxford: Clarendon Press, 2001.

Ratner-Rosenhagen, Jennifer. *American Nietzsche: A History of an Icon and His Ideas*. Chicago: University of Chicago Press, 2012.

Ratzinger, Joseph. "Concerning the Notion of Person in Theology." *Communio* 17, (Fall 1990): 439–54.

———. *Jesus of Nazareth: The Infancy Narratives*. Translated by Philip J. Whitmore. New York: Image, 2012.

Reich, Robert B. *The Common Good*. New York: Alfred A. Knopf, 2018.

Reichley, A. James. *The Art of Government: Reform and Organization Politics in Philadelphia*. New York: Fund for the Republic, 1959.

Rhees, Rush, ed. *Ludwig Wittgenstein: Personal Recollections*. Totowa, NJ: Rowman & Littlefield, 1981.

Rickert, Heinrich. *The Limits of Concept Formation in Natural Science: A Logical Introduction to the Historical Sciences*. Edited and translated by Guy Oakes. Abridged. Cambridge: Cambridge University Press, 1986.

Ringer, Fritz K. *The Decline of the German Mandarins: The German Academic Community, 1890–1933*. Cambridge: Harvard University Press, 1969.

Ritchie, Angus. *Inclusive Populism: Creating Citizens in the Global Age*. Notre Dame: University of Notre Dame Press, 2019.

Roncaglia, Alessandro. *The Wealth of Ideas: A History of Economic Thought*. Cambridge: Cambridge University Press, 2005.

Ross, Iain. *Oscar Wilde and Ancient Greece*. Cambridge: Cambridge University Press, 2013.

Rossides, Daniel W. "The Legacy of Max Weber: A Non-Metaphysical Politics." *Sociological Inquiry* 42, no. 3–4 (1972): 183–210.

Rousseau, Jean-Jacques. *Discourse on the Origins of Inequality (Second Discourse), Polemics, and Political Economy*. Edited by Roger D. Masters and Christopher Kelly. Translated by Judith R. Bush, Roger D. Masters, Christopher Kelly, and Terence Marshall. *The Collected Writings of Rousseau*, vol. 3. Hanover, NH: Dartmouth College Press, 1992.

———. *Discourse on the Sciences and Arts (First Discourse), and Polemics*. Edited by Roger D. Masters and Christopher Kelly. Translated by Judith R. Bush, Roger

D. Masters, and Christopher Kelly. *The Collected Writings of Rousseau*, vol. 2. Hanover, NH: Dartmouth College Press, 1992.

———. *Oeuvres Complètes III: Du Contrat Social, Écrits Politiques*. Edited by Gagnebin Bernard and Raymond Marcel. Paris: Bibliothèque de la Pléiade, 1964.

———. *Social Contract, Discourses on the Virtue Most Necessary for a Hero, Political Fragments, and Geneva Manuscript*. Edited by Roger D. Masters and Christopher Kelly. Translated by Judith R. Bush, Roger D. Masters, and Christopher Kelly. *The Collected Writings of Rousseau*, vol. 4. Hanover, NH: Dartmouth College Press, 1994.

Royce, Josiah. *The Basic Writings of Josiah Royce: Logic, Loyalty, and Community*. Edited by John Joseph McDermott. New York: Fordham University Press, 2005.

Rubin, Isaak Illich. *Essays on Marx's Theory of Value*. Translated by Miloš Samardžija and Fredy Perlman. Detroit: Black & Red, 1972.

Russell, Jeffrey B., and Brooks Alexander. *A History of Witchcraft: Sorcerers, Heretics and Pagans*. 2nd ed. London: Thames & Hudson, 2007.

Ryrie, Alec. *Protestants: The Faith That Made the Modern World*. New York: Viking, 2017.

Safranski, Rüdiger. *Nietzsche: A Philosophical Biography*. Translated by Shelley Frisch. New York: W. W. Norton and Company, 2002.

Santayana, George, and Paul Grimley Kuntz. *Lotze's System of Philosophy*. Edited by Paul Grimley Kuntz. Oxford: Indiana University Press, 1971.

Sawat Selway, Joel. "Cross-Cuttingness, Cleavage Structures and Civil War Onset." *British Journal of Political Science* 41, no. 1 (2011): 111–38.

Schabert, Tilo. *Boston Politics: The Creativity of Power*. Berlin: Walter de Gruyter, 1989.

Scheffler, Samuel. "Morality and Reasonable Partiality." In *Partiality and Impartiality: Morality, Special Relationships, and the Wider World*, edited by Brian Feltham and John Cottingham, 98–130. Oxford: Oxford University Press, 2010.

Scheler, Max. *Formalism in Ethics and Non-Formal Ethics of Values*. Translated by Manfred S. Frings and Roger L. Funk. Evanston: Northwestern University Press, 1973.

———. *Selected Philosophical Essays*. Translated by David R. Lachterman. Evanston: Northwestern University Press, 1973.

Schindler, D. C. *Freedom from Reality: The Diabolical Character of Modern Liberty*. Notre Dame: University of Notre Dame Press, 2017.

———. *The Perfection of Freedom: Schiller, Schelling, and Hegel between the Ancients and the Moderns*. Eugene, Oregon: Cascade, 2012.

———. *The Politics of the Real: The Church Between Liberalism and Integralism*. Steubenville, Ohio: New Polity, 2021.

Schmitt, Carl, Eberhard Jungel, and Sepp Schelz. *Die Tyrannei der Werte*. Hamburg: Lutherisches Verlagshaus, 1979.

Schnädelbach, Herbert. *Philosophy in Germany, 1831–1933*. Translated by Eric Matthews. Cambridge: Cambridge University Press, 1984.

Scott, Jr., Hugh D. *How to Go into Politics*. New York: John Day, 1949.

Scruton, Roger. "Parfit the Perfectionist." *Philosophy* 89, no. 350 (2014): 621–34.

Sennett, Richard. *Authority*. New York: Alfred A. Knopf, 1980.

Shapin, Steven. *A Social History of Truth: Civility and Science in Seventeenth-Century England*. Chicago: University of Chicago Press, 1994.

Shapiro, Barbara J. *A Culture of Fact: England, 1550–1720*. Ithaca: Cornell University Press, 2000.

Sharp, Frank Chapman. "The Ethical System of Richard Cumberland and Its Place in the History of British Ethics." *Mind* 21, no. 83 (1912): 371–98.

Shelley, Trevor. *Globalization and Liberalism: Montesquieu, Tocqueville, and Manent*. Notre Dame: University of Notre Dame Press, 2020.

Sica, Alan. *Max Weber and the New Century*. New Brunswick: Transaction, 2004.

Simons, Peter M. *Philosophy and Logic in Central Europe from Bolzano to Tarski: Selected Essays*. Dordrecht: Springer, 1992.

Skinner, Quentin. *The Foundations of Modern Political Thought: Volume Two, The Age of Reformation*. Cambridge: Cambridge University Press, 1978.

———. *Visions of Politics III: Hobbes and Civil Science*. Cambridge: Cambridge University Press, 2002.

Sluga, Hans D. *Gottlob Frege*. London: Routledge & Kegan Paul, 1980.

Smilansky, Saul. *10 Moral Paradoxes*. Malden, MA: Blackwell, 2007.

Smith, Adam. *An Inquiry into the Nature and Causes of the Wealth of Nations*. Edited by Kathryn Sutherland. Oxford: Oxford University Press, 1993.

Smith, Blake. "Liberalism for Losers: Carl Schmitt's 'The Tyranny of Values.'" *American Affairs* V, no. 1 (2021): 222–40.

Smith, Christian. *Lost in Transition: The Dark Side of Emerging Adulthood*. Oxford: Oxford University Press, 2011.

Smith, Jean Edward. *FDR*. New York: Random House, 2008.

Socci, Antonio. *I Nuovi Perseguitati: Indagine sulla intolleranza anticristiana nel nuovo secolo del martirio*. Milan: Piemme, 2002.

Sokolowski, Robert. *Introduction to Phenomenology*. Cambridge: Cambridge University Press, 2000.

———. *Phenomenology of the Human Person*. Cambridge: Cambridge University Press, 2008.

Spaemann, Robert. "The Dictatorship of Values." Project Syndicate, 2001. Accessed September 2, 2022, https://www.project-syndicate.org/commentary/-the-dictatorship-of-values.

Spruyt, Hendrik. *The Sovereign State and Its Competitors: An Analysis of Systems Change*. Princeton: Princeton University Press, 1996.

Stafford, Richard A., Joseph P. McLaughlin Jr., Michelle J. Atherton, Megan Mullin, and Nathan Shrader. *The Temple Papers on the Pennsylvania General Assembly, vol. IV: A Discussion of Topics Related to the Continuing Evolution of the Pennsylvania General Assembly*. Philadelphia: Temple Institute for Public Affairs, 2012.

Stocker, Michael. *Plural and Conflicting Values*. Oxford: Clarendon Press, 1990.

———. "The Schizophrenia of Modern Ethical Theories." *The Journal of Philosophy* 73, no. 14 (1976): 453–66.

Stover, Justin. "There Is No Case for the Humanities." *American Affairs* I, no. 4 (2017): 210–24.

Straub, Eberhard. *Zur Tyrannei der Werte*. Stuttgart: Klett-Cotta, 2010.

Sullivan, Vickie B. *Machiavelli, Hobbes, and the Formation of a Liberal Republicanism in England*. Cambridge: Cambridge University Press, 2004.

Taleb, Nassim Nicholas. *Skin in the Game: Hidden Asymmetries in Daily Life*. New York: Allen Lane, 2018.

———. *The Black Swan: The Impact of the Highly Improbable*. New York: Random House, 2007.

Taylor, A. J. P. *The Course of German History: A Survey of the Development of German History Since 1815*. London: Routledge, 2005.

Taylor, Charles. *A Secular Age*. Cambridge, Massachusetts: The Belknap Press, 2007.

Telfer, Elizabeth. "Friendship." In *Other Selves: Philosophers on Friendship*, edited by Michael Pakaluk, 250–67. Indianapolis: Hackett, 1991.

Thomas, Evan Edward. *Lotze's Theory of Reality*. London: Longmans, Green, and Co., 1921.

Tilly, Charles. *Contention and Democracy in Europe, 1650–2000*. Cambridge: Cambridge University Press, 2004.

———. *Trust and Rule*. Cambridge: Cambridge University Press, 2005.

Tuck, Richard. *Natural Rights Theories: Their Origin and Development*. Cambridge: Cambridge University Press, 1979.

Tuininga, Matthew J. *Calvin's Political Theology and the Public Engagement of the Church*. Cambridge: Cambridge University Press, 2017.

Türks, Paul. *Philip Neri: The Fire of Joy*. Translated by Daniel Utrecht. New York: Alba House, 1995.

Uslaner, Eric M. *The Moral Foundations of Trust*. Cambridge: Cambridge University Press, 2002.

Valéry, Paul. *History and Politics*. Translated by Denise Folliot and Jackson Mathews. New York: Pantheon, 1962.

van Oyen, H. "Wertethik." In *Die Religion in Geschichte Und Gegenwart: Handwörterbuch Für Theologie Und Religionswissenschaft*, edited by Kurt Galling. Tübingen: J. C. B. Mohr (P. Siebeck), 1962.

Varga, Peter Andras. "The Missing Chapter from the Logical Investigations: Husserl on Lotze's Formal and Real Significance of Logical Laws." *Husserl Studies* 29, no. 3 (2013): 181–209.

Vermeule, Adrian. "Integration from Within." *American Affairs* II, no. 1 (2018): 202–13.

Voegelin, Eric. *The New Science of Politics: An Introduction*. Chicago: University of Chicago Press, 1987.

von Coelln, Hermann. *Von den Gütern zu den Werten: Versuch einer Kritik Aller Wertphilosophie*. Essen: Die Blaue Eule, 1996.

von Heyking, John. *Augustine and Politics as Longing in the World*. Columbia: University of Missouri Press, 2001.

———. "Friendship as Precondition and Consequence of Creativity in Politics." In *The Primacy of Persons in Politics: Empiricism and Political Philosophy*, edited by John von Heyking and Thomas Heilke, 79–106. Washington DC: The Catholic University of America Press, 2013.

———. *The Form of Politics: Aristotle and Plato on Friendship*. Montreal: McGill-Queen's University Press, 2016.

von Heyking, John, and Richard Avramenko. "Introduction: The Persistence of Friendship in Political Life." In *Friendship and Politics: Essays in Political Thought*, edited by John von Heyking and Richard Avramenko. Notre Dame: University of Notre Dame Press, 2008.

von Hildebrand, Dietrich. *What Is Philosophy?* Steubenville, Ohio: Dietrich von Hildebrand Legacy Project, 2021.

Wallerstein, Immanuel. *The Modern World-System I: Capitalist Agriculture and the Origins of the European World-Economy in the Sixteenth Century*, vol. 1. Berkeley: University of California Press, 2011.

Walsh, David. *Politics of the Person as the Politics of Being*. Notre Dame: University of Notre Dame Press, 2016.

Walter, Nigel. "From Values to Narrative: A New Foundation for the Conservation of Historic Buildings." *International Journal of Heritage Studies* 20, no. 6 (2014): 634–50.

Walzer, Michael. *Thick and Thin: Moral Argument at Home and Abroad*. Notre Dame: University of Notre Dame Press, 2019.

Warren, Mark E., ed. *Democracy and Trust*. Cambridge: Cambridge University Press, 1999.

Weber, Max. *From Max Weber: Essays in Sociology*. Edited by C. Wright Mills and H. H. Gerth. Oxford: Oxford University Press, 1958.

———. *The Methodology of the Social Sciences*. Edited by Edward A. Shils and Henry A. Finch. Glencoe, Illinois: The Free Press, 1949.

Weinberger, David. *Too Big to Know*. New York: Basic Books, 2011.

Weir, Robert E. *Workers in America: A Historical Encyclopedia*, vol. 2. Santa Barbara, California: ABC-CLIO, 2013.

Wendling, Amy E. *The Ruling Ideas: Bourgeois Political Concepts*. Lanham: Lexington Books, 2012.

Werner, Folke. *Vom Wert der Werte: Die Tauglichkeit des Wertbegriffs als Orientierung gebende Kategorie menschlicher Lebensführung Eine Studie aus evangelischer Perspektive*. Münster: LIT, 2002.

White, Nicholas. "Indifferenz und der nicht peripatetische stoische Begriff des Guten." In *Zur Ethik der Älteren Stoa*, edited by Barbara Guckes, 180–98. Göttingen: Vandenhoeck & Ruprecht, 2004.

Whittington, Keith E. *Political Foundations of Judicial Supremacy: The Presidency, the Supreme Court, and Constitutional Leadership in U.S. History*. Princeton: Princeton University Press, 2007.

Wieland, G. "Moral, Moralisch, Moralphilosophie: 12. Jahrhundert, Hoch- und Spätscholastik." In *Historisches Wörterbuch der Philosophie*, edited by Joachim Ritter, 3:153–56. Basel/Stuttgart: Schwabe & Co., 1974.

Wilde, Lawrence. *Global Solidarity*. Edinburgh: Edinburgh University Press, 2013.

Willey, Thomas E. *Back to Kant: The Revival of Kantianism in German Social and Historical Thought, 1860–1914*. Detroit: Wayne State University Press, 1978.

Williams, Howard. *Kant's Critique of Hobbes: Sovereignty and Cosmopolitanism*. Cardiff: University of Wales Press, 2003.

Wilson, James Q. *The Moral Sense*. New York: The Free Press, 1993.

Wilson, Peter H. *Absolutism in Central Europe*. London: Routledge, 2000.

———. *The Thirty Years War: Europe's Tragedy*. Cambridge, Massachusetts: Belknap Press, 2009.

Windelband, Wilhelm. *Die philosophischen Richtungen der Gegenwart*. Edited by Ernst von Aster. Leipzig: Quelle & Meyer, 1911.

———. *Präludien*. 3rd ed. Tübingen: J.C.B. Mohr, 1907.

———. "The Principles of Logic." In *Encyclopaedia of the Philosophical Sciences*, edited by Henry Jones, translated by B. Ethel Meyer, 7–66. London: Macmillian and Co., 1913.

———. *Über Willensfreiheit*. Tübingen: J.C.B. Mohr (P. Siebeck), 1904.

Winner, Langdon. "Brandy, Cigars, and Human Values." In *The Whale and the Reactor: The Search for Limits in an Age of High Technology*, 155–63. Chicago: University of Chicago Press, 1986.

Witte, John. *Law and Protestantism: The Legal Teachings of the Lutheran Reformation*. Cambridge: Cambridge University Press, 2002.

Wittgenstein, Ludwig. *Major Works: Selected Philosophical Writings*. New York: HarperCollins, 2009.

Woodruff, Paul. "In Place of Loyalty: Friendship and Adversary Politics in Classical Greece." In *Loyalty*, edited by Sanford Levinson, Joel Parker, and Paul Woodruff. New York: New York University Press, 2013.

Woodward, William R. *Hermann Lotze: An Intellectual Biography*. Cambridge: Cambridge University Press, 2015.

Zagorin, Perez. *Hobbes and the Law of Nature*. Princeton: Princeton University Press, 2009.

Ziche, Paul. "Indecisionism and Anti-Relativism: Wilhelm Windelband as a Philosophical Historiographer of Philosophy." In *From Hegel to Windelband: Historiography of Philosophy in the 19th Century*, edited by Valentin Pluder and Gerald Hartung. Berlin: Walter de Gruyter, 2015.

Zijderveld, Anton C. *Rickert's Relevance: The Ontological Nature and Epistemological Functions of Values*. Leiden: Brill, 2006.

Index

About the Author

Philip J. Harold is professor of politics and dean of the Constantin College of Liberal Arts at the University of Dallas.

www.ingramcontent.com/pod-product-compliance
Lightning Source LLC
Chambersburg PA
CBHW022310280326
41932CB00010B/1046

* 9 7 8 1 5 3 8 1 7 4 1 5 9 *